2017
Computer lab: 8/30, 9/13. 9/27, 10/8, 11/1, 11/15, 11/29

Excellent English 4
Language Skills for Success

Susannah MacKay
Mari Vargo
Pamela Vittorio

Jan Forstrom
Marta Pitt
Shirley Velasco

Excellent English Student Book 4

ISBN 13: 978-0-07-719773-5 (Student Book)
ISBN 10: 0-07-719773-9
6 7 8 9 10 11 12 RMN 17 16 15 14 13 12

Series editor: Nancy Jordan
Developmental editor: Jennifer Bixby
Cover designer: Witz End Design
Interior designer: NETS
Compositor: Thompson Steele

The credits section for this book begins on page 234 and is considered an extension of the copyright page.

The **McGraw·Hill** Companies

Acknowledgements

The authors and publisher would like to thank the following individuals who reviewed the *Excellent English* program at various stages of development and whose comments, reviews, and field-testing were instrumental in helping us shape the series.

Tony Albert • Jewish Vocational Service; San Francisco, CA

Alex Baez • The Texas Professional Development Group; Austin, TX

Katie Blackburn • Truman College; Chicago, IL

Robert Breitbard • Collier County Adult Education; Naples, FL

Jeff Bright • McHenry County College; Crystal Lake, IL

Sherrie Carroll • Montgomery College; Conroe, TX

Georges Colin • Lindsey Hopkins Technical Education Center; Miami, FL

Irene Dennis • Palo Alto College; Palo Alto, CA

Terry Doyle • City College of San Francisco, Alemany Campus; San Francisco, CA

Rolly Fanton • San Diego City College; San Diego, CA

Ingrid Farnbach • City College of San Francisco; San Francisco, CA

Colleen Fitzmaurice • San Diego Community College District, Mid-City; San Diego, CA

Phil Garfinkel • Adult & Family Education of Lutheran Medical Centers; Brooklyn, New York

Ana Maria Guaolayol • Miami-Dade College, Kendall Campus; Miami, FL

Shama Hasib • City College of San Francisco; San Francisco, CA

Margaret Hass • San Diego Community College District, Mid-City; San Diego, CA

Kathleen Hiscock • Portland Adult Education; Portland, ME

Giang Hoang • Evans Community Adult School, Los Angeles Unified School District; Los Angeles, CA

Armenuhi Hovhannes • City College of San Francisco, Mission Campus; San Francisco, CA

Vivian Ikeda • City College of San Francisco, Teacher Resource Center; San Francisco, CA

Sally Ruth Jacobson • San Diego Community College District, Centre City; San Diego, CA

Kathleen Jimenez • Miami-Dade College, Kendall Campus; Miami, FL

Nancy Johansen • San Diego Community College District, Mid-City; San Diego, CA

Mary Kapp • City College of San Francisco, Chinatown Campus; San Francisco, CA

Caryn Kovacs • Brookline Adult Education; Brookline, MA

Linda Kozin • San Diego Community College District, North City Center; San Diego, CA

Gretchen Lammers-Ghereben • Martinez Adult Education School; Martinez, CA

Paul Mayer • Glendale Community College; Glendale, CA

Cathleen McCargo • Arlington Education and Employment Program (REEP); Arlington, VA

Lee Mosteller • San Diego Community College District, North City; San Diego, CA

Virginia Parra • Miami Dade College; Miami, FL

Iliana Pena • Lindsey Hopkins Technical Education Center; Miami, FL

Howard Riddles • Tomlinson Adult Learning Center; St. Petersburg, FL

Lisa Roberson • Mission Language and Vocational School; San Francisco, CA

Renata Russo Watson • Harris County Department of Education; Harris County, TX

Francisco Sanchez • Miami-Dade College, Kendall Campus; Miami, FL

Curt Sanford • City College of San Francisco, Alemany Campus; San Francisco, CA

Laurie Shapero • Miami-Dade College, Kendall Campus; Miami, FL

Eileen Spada • Max Hayes Adult School; Detroit, IL

Margaret Teske • Mt. San Antonio College; Walnut, CA

Theresa Warren • East Side Independence Adult Center; San Jose, CA

D. Banu Yaylali • Miami-Dade College, Kendall Campus; Miami, FL

Scope and Sequence

Unit	Grammar Point	Vocabulary	Listening/ Speaking/ Pronunciation	Reading	Writing
Pre-unit *page 2*	• Spelling • Punctuation • Verb form • Subject verb agreement • Capitalization	• Classroom language • Appointments	• Listen to introductions • Request clarification • Answer personal information questions	• Read a daily schedule	• Complete a conversation dialogue • Write a paragraph about a daily schedule
1 **Education Matters** *page 6*	• Simple present and present continuous • Correlative conjunctions • Expressing future time with *will, be, going to,* and the present continuous	• Adult education • Coursework • Job skills	• Listen to information about school • Express encouragement • Talk about programs and courses • Reductions with *n't* • Listen to a conversation between an employer and an employee	• Examine college transcripts • Read a career school advertisement • Read an email from a teacher	• Write statements about yourself • Make a list of programs and courses of interest to you • Write a letter to a professor
2 **Aiming for Excellence** *page 22*	• Part time clauses with *after, when, as soon as, before,* and *until* • Simple past and present perfect • Express similarities with *so, too, either,* and *neither*	• Feelings • Work communication • Job training	• Listen to a conversation between two coworkers • Role play a conversation between a parent and a child	• Read a job evaluation form • Read notes from an interview • Read a letter requesting a raise	• Fill out a work schedule • List personal qualities on a chart • Write a persuasive letter
3 **That's Entertainment!** *page 38*	• Past perfect • Past perfect continuous	• Dating • Outings • Media	• Listen to information about a TV schedule • Listen to a dialogue about a movie • Talk about activities with surprise and sympathy • Discuss your childhood	• Read a journal about a trip • Read magazine descriptions • Read an article about a politician • Read an autobiography	• Take conversation notes • Complete a personal timeline • Write an autobiography
4 **Focus on Finance** *page 54*	• Past modals; *should (not) / must (not) + have + the past participle* • Tag questions	• Banking • Personal finances	• Give advice about money • Talk about money mistakes • Describe a problem you have had in the past • Intonation of Tag questions	• Read an online banking email message • Interpret a monthly budget • Read a credit card statement • Read an article about credit card reports • Read a letter from a hotel • Read a business letter	• Write advice about money • Write a business letter • Complete a customer survey

Correlations

Civics/ Lifeskills	Math	Critical Thinking	CASAS	SCANS	EFF Content Standards
• Recognize cultural differences • Keep a medical appointment and daily schedule	• Practice time on a schedule • Review dates and telephone numbers	• Observe mistakes • Manage daily tasks	• 0.1.4 • 0.1.5 • 0.2.1 • 0.1.6	• Acquires and evaluates information • Interprets and communicates information • Participates as a member of a team	• Read with understanding • Convey ideas in writing • Speak so others can understand • Listen actively
• Discuss job skills needed for a day care worker • Role play a conversation with a parent and day care center worker	• Calculate grade point average • Scheduling classes	• Plan for future goals • Decide how to proceed based on factual information	• **1:** 0.1.5 • **2:** 7.4.8 • **3:** 7.5.6, 0.1.4 • **4:** 7.1.2 • **5:** 1.1.8, 6.0.3, 6.0.4, 6.7.5, 7.1.1 • **6:** 0.1.3, 2.5.5, 7.4.1 • **7:** 0.1.4, 0.2.3, 4.5.5 • **8:** 4.4.5, 7.1.1, 7.1.4, 7.2.3, 7.4.7	• Interprets and communicates information • Exercises leadership • Participates as a member of a team • Organizes and maintains information • Understands systems • Applies technology to task • Selects technology • Monitors and corrects performance	• Take responsibility for learning • Plan • Cooperate with others • Use math to solve problems and communicate • Reflect and evaluate • Use information and communications technology
• Read and discuss an annual benefits review • Have an active voice to initiate improvement	• Figuring salary increases • Review an annual benefits statement • Vacation time • Retirement vesting	• Compare and contrast personal qualities • Weigh options between job benefits	• **1:** 4.4.1, 4.4.6 • **2:** 4.6.2, 7.4.8 • **3:** 0.1.4, 4.6.4, 4.7.3, 4.8.1, 7.5.6 • **4:** 4.1.7, 4.4.2, 4.6.1 • **5:** 4.2.1, 4.4.4, 6.1.1, 6.2.3, • **6:** 4.1.7, 4.8.6 • **7:** 0.1.3, 4.1.7, 4.1.9, 4.6.5, 7.2.6, 7.2.7 • **8:** 4.4.3, 4.6.2, 7.1.4, 7.4.7	• Allocates time • Acquires and evaluates information • Uses computers to process information • Applies technology to task • Organizes and maintains information • Monitors and corrects performance • Allocates money • Improves and designs systems • Exercises leadership	• Read with understanding • Observe critically • Convey ideas in writing • Reflect and evaluate • Listen actively • Solve problems and make decisions • Use math to solve problems and communicate • Advocate and influence • Take responsibility for learning
• File a security report	• Calculate sales tax • Write dates on a timeline	• Discriminate types of feelings in conversations • Reflect on a past experience	• **1:** 0.2.1, 0.2.4 • **2:** 7.2.4, 7.2.5 • **3:** 2.6.2, 2.6.3 • **4:** 0.1.5, 7.5.6, 0.1.2, 0.1.3 • **5:** 1.2.4, 6.0.5, 6.2.3, 6.5.1 • **6:** 4.8.1, 7.2.2, 7.4.1 • **7:** 0.2.3, 7.2.6, 7.4.1, 7.4.2 • **8:** 4.6.2, 7.1.4, 7.4.7,	• Interprets and communicates information • Allocates human resources • Allocates money • Organizes and maintains information • Teaches others • Monitors and corrects performance	• Speak so others can understand • Observe critically • Listen actively • Use math to solve problems and communicate • Read with understanding • Solve problems and make decisions
• Guard against fraud • Make careful choices about finances	• Calculate interest earned	• Make financial decisions based on income	• **1:** 1.3.1, 1.5.1 • **2:** 1.8.1, 1.8.2 • **3:** 1.8.5, 6.1.5, 6.4.3, 6.4.4, 6.4.5, 7.2.2, 7.3.2, 7.5.6 • **4:** 0.1.6 • **5:** 0.1.6, 1.3.2, 1.5.1, 1.5.3, 6.1.1 • **6:** 7.2.4, 7.4.1 • **7:** 1.2.5, 1.6.3, 7.2.5, 7.5.5 • **8:** 1.2.5, 7.1.4, 7.3.1, 7.3.2, 7.4.7	• Allocates money • Serves clients/customers • Negotiates • Improves and designs systems • Acquires and evaluates information • Participates as a member of a team • Exercises leadership	• Solve problems and make decisions • Use math to solve problems and communicate • Resolve conflict and negotiate • Observe critically • Reflect and evaluate • Read with understanding

Unit	Grammar Point	Vocabulary	Listening/ Speaking/ Pronunciation	Reading	Writing
5 **Law and Society** *page 70*	• Active and passive voices (simple present and simple past) • *Yes/No* and information in the passive voice	• Federal government • Community services • USA holidays • Legal terms	• Listen to information about community services • Content word stress • Role play a conversation with a partner about legal aide	• Read about branches of the government • Read a W-2 form • Read information about taxes • Read about federal holidays	• Write a list of services that are available to the public • Write personal information questions • Write about a special holiday
6 **House and Home** *page 86*	• Articles • Adjective clauses with relative pronouns as subjects • Embedded questions with *if, whether,* and other question words	• Home maintenance • Phone etiquette • Tenant rights • Rental agreement	• Talk with a partner about fixing or updating your house • Make a call to a phone company • Pronounce *a* and *an* with adjectives • Role play a problem with a caller and a radio host	• Read about tenants rights • Read an advice column about renting • Examine a rental agreement • Read a letter of request	• Write about a problem with household utilities • Write solutions to problems while listening to a radio program • Write a letter of complaint
7 **In the News** *page 102*	• Adjective clauses with relative pronouns as subjects • Adjective clauses with relative pronouns as objects	• News • Opinions • Reasons • Food safety	• Listen to the news • Linking with (*that*) • Tell your opinion to a partner • Talk about food safety • Discuss food illness experiences	• Analyze parts of a newspaper • Read a controversial article • Read a parents' news story	• Write ideas for a blog • Take notes about opinions • Write in support of an issue
8 **The World Around Us** *page 118*	• Gerunds as objects • Gerund as objects of verb + preposition	• Weather • Maps • Temperature • National disaster agencies	• Talk about the weather • Discuss weather concerns • Listen to statements about a map • Give a weather report • Link final consonant sounds with vowels	• Read a USA map • Read about national disaster agencies • Read an article about environmental issues • Read a letter from a senator	• Write about severe weather conditions • Complete a Red Cross volunteer form • Complete a chart from a TV talk show • Write a letter to a local government to assert your opinion

Correlations

Civics/Lifeskills	Math	Critical Thinking	CASAS	SCANS	EFF Content Standards
• Discuss size of workplace and management	• Calculate refunds and taxes owed	• Research a holiday on the Internet • Communicate workplace preferences through reasoning	• **1:** 5.2.1, 5.5.2, 5.5.3, 5.5.4, 5.5.8, 5.6.3 • **2:** 2.5.3, 5.6.1, 5.6.2 • **3:** 5.3.2, 5.3.6, 5.5.6 • **4:** 5.3.1, 5.3.2, 5.3.3, 5.6.3 • **5:** 5.4.1, 5.4.3, 5.4.4 • **6:** 2.7.1, 2.7.3, 7.4.5 • **7:** 2.7.1, 7.4.4, 7.4.5 • **8:** 4.1.1, 7.1.4, 7.4.7	• Exercises leadership • Monitors and corrects performance • Organizes and maintains information • Interprets and communicates information • Works with cultural diversity • Improves and designs systems	• Listen actively • Convey ideas in writing • Speak so others can understand • Take responsibility for learning • Read with understanding • Learn through research • Observe critically • Cooperate with others • Use math to solve problems and communicate • Reflect and evaluate • Use information and communications technology
• Find errors in telephone bills • Question rental options • Use email at work	• Calculate a work estimate • Use multiplication to solve money problems	• Dispute a phone bill • Advocate to solve problems	• **1:** 1.4.4, 1.7.4, 1.7.5, 2.5.1 • **2:** 1.4.4, 1.4.7, 1.7.4, 1.7.5, 8.2.6, 4.7.1, 6.4.6 • **3:** 2.1.4, 7.5.6 • **4:** 1.4.1, 1.4.3, 1.4.5 • **5:** : 1.4.5, 7.3.2, 8.2.3, 8.2.4 • **6:** 1.4.3, 7.4.4 • **7:** 5.1.6, 7.3.1 • **8:** 7.1.4, 7.4.7, 7.5.6	• Allocates human resources • Maintains and troubleshoots technology • Acquires and evaluates information • Participates as a member of a team	• Resolve conflict and negotiate • Advocate and influence • Read with understanding • Observe critically • Convey ideas in writing • Take responsibility for learning
• Listen to a food safety presentation	• Interpret a bar graph	• Locate newspaper sections • Identify opinions and reasons	• **1:** 0.1.2 • **2:** 5.3.7, 5.3.8 • **3:** 0.1.2, 7.5.6 • **4:** 1.2.5, 4.1.3 • **5:** 6.7.2 • **6:** 1.2.5, 7.4.1, 7.5.5 • **7:** 0.1.3, 0.2.3, 1.2.5 • **8:** 3.5.5, 4.3.3, 4.3.4, 7.1.4, 7.4.7	• Exercises leadership • Organizes and maintains information • Participates as a member of a team • Allocates material and facility resources • Interprets and communicates information • Acquires and evaluates information • Monitors and corrects performance	• Speak so others can understand • Convey ideas in writing • Read with understanding • Use information and communications technology • Use math to solve problems and communicate • Reflect and evaluate • Cooperate with others
• Discuss on-the-job hazards	• Convert Fahrenheit and Celsius temperature • Use multiplication and division	• Decide what to do in a weather emergency	• **1:** 2.3.3 • **2:** 1.1.3, 2.3.3, 5.7.3 • **3:** 1.1.3, 1.1.5, 6.1.2, 6.1.3, 6.1.4, 6.6.4, 6.6.7, 7.5.6 • **4:** 5.7.1, 5.7.2, 5.7.4 • **5:** 5.1.5, 2.5.2 • **6:** 5.7.1, 7.4.1 • **7:** 5.7.4, 7.5.7 • **8:** 2.5.1, 3.4.2, 7.1.4, 7.4.7	• Interprets and communicates information • Organizes and maintains information • Exercises leadership • Participates as a member of a team • Monitors and corrects performance	• Use information and communications technology • Listen actively • Convey ideas in writing • Take responsibility for learning • Reflect and evaluate • Read with understanding • Cooperate with others • Solve problems and make decisions

Correlations

Civics/Lifeskills	Math	Critical Thinking	CASAS	SCANS	EFF Content Standards
• Collaborate to solve a work problem	• Interpret statistical information • Work with percentages	• Devise a plan to start a business • Propose solutions to neighborhood problems	• **1:** 2.2.3, 2.5.4, 2.2.2 • **2:** 5.3.1 • **3:** 1.9.2, 2.2.2 • **4:** 1.9.2, 1.9.7, 7.5.1 • **5:** 2.3.1, 6.4.2, 6.8.1, • **6:** 0.1.2, 7.4.1 • **7:** 1.9.7, 1.9.8 • **8:** 7.1.4, 7.3.4, 7.4.7	• Interprets and communicates information • Negotiates • Understands systems • Selects technology • Applies technology to task • Acquires and evaluates information • Monitors and corrects performance	• Reflect and evaluate • Observe critically • Cooperate with others • Speak so others can understand • Use math to solve problems and communicate • Take responsibility for learning • Convey ideas in writing
• Read an online job advertisement • Plan for a safe environment	• Subtract decimals • Read a bar graph	• Examine job skills and qualifications • Make wise choices	• **1:** 1.4.8, 3.4.2 • **2:** 3.4.2, 6.1.2, 6.2.2, 6.7.2 • **3:** 3.4.2, 8.3.1 • **4:** 3.5.9 • **5:** 3.5.8, 3.5.9 • **6:** 3.4.1, 3.4.5, 7.4.1 • **7:** 0.1.3, 7.5.7 • **8:** 4.1.3, 4.4.2, 7.1.4, 7.4.7	• Understands systems • Interprets and communicates information • Allocates human resources • Teaches others • Exercises leadership • Improves and designs systems • Monitors and corrects performance	• Guide others • Plan • Observe critically • Advocate and influence • Read with understanding • Reflect and evaluate • Convey ideas in writing
• Role play with a partner to negotiate better benefits • Observe an interview	• Read a bar graph • Work with percentages	• Self-reflect on your strengths and weaknesses • Analyze a document for detailed information	• **1:** 4.1.2 • **2:** 4.1.3, 4.1.8 • **3:** 4.4.1, 4.1.7, 7.5.6 • **4:** 4.4.5, 4.4.7 • **5:** 4.4.3, 6.4.2, 6.7.2 • **6:** 4.1.2, 4.1.3, 4.1.5, 7.4.1 • **7:** 4.1.2, 7.5.1 • **8:** 7.1.1, 7.1.2, 7.1.4, 7.4.7	• Allocates human resources • Exercises leadership • Improves and designs systems • Monitors and corrects performance • Organizes and maintains information • Selects technology • Applies technology to task • Negotiates	• Plan • Listen actively • Reflect and evaluate • Convey ideas in writing • Advocate and influence • Cooperate with others • Guide others • Observe critically • Take responsibility for learning
• Write ideas for a city improvement plan • Write about how employees feel at work • Write notes about things you plan to change in your life • Write a paragraph with your goals for the next five years	• Use the Internet to find information • Make a list of pros and cons about two job offers	• Find problems in your community, city, or country • Compare and contrast the lives and goals of others	• **1:** 0.1.5 • **2:** 5.1.4, 5.1.6, 7.2.4, 7.2.6, 7.3.1 • **3:** 4.8.1, 5.1.4, 7.3.1, 7.3.2 • **4:** 6.8.2, 7.5.7 • **5:** 4.2.4, 6.4.2, 6.7.4, 7.4.8 • **6:** 7.1.1, 7.2.1, 7.4.1 • **7:** 7.2.3, 7.2.6, 7.4.8, 7.5.5, 7.5.7 • **8:** 7.1.4, 7.2.5, 7.4.7, 7.5.5, 7.5.7	• Exercises leadership • Interprets and communicates information • Improves and designs systems • Negotiates • Acquires and evaluates information • Allocates time • Monitors and corrects performance	• Plan • Advocate and influence • Listen actively • Use math to solve problems and communicate • Read with understanding • Convey ideas in writing • Take responsibility for learning

To The Teacher

PROGRAM OVERVIEW

> **Excellent English: Language Skills for Success** equips students with the grammar and skills they need to access community resources, while developing the foundation for long-term career and academic success.

Excellent English is a four-level, grammar-oriented series for English learners featuring a *Grammar Picture Dictionary* approach to vocabulary building and grammar acquisition. An accessible and predictable sequence of lessons in each unit systematically builds language and math skills around life-skill topics. *Excellent English* is tightly correlated to all of the major standards for adult instruction.

What has led the *Excellent English* team to develop this new series? The program responds to the large and growing need for a new generation of adult materials that provide a more academic alternative to existing publications. *Excellent English* is a natural response to the higher level aspirations of today's adult learners. Stronger reading and writing skills, greater technological proficiency, and a deeper appreciation for today's global economy—increasingly, prospective employees across virtually all industries must exhibit these skill sets to be successful. Interviews with a wide range of administrators, instructors, and students underscore the need for new materials that more quickly prepare students for the vocational and academic challenges they must meet to be successful.

The Complete Excellent English Program

- The **Student Book** features twelve 16-page units that integrate listening, speaking, reading, writing, grammar, math, and pronunciation skills with life-skill topics, critical thinking activities, and civics concepts.

- The **Student Book with Audio Highlights** provides students with audio recordings of all of the Grammar Picture Dictionary, pronunciation, and conversation models in the Student Book.

- The **Workbook with Audio CD** is an essential companion to the Student Book. It provides:
  - Supplementary practice activities correlated to the Student Book.

- Application lessons that carry vital, standards-based learning objectives through its *Family Connection*, *Community Connection*, *Career Connection*, and *Technology Connection* lessons.
- Practice tests that encourage students to assess their skills in a low-stakes environment, complete with listening tasks from the Workbook CD.

- The **Teacher's Edition with Tests** provides:
  - Step-by-step procedural notes for each Student Book activity.
  - Expansion activities for the Student Book, many of which offer creative tasks tied to the "big picture" scenes in each unit, including photocopiable worksheets.
  - Culture, Grammar, Academic, Vocabulary, and Pronunciation Notes.
  - A two-page written test for each unit.
  - Audio scripts for audio program materials.
  - Answer keys for Student Book, Workbook, and Tests.

- The **Interactive Multimedia Program** in *Excellent English* Levels 1 and 2 incorporates and extends the learning goals of the Student Book by integrating language, literacy, and numeracy skill-building with multimedia practice on the computer. A flexible set of activities correlated to each unit builds vocabulary, listening, reading, writing, and test-taking skills.

- The **Color Overhead Transparencies** encourage instructors to present new vocabulary and grammar in fun and meaningful ways. This component provides a full color overhead transparency for each "big picture" scene, as well as transparencies of the grammar charts in each unit.

- The **Big Picture PowerPoint® CD-ROM** includes the "big picture" scenes for all four Student Books. Instructors can use this CD-ROM to project the scenes from a laptop through an LCD or data projector in class.

- The **Audio CDs** and **Audiocassettes** contain recordings for all listening activities in the Student Book. Listening passages for the unit tests are provided on a separate Assessment CD or cassette.

- The **EZ Test® CD-ROM Test Generator** provides a databank of assessment items from which instructors can create customized tests within minutes. The EZ Test assessment materials are also available online at www.eztestonline.com.

Student Book Overview

Consult the *Welcome to Excellent English* guide on pages xiv-xix. This guide offers instructors and administrators a visual tour of one Student Book unit.

Excellent English is designed to maximize accessibility and flexibility. Each unit in Levels 3 and 4 contain the following sequence of eight, two-page lessons that develop vocabulary and build language, grammar, and math skills around life-skill topics:

- Lesson 1: Grammar and Vocabulary (1)
- Lesson 2: Grammar Practice Plus
- Lesson 3: Listening and Conversation
- Lesson 4: Grammar and Vocabulary (2)
- Lesson 5: Grammar Practice Plus
- Lesson 6: Reading
- Lesson 7: Writing
- Lesson 8: Career Connection and Check Your Progress

Each lesson in *Excellent English* is designed as a two-page spread. Lessons 1 and 4 introduce new grammar points and vocabulary sets that allow students to practice the grammar in controlled and meaningful ways. Lessons 2 and 5—the Grammar Practice Plus lessons—provide more opened-ended opportunities for students to use their new language productively. Lesson 3 allows students to hear a variety of listening inputs and to use their new language skills in conversation. In Lessons 6 and 7, students develop the more academic skills of reading and writing through explicit teaching of academic strategies and through exposure to multiple text types and writing tasks. Each unit ends with Lesson 8, an exciting capstone that offers both Career Connection—a career-oriented lesson that presents a variety of workplace situations and provides language-oriented problem-solving tasks—and Check Your Progress—a self-evaluation task. Each lesson addresses a key adult standard, and these standards are indicated in the scope and sequence and in the footer at the bottom of the left-hand page in each lesson.

SPECIAL FEATURES IN EACH STUDENT BOOK UNIT

- **Grammar Picture Dictionary**. Lessons 1 and 4 introduce students to vocabulary and grammar through a picture dictionary approach. This context-rich approach allows students to acquire grammatical structures as they build vocabulary.

- **Grammar Charts**. Also in Lessons 1 and 4, new grammar points are presented in clear paradigms, providing easy reference for students and instructors.

- **"Grammar Professor" Notes**. Additional information related to key grammar points is provided at point of use through the "Grammar Professor" feature. A cheerful, red-haired character appears next to each of these additional grammar points, calling students' attention to learning points in an inviting and memorable way.

- **Math**. Learning basic math skills is critically important for success in school, on the job, and at home. As such, national and state standards for adult education mandate instruction in basic math skills. In each unit, a Math box is dedicated to helping students develop the functional numeracy and language skills they need for success with basic math.

- **Pronunciation**. This special feature has two major goals: (1) to help students hear and produce specific sounds, words, and phrases so they become better listeners and speakers; and (2) to address issues of stress, rhythm, and intonation so that students' spoken English becomes more comprehensible.

- ***What about you?*** Throughout each unit of the Student Book, students are encouraged to apply new language to their own lives through personalization activities.

- **"Big Picture" scenes**. Lesson 2 in each unit introduces a "big picture" scene. This scene serves as a springboard to a variety of activities provided in the Student Book, Teacher's Edition, Color Overhead Transparencies package and the Big Picture PowerPoint CD-ROM. In the Student Book, the "big picture" scene features key vocabulary and serves as a prompt for language activities that practice the grammar points of the unit. The scene features characters with distinct personalities for students to enjoy, respond to, and talk about.

CIVICS CONCEPTS

Many institutions focus direct attention on the importance of civics instruction for English language learners. Civics instruction encourages students to become active and informed community members. The Teacher's Edition includes multiple *Community Connection* activities in each unit. These activities encourage learners to become more active and informed members of their communities.

ACADEMIC SKILL DEVELOPMENT

Many adult programs recognize the need to help students develop important academic skills that will facilitate lifelong learning. The *Excellent English* Student Book addresses this need through explicit teaching of reading and writing strategies, explicit presentation and practice of grammar, and academic notes in the Teacher's Edition. The Teacher's Edition also includes multiple *Academic Connection* activities in each unit. These activities encourage learners to become more successful in an academic environment.

CASAS, SCANS, EFF, AND OTHER STANDARDS

Instructors and administrators benchmark student progress against national and/or state standards for adult instruction. With this in mind, *Excellent English* carefully integrates instructional elements from a wide range of standards including CASAS, SCANS, EFF, TABE CLAS-E, the Florida Adult ESOL Syllabi, and the Los Angeles Unified School District Course Outlines. Unit-by-unit correlations of some of these standards appear in the Student Book scope and sequence on pages iv-ix. Other correlations appear in the Teacher's Edition. Here is a brief overview of our approach to meeting the key national and state standards:

- **CASAS.** Many U.S. states, including California, tie funding for adult education programs to student performance on the Comprehensive Adult Student Assessment System (CASAS). The CASAS (www.casas.org) competencies identify more than 30 essential skills that adults need in order to succeed in the classroom, workplace, and community. *Excellent English* comprehensively integrates all of the CASAS Life Skill Competencies throughout the four levels of the series.

- **SCANS.** Developed by the United States Department of Labor, SCANS is an acronym for the Secretary's Commission on Achieving Necessary Skills (wdr.doleta.gov/SCANS/). SCANS competencies are workplace skills that help people compete more effectively in today's global economy. A variety of SCANS competencies is threaded throughout the activities in each unit of *Excellent English*.

The incorporation of these competencies recognizes both the intrinsic importance of teaching workplace skills and the fact that many adult students are already working members of their communities.

- **EFF.** Equipped for the Future (EFF) is a set of standards for adult literacy and lifelong learning, developed by The National Institute for Literacy (www.nifl.gov). The organizing principle of EFF is that adults assume responsibilities in three major areas of life – as workers, as parents, and as citizens. These three areas of focus are called "role maps" in the EFF documentation. Each *Excellent English* unit addresses all three of the EFF role maps in the Student Book or Workbook.

- **Florida Adult ESOL Syllabi** provide the curriculum frameworks for all six levels of instruction; Foundations, Low Beginning, High Beginning, Low Intermediate, High Intermediate, and Advanced. The syllabi were developed by the State of Florida as a guide to include the following areas of adult literacy standards: workplace, communication (listen, speak, read, and write), technology, interpersonal communication, health and nutrition, government and community resources, consumer education, family and parenting, concepts of time and money, safety and security, and language development (grammar and pronunciation). *Excellent English* Level 3 incorporates into its instruction the vast majority of standards at the Low Intermediate level.

- **TABE Complete Language Assessment System— English (CLAS-E)** has been developed by CTB/McGraw-Hill and provides administrators and teachers with accurate, reliable evaluations of adult students' English language skills. TABE CLAS-E measures students' reading, listening, writing, and speaking skills at all English proficiency levels and also assesses critically important grammar standards. TABE CLAS-E scores are linked to TABE 9 and 10, providing a battery of assessment tools that offer seamless transition from English language to adult basic education assessment.

- **Los Angeles Unified School District (LAUSD) Course Outlines**. LAUSD Competency-Based Education (CBE) Course Outlines were developed to guide teachers in lesson planning and to inform students about what they will be able to do after successful completion of their course. The CBE Course outlines focus on acquiring skills in listening, speaking, reading and writing in the context of everyday life. *Excellent English* addresses all four language skills in the contexts of home, community and work, appropriately targeting Intermediate Low adult ESL students.

TECHNOLOGY

Technology plays an increasingly important role in our lives as students, workers, family members, and citizens. Every unit in the Workbook includes a one-page lesson titled *Technology Connection* that focuses on some aspect of technology in our everyday lives.

The EZ Test® CD-ROM Test Generator—and its online version, available at www.eztestonline.com—allow instructors to easily create customized tests from a digital databank of assessment items.

NUMBER OF HOURS OF INSTRUCTION

The *Excellent English* program has been designed to accommodate the needs of adult classes with 100–180 hours of classroom instruction. Here are three recommended ways in which various components in the *Excellent English* program can be combined to meet student and instructor needs.

- **80–100 hours**. Instructors are encouraged to work through all of the Student Book materials. The Color Overhead Transparencies can be used to introduce and/or review materials in each unit. Instructors should also look to the Teacher's Edition for teaching suggestions and testing materials as necessary. *Time per unit: 8–10 hours.*

- **100–140 hours**. In addition to working through all of the Student Book materials, instructors are encouraged to incorporate the Workbook activities for supplementary practice. *Time per unit: 10–14 hours.*

- **140–180 hours**. Instructors and students working in an intensive instructional setting can take advantage of the wealth of expansion activities threaded through the Teacher's Edition to supplement the Student Book, and Workbook. *Time per unit: 14–18 hours.*

ASSESSMENT

The *Excellent English* program offers instructors, students, and administrators the following wealth of resources for monitoring and assessing student progress and achievement:

- **Standardized testing formats.** *Excellent English* is comprehensively correlated to the CASAS competencies and all of the other major national and state standards for adult learning. Students have the opportunity to practice answering CASAS-style listening questions in Lessons 3 of each Student Book unit, and both listening and reading questions in the Unit tests in the Teacher's Edition and practice tests in the Workbook. Students practice with the same items types and bubble-in answer sheets they encounter on CASAS and other standardized tests.

- **Achievement tests.** The *Excellent English* Teacher's Edition includes paper-and-pencil end-of-unit tests. In addition, the *EZ Test® CD-ROM Test Generator* provides a databank of assessment items from which instructors can create customized tests within minutes. The EZ Test assessment materials are also available online at www.eztestonline.com. These tests help students demonstrate how well they have learned the instructional content of the unit. Adult learners often show incremental increases in learning that are not always measured on the standardized tests. The achievement tests may demonstrate learning even in a short amount of instructional time. Twenty percent of each test includes questions that encourage students to apply more academic skills such as determining meaning from context, making inferences, and understanding main ideas. Practice with these question types will help prepare students who may want to enroll in academic classes.

- **Performance-based assessment.** *Excellent English* provides several ways to measure students' performance on productive tasks, including the Writing tasks in Lesson 7 of each Student Book unit. In addition, the Teacher's Edition suggests writing and speaking prompts that instructors can use for performance-based assessment.

- **Portfolio assessment.** A portfolio is a collection of student work that can be used to show progress. Examples of work that the instructor or the student may submit in the portfolio include writing samples, speaking rubrics, audiotapes, videotapes, or projects.

- **Self-assessment.** Self-assessment is an important part of the overall assessment picture, as it promotes student involvement and commitment to the learning process. When encouraged to assess themselves, students take more control of their learning and are better able to connect the instructional content with their own goals. The Student Book includes Check Your Progress activities at the end of each unit, which allow students to assess their knowledge of vocabulary and grammar. Students can chart their mastery of the key language lessons in the unit, and use this information to set new learning goals.

Welcome to Excellent English!

A **Grammar Professor** calls students' attention to additional grammar points in an inviting and memorable way.

Grammar Picture Dictionary uses engaging illustrations to showcase target grammar and vocabulary.

Clear and thorough **grammar charts** make target grammar points accessible and easily comprehensible.

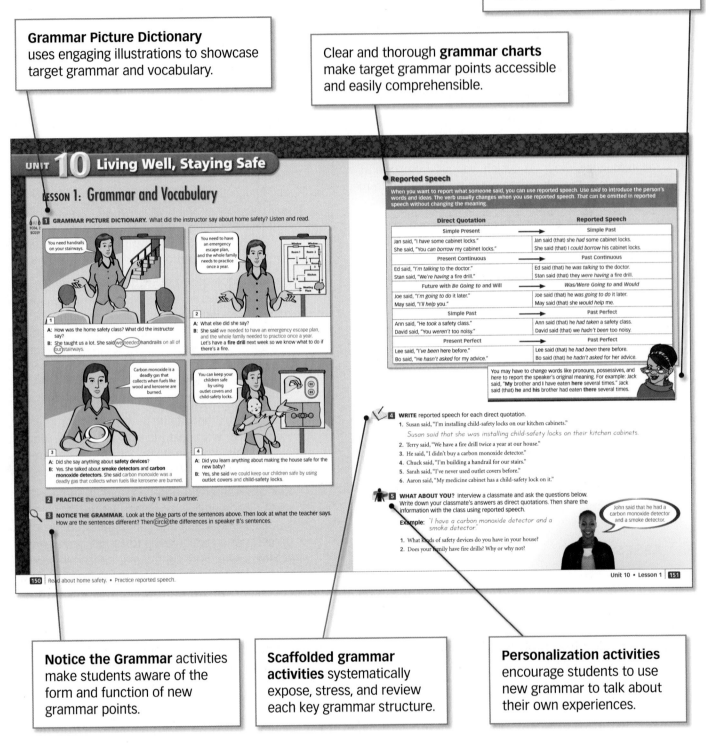

Notice the Grammar activities make students aware of the form and function of new grammar points.

Scaffolded grammar activities systematically expose, stress, and review each key grammar structure.

Personalization activities encourage students to use new grammar to talk about their own experiences.

Grammar Practice Plus lessons introduce additional vocabulary while recycling and practicing the target grammar.

Notebook Writing Activities encourage students to write more freely.

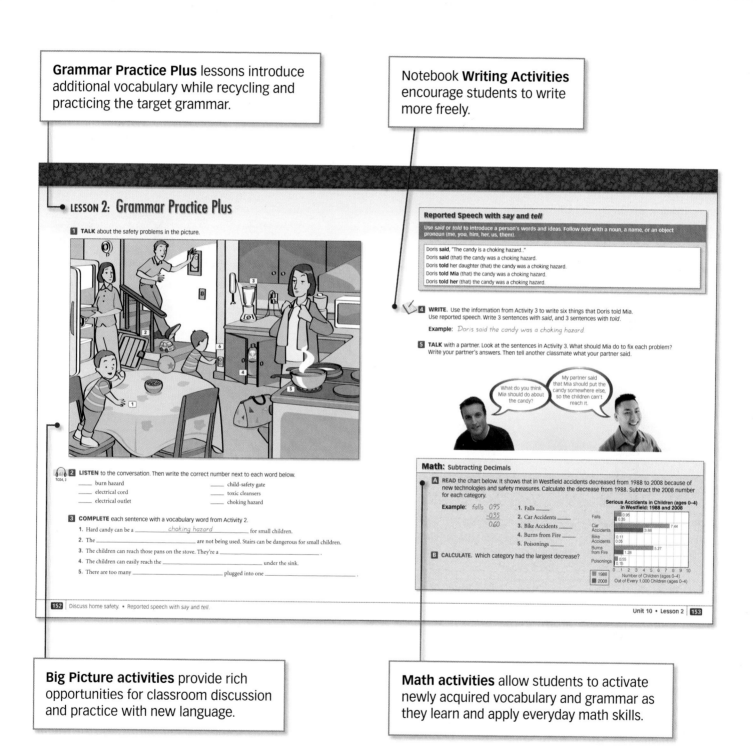

LESSON 2: Grammar Practice Plus

1 TALK about the safety problems in the picture.

2 LISTEN to the conversation. Then write the correct number next to each word below.

_____ burn hazard

_____ electrical cord

_____ electrical outlet

_____ child-safety gate

_____ toxic cleansers

_____ choking hazard

3 COMPLETE each sentence with a vocabulary word from Activity 2.

1. Hard candy can be a _____ choking hazard _____ for small children.

2. The _____ are not being used. Stairs can be dangerous for small children.

3. The children can reach those pans on the stove. They're a _____ .

4. The children can easily reach the _____ under the sink.

5. There are too many _____ plugged into one _____ .

Reported Speech with say and tell

Use *said* or *told* to introduce a person's words and ideas. Follow *told* with a noun, a name, or an object pronoun (me, you, him, her, us, them).

Doris **said**, "The candy is a choking hazard.."
Doris **said** (that) the candy was a choking hazard.
Doris **told** her daughter (that) the candy was a choking hazard.
Doris **told Mia** (that) the candy was a choking hazard.
Doris **told her** (that) the candy was a choking hazard.

4 WRITE. Use the information from Activity 3 to write six things that Doris told Mia. Use reported speech. Write 3 sentences with *said*, and 3 sentences with *told*.

Example: *Doris said the candy was a choking hazard.*

5 TALK with a partner. Look at the sentences in Activity 3. What should Mia do to fix each problem? Write your partner's answers. Then tell another classmate what your partner said.

What do you think Mia should do about the candy?

My partner said that Mia should put the candy somewhere else, so the children can't reach it.

Math: Subtracting Decimals

A READ the chart below. It shows that in Westfield accidents decreased from 1988 to 2008 because of new technologies and safety measures. Calculate the decrease from 1988. Subtract the 2008 number for each category.

Example: falls 0.95
−0.35
0.60

1. Falls _____
2. Car Accidents _____
3. Bike Accidents _____
4. Burns from Fire _____
5. Poisonings _____

B CALCULATE. Which category had the largest decrease?

Serious Accidents in Children (ages 0–4) in Westfield: 1988 and 2008

Falls 0.95 / 0.35
Car Accidents 7.44 / 3.88
Bike Accidents 0.11 / 0.05
Burns from Fire 5.27 / 1.28
Poisonings 0.55 / 0.15

0 1 2 3 4 5 6 7 8 9 10
Number of Children (ages 0–4)
Out of Every 1,000 Children (ages 0–4)

■ 1988
■ 2008

Big Picture activities provide rich opportunities for classroom discussion and practice with new language.

Math activities allow students to activate newly acquired vocabulary and grammar as they learn and apply everyday math skills.

Listening comprehension activities provide students with opportunities to build practical listening skills.

Life skills-based listening activities integrate grammar and vocabulary to provide students with models of everyday conversation.

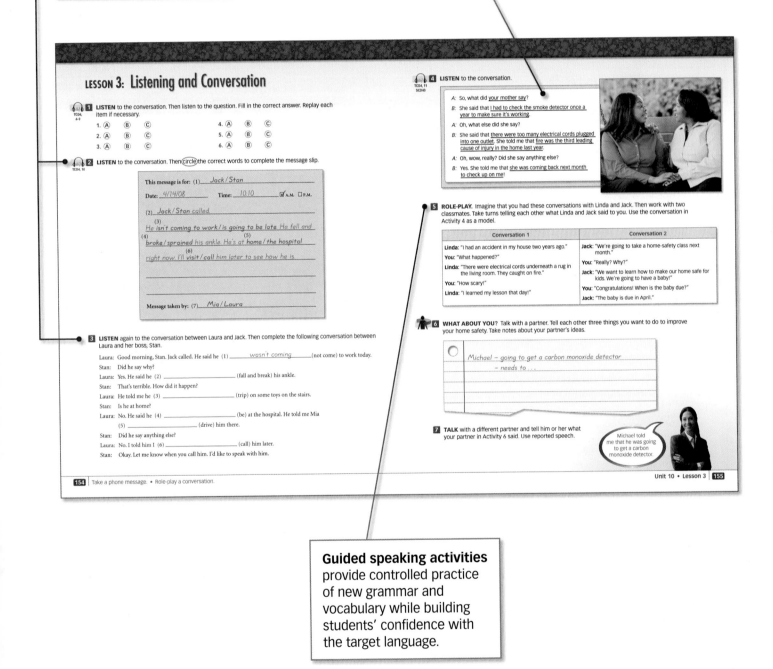

LESSON 3: Listening and Conversation

1 **LISTEN** to the conversation. Then listen to the question. Fill in the correct answer. Replay each item if necessary.

TCD4, 4–9

1. Ⓐ Ⓑ Ⓒ   4. Ⓐ Ⓑ Ⓒ
2. Ⓐ Ⓑ Ⓒ   5. Ⓐ Ⓑ Ⓒ
3. Ⓐ Ⓑ Ⓒ   6. Ⓐ Ⓑ Ⓒ

2 **LISTEN** to the conversation. Then circle the correct words to complete the message slip.

TCD4, 10

This message is for: (1) __Jack / Stan__

Date: __4/14/08__   Time: __10:10__   ☑ A.M. ☐ P.M.

(2) __Jack / Stan called.__

(3)
He isn't coming to work / is going to be late He fell and
(4)   (5)
broke / sprained his ankle. He's at home / the hospital
(6)
right now. I'll visit / call him later to see how he is.

_____

_____

Message taken by: (7) __Mia / Laura__

3 **LISTEN** again to the conversation between Laura and Jack. Then complete the following conversation between Laura and her boss, Stan.

Laura: Good morning, Stan. Jack called. He said he (1) ___wasn't coming___ (not come) to work today.
Stan: Did he say why?
Laura: Yes. He said he (2) _____ (fall and break) his ankle.
Stan: That's terrible. How did it happen?
Laura: He told me he (3) _____ (trip) on some toys on the stairs.
Stan: Is he at home?
Laura: No. He said he (4) _____ (be) at the hospital. He told me Mia
        (5) _____ (drive) him there.
Stan: Did he say anything else?
Laura: No. I told him I (6) _____ (call) him later.
Stan: Okay. Let me know when you call him. I'd like to speak with him.

154 Take a phone message. • Role-play a conversation.

4 **LISTEN** to the conversation.

TCD4, 11
SCD40

A: So, what did your mother say?
B: She said that I had to check the smoke detector once a year to make sure it's working.
A: Oh, what else did she say?
B: She said that there were too many electrical cords plugged into one outlet. She told me that fire was the third leading cause of injury in the home last year.
A: Oh, wow, really? Did she say anything else?
B: Yes. She told me that she was coming back next month to check up on me!

5 **ROLE-PLAY.** Imagine that you had these conversations with Linda and Jack. Then work with two classmates. Take turns telling each other what Linda and Jack said to you. Use the conversation in Activity 4 as a model.

Conversation 1	Conversation 2
Linda: "I had an accident in my house two years ago." **You:** "What happened?" **Linda:** "There were electrical cords underneath a rug in the living room. They caught on fire." **You:** "How scary!" **Linda:** "I learned my lesson that day!"	**Jack:** "We're going to take a home-safety class next month." **You:** "Really? Why?" **Jack:** "We want to learn how to make our home safe for kids. We're going to have a baby!" **You:** "Congratulations! When is the baby due?" **Jack:** "The baby is due in April."

6 **WHAT ABOUT YOU?** Talk with a partner. Tell each other three things you want to do to improve your home safety. Take notes about your partner's ideas.

Michael – going to get a carbon monoxide detector
– needs to . . .

7 **TALK** with a different partner and tell him or her what your partner in Activity 6 said. Use reported speech.

Michael told me that he was going to get a carbon monoxide detector.

Unit 10 • Lesson 3 155

Guided speaking activities provide controlled practice of new grammar and vocabulary while building students' confidence with the target language.

Pre-reading tasks activate prior knowledge and introduce the reading passage.

LESSON 6: Reading

1 THINK ABOUT IT. When your doctor gives you a new medication, what questions do you ask him or her? Write your ideas here.

1. _____
2. _____
3. _____

Reading Strategy Summary

| Preview the text. |
| Make inferences. |
| **Use context to guess the meaning of new words.** |

2 BEFORE YOU READ. Preview the advertisement. Look at the picture and the different parts of the advertisement. What product is advertised?

3 READ the advertisement on the next page. Did you correctly guess what the advertisement is about?

4 AFTER YOU READ.

A. ANSWER the questions with a partner.

1. What is the name of the medication in the advertisement?
2. What is the medication for?
3. Why did the man go to see his physician?
4. What advice did the physician give to the man?
5. How often should a person take this medication?
6. What are some possible side effects of this medication?
7. What might happen if someone has an allergic reaction to Fumenol?

B. REREAD the advertisement and underline any words you do not know. With a partner, choose five words from the advertisement. Write them below, and use the context to guess the meaning of each word. Write your guesses below. Then use a dictionary to look up the word and find out if you were correct.

READING FOCUS: Use context to guess the meaning of new words

When you don't know the meaning of a word, read the complete sentence with the word in it, and one or two sentences before and after it. Then try to guess the meaning.

1. _____
2. _____
3. _____
4. _____
5. _____

" I was only 43—I didn't want to die! I decided to make a change . . . with *Fumenol*. "

When I was in my 20s, I used to eat whatever I wanted. I used to smoke a lot, too. I didn't worry about my health at all.

But then when I was 43, I had a heart attack. My physician said that I had to change my lifestyle*. He wanted me to give up fatty foods, alcohol, and cigarettes. I took some time to think over what he had said. I was only 43—I didn't want to die! I decided to make a change.

The first thing I wanted to do was to find out about ways to quit smoking. I was used to smoking about two packs a day. I had tried a dozen* different programs to quit smoking, but I could never follow through with them.

I asked my physician what to do. He said that I should try this new drug, Fumenol. My doctor's advice* has really paid off for me. Fumenol helped me stop smoking in just three weeks. Maybe it can help you, too.

Don't let your life slip away from you. Find out about *Fumenol,* **and stop smoking today.**

WARNING: If you experience chest pain when taking Fumenol, call your physician immediately.
HOW TO USE: Take Fumenol three times each day. Take with meals and a full glass of water to prevent nausea.
SIDE EFFECTS: Some patients experience nausea*, dizziness*, or tiredness when they begin taking Fumenol. If these symptoms last longer than three days, contact your physician.
PRECAUTIONS: Fumenol should not be taken by people who have chronic* liver or kidney problems. Some users experience an allergic reaction to this drug. Symptoms include: rash*, itching, swelling*, and shortness of breath*. If you experience an allergic reaction to this drug, seek medical help immediately.

lifestyle (n.): the way that a person lives
dozen (n.): twelve
advice (n.): an idea or ideas to help make something better
nausea (n.): a feeling of sickness in the stomach
dizziness (n.): a spinning feeling in the head

chronic (adj.): lasting a long time
rash (n.): a red or bumpy area on the body
swelling (n.): area of the body that becomes bigger
shortness of breath (n.): difficulty breathing

Reading comprehension activities allow students to exercise their understanding of new content and grammar.

Reading Focus boxes help students develop the reading strategies necessary for career and academic success.

Reading passages provide students with community- or school-based texts they will encounter in daily life.

Students write a **variety of text types** such as accident reports, applications, letters, and essays.

Writing Focus boxes help students develop critical academic skills.

LESSON 7: Writing

1 WARM UP. Every January, people make New Year's resolutions, or promises to themselves. These promises are often about a healthier lifestyle. Have you ever made a New Year's resolution about your health? What was it?

2 BEFORE YOU WRITE

A. **THINK** about health habits that people often want to change. Make notes about ways that people can improve their health.

THINGS TO CHANGE OR STOP	THINGS TO DO MORE
stop smoking	eat more fruit

B. **WRITE.** Imagine that a friend (or family member) wants to live a healthier lifestyle. He or she asks for your advice. Write your ideas in the chart. Give several suggestions.

What change should your friend make?	Why should he or she make this change?	How can he or she make this change?
You should eat more fruit.	Fruit has vitamins that the body needs.	You should eat an apple instead of potato chips.

C. **READ** the New Year's resolution that Victor wrote. Underline the sentences that answer these questions:
- What?   - Why?   - How?

This year, I must exercise more. I can't do all the things I used to do. I used to lift weights, but now I can hardly pick up my son. I used to have lots of energy, but now I'm tired all the time. I have to make a fitness plan and follow through with it. My doctor said that I should sign up for the gym. I'll have to find out how much a gym membership costs and pick up an application. Then I'll talk it over with my friend Ray. If he signs up, too. I won't give up so easily. It's easier to work out when you do it with a friend.

3 WRITE three New Year's resolutions about your own health. Follow the steps below.

1. In the first column, write about health habits that you want to improve or change. Begin your sentence with I must / I should / I have to.
2. In the second column, give reasons about why you should change each health habit.
3. In the final column, tell what you can do to make each change happen.
4. When you have finished the chart, write a paragraph for each resolution.

> **WRITING FOCUS: Identify problems and solutions**
>
> One way to organize writing is by presenting problems and solutions. First, tell *what* the problem is and explain *why* it is a problem. Then tell *how* to fix the problem. That is the solution.

What to change/improve	Why change/improve	How to change/improve
Resolution 1		
Resolution 2		
Resolution 3		

4 AFTER YOU WRITE

A. **EDIT** your paragraphs. Ask yourself these questions.
1. Are the problem and solution stated clearly?
2. Is there any information that is not about the topic?
3. Is the information in the right order?
4. Do I need to add any information?
5. Is the punctuation correct? Check commas, apostrophes, and periods.
6. Did you use phrasal verbs? If so, are they correct?
7. Did you use reported speech? If so, is it correct?

B. **REWRITE** your paragraphs with corrections.

C. **DISCUSS** your work with a partner. Read each other's resolutions. Then ask and answer questions about each other's ideas.

A series of **highly-scaffolded tasks** culminates in an academic or practical writing task.

Editing and **revising activities** encourage students to be more effective and accurate writers.

The **Career Connection** develops students' problem-solving skills in a variety of workplace situations.

Check Your Progress ensures student comprehension and retention of each unit's target grammar and vocabulary.

Career Connection

1 THINK ABOUT IT. What kinds of things do nurses do at a hospital? What kinds of skills do you think a nurse has that can transfer to other departments in a hospital or private doctor's office?

2 READ this online job advertisement and application form. Nina is applying for a case manager's position at Children's Hospital. As you read, match the numbered words to the correct definition.

CASE MANAGER, Children's Hospital.
Description: Coordinates patient care from admission to (1)**discharge**. Acts as a (2)**liaison** between patient's family and medical team.

Requirements: Registered Nurse (RN) with 3+ years of case management experience. Administrative experience required. Experience preferred in the following clinical areas: (3)**Intensive** Care/Critical Care Unit; Emergency/(4) **Trauma**; Pediatric Care.

APPLICATION FORM
NAME: Nina Escobar
Describe your nursing experience.

I was an RN for 4 years at University Hospital, where I worked in the following departments: Cardiology, Pediatrics, Pediatrics Intensive Care Unit, Respiratory Acute Care Unit.

Describe your previous case management experience.

I worked as a case manager for 3 years at City Hospital, where I served as a patient liaison in the Pediatrics Department. In that position, I helped families fill out insurance paperwork, and I followed up on patient complaints. Often, the families wanted to talk over their options with me. This was the most (5)**rewarding** part of the job—I like helping people during difficult times.

What skills and qualities make you a good candidate for this position?

My manager at City Hospital said that I was the person she counted on most in times of crisis. She trusted me to make important decisions on my own, when needed. I am used to working independently and I am able to make decisions quickly. These are the strengths that I can offer Children's Hospital.

___ A. a wound or shock to the body caused suddenly
___ B. release from the hospital
___ C. someone who helps with communication between two people or groups
___ D. serious, extreme
___ E. satisfying, bringing happiness for something a person has done

3 WRITE. Compare three things from Nina's experience and qualifications to the job description in the advertisement. Do you think Nina's qualifications match those asked for in the job description?

Nina's Experience	Job Description
Nina wrote that she had 3 years of case management experience.	The ad stated that it required 3 or more years of case management experience.

4 ROLE-PLAY a scene between Nina and the hiring supervisor at Children's Hospital. Interview Nina. Ask her how her qualifications will transfer to this job.
Supervisor: Nina, tell me about your work as a case manager.
Nina: I worked for 3 years as a patient liaison in the Pediatrics Department at City Hospital. I helped explain medical options to the children's parents.

5 WHAT ABOUT YOU? What skills do you have from your previous experience or from your educational background that could transfer easily to a job you would like to have? Talk with a partner.

Check Your Progress!

Skill	Circle the answers.	Is it correct?
A. Use reported speech.	1. Ann: "I have some." Ann said she **had** / **have** some. 2. Joe: "I didn't see you." Joe said he **hadn't seen** / **didn't see** me. 3. Ed: "I'm waiting for Sue." Ed said **he** / **I** was waiting for Sue. 4. Kim: "We're going to your house." Kim said they were going to **her** / **my** house.	☐ ☐ ☐ ☐
	Number Correct	0 1 2 3 4
B. Use phrasal verbs.	5. Did they talk **into you** / **you into** buying expensive equipment? 6. The number was easy to find. We looked **it up** / **up it** online. 7. Let's start **over the exercises** / **the exercises over**. I'm not tired yet. 8. I can count **her on** / **on her** to be on time.	☐ ☐ ☐ ☐
	Number Correct	0 1 2 3 4
C. Talk about safety.	9. Hold onto the **locks** / **handrails** when you walk down the stairs. 10. **Outlet covers** / **cabinet locks** protect kids from getting shocked. 11. Carbon monoxide is a deadly **gas** / **smoke**. 12. We have a baby, so we need new safety **devices** / **detectors**.	☐ ☐ ☐ ☐
	Number Correct	0 1 2 3 4
D. Talk about health.	13. I found out **about** / **on** a yoga class that I want to take. 14. Ken signed **in** / **up** for an exercise class that starts next week. 15. That class really paid **out** / **off**. I've lost 10 pounds already. 16. You should **follow through with** / **look forward to** your exercise plan if you want to lose weight.	☐ ☐ ☐ ☐
	Number Correct	0 1 2 3 4

COUNT the number of correct answers above. Fill in the bubbles.

Chart Your Success

Skill	Need Practice	Okay	Good	Very Good	Excellent!
A. Use reported speech.	⓪	①	②	③	④
B. Use phrasal verbs.	⓪	①	②	③	④
C. Talk about safety.	⓪	①	②	③	④
D. Talk about health.	⓪	①	②	③	④

Language in the Classroom

TCD1, 2 **1** **LISTEN.** Complete the sentences with the words below.

| Korea | Peru | Russia | for her job | to go to community college | to take an exam |

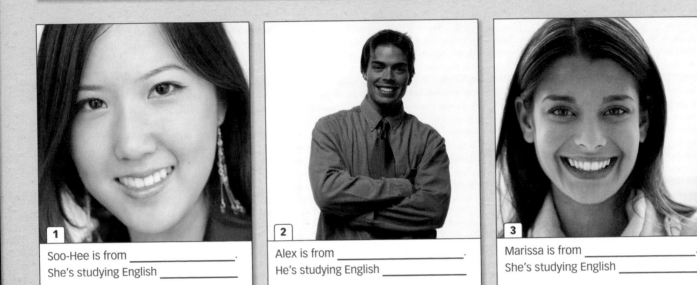

1
Soo-Hee is from _____.
She's studying English _____
_____

2
Alex is from _____.
He's studying English _____
_____

3
Marissa is from _____.
She's studying English _____
_____

TCD1, 3 **2** **LISTEN** and read.

Jose: Hi. I'm <u>Jose</u>. Are you a new student?

Anna: Yes, I am. My name is <u>Anna</u>. Nice to meet you.

Jose: Nice to meet you, too.

Anna: Where are you from?

Jose: I'm from <u>Colombia</u>.

Anna: Oh. Why are you studying English?

Jose: I <u>need it for my job</u>. How about you?

Anna: I <u>want to study at the community college next year</u>.

Jose: Great. You'll like it here. It's a great class.

TCD1, 4 **3** **LISTEN** again and repeat. Then practice the conversation with a partner.

4 **TALK.** Introduce your partner to other students in your class.

His name is Manuel. He's from Mexico.

Her name is Kasia. She's from Poland.

Get to know your classmates. • Make introductions. • Practice classroom language.

5 COMPLETE the classroom conversations with the words below.

Actually	you	Should	No	Yes
right	think	I'll	answer	understand

1. *A:* I _____ the answer is *B*.

   B: _____, I think you're _____.

2. *A:* I think the _____ is *True*. How about _____?

   B: _____, I think it's *False*.

3. *A:* _____ I be Student A?

   B: Sure. Then _____ be Student B.

4. *A:* Do you _____ what this means?

   B: _____, not exactly.

6 LISTEN and read the conversations. They show four things you can do in class to help you learn. Pay attention to the <u>underlined</u> expressions.

TCD1, 5

1. Repeat to check understanding

Teacher: Please write your answers in full sentences.

Student: <u>Write in full sentences?</u>

Teacher: Yes.

2. Say when you don't understand

Teacher: I want you to work in pairs.

Student: <u>I'm sorry. I didn't understand that.</u>

Teacher: Oh. I'd like you to work with another student—with a partner.

3. Ask to hear something again

Teacher: Please turn to page 48.

Student: <u>Excuse me. Could you repeat that, please?</u>

Teacher: I said turn to page 48.

4. Ask for spelling

Teacher: <u>Could you spell that, please?</u>

Student: It's M-A-R-T-I-N-E-Z.

7 LISTEN again and repeat the classroom expressions.

TCD1, 6

8 WHAT ABOUT YOU? Work with a partner. Take turns asking and answering these questions. Practice using the <u>underlined</u> expressions in Activity 6.

1. What's your name?
2. Where are you from?
3. Is this your first time here?
4. Why are you studying English?

Grammar Review

1 **COMPLETE** each question. Write the missing words.

1. What time _does he wake up every day_____?
   He wakes up at 6:30 every day.

2. Where _____?
   They're taking the class at Central College.

3. When _____?
   We're going to pick her up after work.

4. How many _____?
   She ate three pieces of pizza last night.

5. What _____?
   I was taking a shower when the phone rang.

6. _____ to Australia?
   No, I've never been to Australia.

7. How long _____?
   I've been studying English for three years.

8. What _____ if he gets the job?
   If he gets the job, he'll move to another apartment.

2 **WRITE** a different answer for each question in Activity 1. Write in your notebook.

1. _He wakes up at 7:00 on weekdays, and 8:30 on weekends._

3 **READ** the paragraph. Correct the mistake in each sentence.

name's
(1) My ~~names~~ Luis Delgado. (2) I've been study English for a year and a half.

(3) I really likes the classes here. (4) I want to take computer classes at Lincoln

community College next year. (5) I'm looking forward to a grate class!

4 **MATCH** each sentence in Activity 3 with the mistake below.

a. _____ spelling
b. __1__ punctuation
c. _____ verb form
d. _____ subject-verb agreement
e. _____ capitalization

5 **WRITE** a paragraph about yourself in your notebook. Use the paragraph in Activity 3 as a model.

Managing Your Time

1 **READ** Alfonso's schedule and his medical appointment notice below. Then answer the questions.

Wednesday, May 15		
7	00	
	30	
8	00	
	30	
9	00	
	30	Work
10	00	
	30	
11	00	
	30	
12	00	
	30	
1	00	
	30	
2	00	
	30	
3	00	
	30	
4	00	Dr. Stevenson
	30	
5	00	pick up kids at daycare
	30	(tuition due: $600)
6	00	
	30	
7	00	English class
	30	
8	00	
	30	
9	00	
	30	

1. What time does Alfonso work today?

   _____

2. What time does he have English class today?

   _____

3. What else is Alfonso doing today?

   _____

   _____

4. What things does Alfonso need to take with him when he leaves his house today? Circle all that apply:

car keys	insurance card	checkbook
ATM card	dinner	textbook

5. Can he go to the gym today? When?

   _____

2 **TALK** to a partner. Check your answers.

Health Partners Clinic

APPOINTMENT NOTICE

This is to confirm your appointment

WEDNESDAY   MAY 15

3:45 p.m.

DR. MARCIA STEVENSON

Please come to the 5th floor of the Main Pavilion at least 15 minutes before your appointment. If you have any questions or need to change your appointment, call us at (619) 555-2022.

Please don't forget your insurance card and co-payment, if any.

---

3 **WRITE** a paragraph about Alfonso's schedule today. Write in your notebook.

Alfonso is very busy today. First, he has to work from 8 a.m. to 2:30 p.m.

4 **WHAT ABOUT YOU?** Read the questions below. Then ask and answer the questions with a partner.

1. What's your daily schedule?
2. What do you do to remember important appointments?
3. Have you ever missed an important appointment? What did you do?

LESSON 1: Grammar and Vocabulary

TCD1, 7
SCD2

1 GRAMMAR PICTURE DICTIONARY. What are the people doing at this school? Listen and read.

1
Erika **is researching** an **online course** this semester. She needs flexibility with her schedule.

2
Tina is **submitting** her application to the **admissions office**. The admissions office accepts online applications, too.

3
Carrie is applying for financial aid. Her salary doesn't **cover** all of her school expenses.

4
Sam is taking history this term. The course **is a requirement** for his major.

5
Rick and James are taking a **continuing education course**. They attend classes in the evening.

6
José is taking a **placement test** this morning. He wants to **test out** of some of his required courses.

2 READ the sentences in Activity 1 with a partner.

3 NOTICE THE GRAMMAR. Circle the verbs in the simple present. Underline the verbs in the present continuous. If there is a time expression, draw a rectangle around it.

Simple Present and Present Continuous Review

- Use the simple present to make general statements of fact and to talk about repeated actions or habits.
- Use the present continuous to talk about actions in progress right now, or actions that are temporary.

Simple Present

I **enroll** for classes every semester.
Do you **register** online?
He **doesn't study** on the weekends.
The office **accepts** online applications.
Twice a week, we **practice** pronunciation.
Where **do** they **study** at night?

Present Continuous

I'm **not using** the computer right now.
He **isn't eating** lunch now.
We're **writing** an email to our teacher.
Is she **studying** for finals this week?
Are you **working** a lot these days?
Where **are** they **going**?

Time Expressions

Time expressions usually come at the beginning or the end of a sentence. If the time expression comes at the beginning, it is usually followed by a comma. If it comes at the end, do not use a comma.

Every day, she goes to class.
These days, I'm studying French.

She goes to class **every day.**
I'm studying French **these days.**

---

4 COMPLETE the paragraph. Circle the correct form of the verb.

Rosa is a new student at East Mountain Community College. Today she (1) **enrolls / is enrolling** in the business management program. This morning, she (2) **takes / is taking** a placement test in the admissions office. She (3) **tries / is trying** to test out of some of the introductory courses. Later today, Rosa is going to register for "Principles of Management." The course (4) **satisfies / is satisfying** a requirement for her program. To help her pay for school, Rosa (5) **applies / is applying** for financial aid, too.

5 WHAT ABOUT YOU? Complete the sentences about yourself. Use the simple present or the present continuous.

1. Today, I _____ .

2. Every day, I _____ .

3. This week, I _____ .

4. This month, I _____ .

5. Every week, I _____ .

6. Once a day, I _____ .

7. Once a month, I _____ .

8. In our class, I _____ .

LESSON 2: Grammar Practice Plus

1 **TALK** about the picture. What are people interested in? What are they doing?

Script on page 213

NOT ON CD!!

2 **LISTEN** and write the correct number next to each name.

_____ **Paulo**   _____ **Rebecca**   _____ **Luis**   _____ **Carlos**   _____ **Ana**

3 **LISTEN** again. Which programs and courses are Carlos and Rebecca interested in?
Check ☑ them in the box below.

missing

☐ accounting
☐ auto body repair
☑ business
☐ business management

☐ computer programming
☐ early childhood education
☐ electrical work
☐ health care

☐ hotel and hospitality
☐ medical assisting
☐ nursing
☐ restaurant management

4 **WRITE** sentences about the people in the picture. Use simple present and present continuous.

1. Carlos / be / business program. He / take / accounting courses.

Carlos is in a business program. He's taking accounting classes.

2. Rebecca / attend / community college. She / be / nursing program.

3. Ana / be / high school. She / look into / early childhood education.

4. Luis / be / middle school. He / look through / two books.

5. Paulo / like / computers and cars. He / hold / book about computer programming.

Correlative Conjunctions

Both . . . and, either . . . or, and *neither . . . nor* are correlative conjunctions. Use them to link similar types of phrases in a sentence.

Sam dislikes **both** algebra **and** accounting.
Both Jorge **and** Maria like algebra.

Erica takes **either** the bus **or** the train.
Either Ms. Jones **or** Mr. Lopez teaches accounting. I can't remember.

Paulo reads **neither** magazines **nor** newspapers.
Neither Wei **nor** Gina is in my nursing class.

> *Neither . . . nor* is used more often in writing than in speaking.

5 **WRITE.** Complete the sentences about the picture in Activity 1 with *either . . . or, neither . . . nor,* or *both . . . and.*

1. _Neither_ Luis _nor_ Paulo is reading about business.

2. Carlos is getting books for _____ business management _____ accounting.

3. Paulo is looking at _____ auto body repair _____ computer programming books.

4. Ana wants to study _____ early childhood education _____ restaurant management. She hasn't decided yet.

5. _____ Luis _____ Ana is in college yet. They're too young.

6 **WRITE** sentences by putting the words in the correct order.

1. Alejandro / both / is taking / management / hotel and hospitality courses / and /.
   Alejandro is taking both management and hotel and hospitality courses.

2. neither / electrical work / Tina / nor / is studying / air conditioning science /.
   _____

3. or / Robert / health care / is looking into / computer programming / either /.
   _____

4. Susan / business / is registering for / Neither / Berta / nor /.
   _____

5. Both / are taking / Clara / and / medical assisting classes / Manuel /.
   _____

 7 **WHAT ABOUT YOU?** Think about the programs and courses in Activity 3 on page 8. Make a list of the ones you are interested in and the ones you are not interested in. Exchange your list with a partner and write sentences about your partner's list using correlative conjunctions.

Example: *Nadia is interested in neither accounting nor computer programming. She likes both early childhood education and health care.*

LESSON 3: Listening and Conversation

P213
missing

1 **LISTEN** to the question. Then listen to a husband and wife talk about schedules. Listen to the question again. Fill in the correct answer. Replay each item if necessary.

TCD1,
10–15

1. Ⓐ   Ⓑ   Ⓒ   4. Ⓐ   Ⓑ   Ⓒ
2. Ⓐ   Ⓑ   Ⓒ   5. Ⓐ   Ⓑ   Ⓒ
3. Ⓐ   Ⓑ   Ⓒ   6. Ⓐ   Ⓑ   Ⓒ

missing

2 **LISTEN** to the whole conversation. Check ☑ the correct box.

TCD1, 16

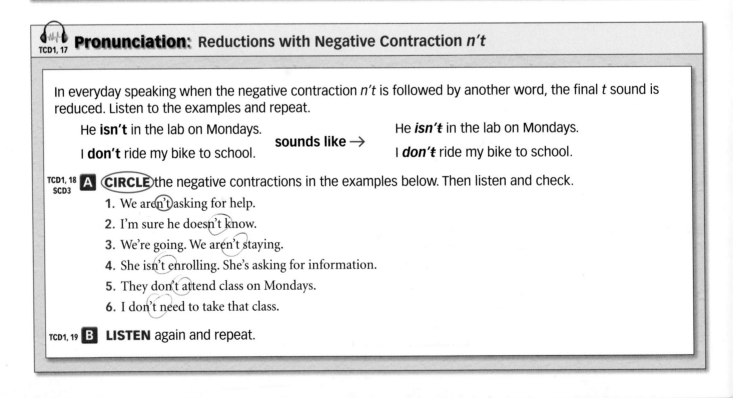

	LINDA	TOM	
1.	☑	☐	is signing up for an English class on Monday and Wednesday nights.
2.	☐	☑	is taking a continuing education course on Tuesday and Thursday afternoons.
3.	☑	☐	wants to take an American history course on Friday afternoons.
4.	☐	☑	suggests that Sam could take the bus to swim class on Friday afternoons.
5.	☑	☐	doesn't have much flexibility in his/her schedule.

Pronunciation: Reductions with Negative Contraction *n't*

TCD1, 17

In everyday speaking when the negative contraction *n't* is followed by another word, the final *t* sound is reduced. Listen to the examples and repeat.

He **isn't** in the lab on Mondays.   **sounds like** →   He **isn't** in the lab on Mondays.

I **don't** ride my bike to school.   I **don't** ride my bike to school.

A **CIRCLE** the negative contractions in the examples below. Then listen and check.

TCD1, 18
SCD3

1. We aren't asking for help.
2. I'm sure he doesn't know.
3. We're going. We aren't staying.
4. She isn't enrolling. She's asking for information.
5. They don't attend class on Mondays.
6. I don't need to take that class.

B **LISTEN** again and repeat.

TCD1, 19

3 **LISTEN** and read.

A: How is <u>Carlos</u> doing?

B: Oh, <u>he's</u> great, but <u>he's</u> very busy! <u>He's</u> taking <u>Accounting 101</u> this semester at the community college.

A: Really? That's great!

B: Yes, <u>he's</u> in a <u>business</u> program at the college.

A: Good for <u>him</u>.

4 **PRACTICE** the conversation from Activity 3 with a partner. Use the information in the chart. For item 5, fill in the name and information for someone you know.

Name	Course	Program
1. Linda	Introduction to Health Care 101	nursing
2. Hector	Auto Body Repair 124	automotive technology
3. Robert	Early Childhood Education 182	child care
4. Alice	Principles of Management 137	business
5. _____	_____	_____

5 **WHAT ABOUT YOU?** Talk with a partner. Use the expressions in the Conversation Strategy box below. What classes are you taking? What new or interesting things are you doing?

Example: A: How're you doing?

B: I'm fine! I'm taking a computer class this semester.

A: Really? That's great!

B: Yes, I'm learning an accounting program on the computer.

A: Good for you!

Conversation Strategy	
Expressing Encouragement	
A: That sounds interesting.	B: Yes. It is!
A: That's great.	B: Thank you. I'm enjoying it.
A: Congratulations!	B: Thank you.
A: That's terrific!	B: Thank you.
A: I'm so happy for you.	B: Thanks so much. I appreciate that.
A: Wonderful!	B: Thank you. It's been really interesting.
A: Good for you!	B: Thanks!

LESSON 4: Grammar and Vocabulary

1 **GRAMMAR PICTURE DICTIONARY.** What are these people thinking about? Listen and read.

TCD1, 21
SCD5

1 Gabby will earn three **credits** for taking a computer science class. She is **on track** for her graduation in May.

2 Thomas is **contacting** a **school administrator** tomorrow. He is going to talk to her about his problem with financial aid.

3 Alex is going to **make improvements**. He will **prioritize** his **tasks** and **organize** his time more efficiently.

4 Patricia is taking a **personality test** in the career center on Tuesday. Then she is going to **meet with** a career advisor.

2 **READ** the sentences in Activity 1 with a partner.

3 **NOTICE THE GRAMMAR.** Underline the verbs in present continuous in Activity 1. Circle the future verb forms with will. Draw a rectangle around future verb forms with be going to

Expressing Future Time with *Will, Be Going To,* and the Present Continuous

Use *will, be going to,* or the present continuous to talk about the future.

Use *will* to make plans, commitments, and offers at the moment of speaking.

> We'**ll work** on the applications tonight.
> I'**ll be** home at six o'clock every night.
> Sure, I'**ll help** you carry it.

Use *will* to ask for favors.

> **Will** you **help** me with this?
> **Will** you **study** with me tonight?

Use *will* to talk about definite future events or results.

> She **will** earn three credits for her class.
> If she takes this class, she'**ll** have enough credits to graduate.

Use *will* and *be going to* to make predictions about the future.

> They **will do** well on the test next week.
> The library **will be** full this weekend.

> They'**re going to do** well on the test next week.
> The library **is going to be** full this weekend.

Use the present continuous or *be going to* to talk about plans you've already made.

> A: What **are** you **doing** tomorrow?
> B: I'**m studying** for my history test.

> A: What **are you going to do** tomorrow?
> B: I'm **going to study** for my history test.

Use *be going to* when plans are already made, or something is sure to happen: *I'm going to attend class tomorrow.*

Use *will* when you're not sure if it will happen, or if it's only possible or probable: *I*

4 COMPLETE. Circle the correct words to complete the sentences.

1. A: Did you make an appointment with the school administrator?
   B: Yes, I **'m going to** / **will** meet with her at 3:00 tomorrow.

2. I think it **is raining** / **is going to rain** tomorrow.

3. A: These books are heavy!
   B: I **'ll** / **'m going to** help you carry them.

4. A: What **will you** / **are you going to** do tomorrow?
   B: I **will play** / **'m playing** tennis with Susan.

5 WHAT ABOUT YOU? Talk with a partner about what you are going to do in the future, for example, next semester, next week, or next year. Use the verbs below.

1. register for
2. meet with
3. work hard
4. organize
5. look into
6. make improvements to

Are you going to register for classes next semester?

Yes, I think I'll register next week, on Tuesday.

LESSON 5: Grammar Practice Plus

1 **READ.** Compare the list of required courses with Rebecca's transcript. Check ☑ the required courses that Rebecca has taken.

Tip
An **internship** is a short-term job that you do to get experience. Usually you work without pay.

MEDICAL ASSISTANT PROGRAM REQUIREMENTS

BASIC REQUIRED COURSES:
- ☑ English 101
- ☐ Biology 181: The Human Body
- ☐ Mathematics 201

REQUIRED MEDICAL COURSES:
- ☐ Introduction to Health Care
- ☐ Medical Assisting Skills I
- ☐ Medical Assisting Skills II
- ☐ Child Care
- ☐ Introduction to Illness
- ☐ Medical Office Procedures
- ☐ Medical Technology
- ☐ Basics of Medicine Doses
- ☐ Patient Information
- ☐ Medical Assisting Internship

VALLEY COLLEGE
PROSPICIAM AD VALLESE

OFFICIAL TRANSCRIPT
Rebecca G. Martin
Student ID: 000033467

SPRING SEMESTER 2007		FALL SEMESTER 2007	
English 101	A-	Medical Assisting Skills I	B+
The Human Body	C+	Introduction to Illness	B-
Introduction to Health Care	A-	Patient Information	A

SUMMER TERM 2007		SPRING SEMESTER 2008	
Mathematics 201	B+	Medical Assisting Skills II	A
		Child Care	B

2 **LISTEN** to the conversation between Rebecca and her advisor. On the list of program requirements above, underline the classes you hear.

TCD1, 22

3 **LISTEN** again. Match.

1. __*a*__ Rebecca
2. _____ The internship
3. _____ Her advisor
4. _____ Her favorite professor

a. is going to finish in three semesters.
b. will help her find an internship.
c. is teaching her course next semester.
d. will be her last requirement for the program.

4 **WHAT ABOUT YOU?** Think about your class(es). What plans do you have? What improvements do you want to make? Write four sentences about your plans for school. Then talk with a partner about your plans.

Example: *I'm going to complete my homework on time.*

_____

_____

_____

_____

_____

5 COMPLETE the letter from Rebecca to her friend Mari. Use the correct form of these verbs. Be prepared to say why you chose each verb tense.

contact	make	try	study	take

Dear Mari,

It was so good to hear from you! Guess what! My whole family is in school right now. We really have to organize our time carefully. (1) I __Study__ medical assisting, and Carlos is in a business program. I'm on track to graduate in one year. Ana is looking into her choices for college. She (2) __take__ a placement test in a few weeks, and she (3) __Contact__ a school administrator at the community college to learn about different programs, too. Luis isn't doing as well in school, but I'm sure he (4) __make__ improvements. He (5) __try__ really hard and he's doing well in science. Little Paulo is doing well too. How is your family? I'd love to know more.

Rebecca

6 READ the letter again. Then read each sentence below. Write *N* if it is happening now. Write *F* for something happening in the future.

___ 1. Rebecca's medical assisting program   ___ 4. Ana's placement test

___ 2. Rebecca's graduation   ___ 5. Carlos's business program

___ 3. Luis's academic improvements

Math: Calculating Grade Point Average (GPA)

CALCULATE Luis's grade point average (GPA). Luis needs a good GPA to apply for college. Follow the steps below to calculate his GPA. Note that some classes have more units (credits) than others. Also, each letter grade (A, B, C, D, F) has a numerical value.

Step 1 Write the grade point value for each class.

Step 2 Multiply the units for each class by the grade point value for the class to get the total grade points for that class.

Step 3 Add the total grade points for all of the classes.

Step 4 Add the total units for all of the classes.

Step 5 Divide the total grade points by the total units.

Step 6 Write Luis's GPA: __2.33__.

Class	Units	Grade	Grade Point Value	Grade Points
Math	4	C	2	8
Science	4	A	4	16
English	4	C	2	8
History	4	D	1	4
P.E.	2	B	3	6
Totals	18			42
Total grade points ÷ Total units = GPA				2.33

A = 4	B = 3	C = 2	D = 1

LESSON 6: Reading

1 **THINK ABOUT IT.** Discuss these questions in a group. Use your prior knowledge.

1. What schools for adults are in or near your city?
2. What kind of classes do these schools offer?
3. Have you been to one of the schools? What was it like?
4. What do you know about online courses? What kinds of courses can you take online?

READING FOCUS: Use prior knowledge

Before you read, think about what you already know about the topic. Your prior knowledge and experience will help you understand what you read.

2 **BEFORE YOU READ.** Look at the brochure on the next page. Preview the brochure. Look at each heading and skim the text under it. What kind of information does each section give?

READING FOCUS: Preview a reading

Articles, brochures, and books have headings at the beginning of sections. A heading is usually one line of text that is in big, bold, or colored letters. To preview, read each heading to get a general idea of what the text is about. Illustrations and photos can also help you preview.

3 **READ** the brochure on the next page. Which course is the most interesting to you?

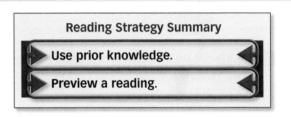

Reading Strategy Summary

➤ Use prior knowledge.

➤ Preview a reading.

4 **AFTER YOU READ.**

A. VOCABULARY. Find and circle these words in the reading. Then match the word with the definition. Use a dictionary to check your answers.

1. ___c___ give up
2. ___a___ format
3. ___e___ download
4. ___d___ basics
5. ___b___ earn a living

a. the way something is organized or arranged
b. work for money to live
c. stop doing something
d. the simplest or most important ideas
e. transfer information from the Internet to a computer

B. DISCUSS the questions with a partner.

1. Are classes taken at the school or online?
2. When can you enroll in a course?
3. Which course teaches about animal health?
4. In which course will you learn about fixing ovens?
5. Which course would be good for someone who likes the outdoors?
6. Why should someone take the Computer Basics course?

C. TALK with a partner.

1. Would you like to take an online course? What subject?
2. Would you prefer to take an online course or a classroom course? List advantages and disadvantages for each.

NEW HORIZONS CAREER SCHOOL

At New Horizons, we know that you have plans for your future. We can help you achieve your dreams! We offer online courses that give you the job skills you need, on a schedule that works for you. You can enroll anytime and complete a course at your own pace. You don't have to give up time at work or with your family.

Our courses are convenient*, too. We ship course materials directly to your home. Our online course format makes it easy for you to complete your course from anywhere. You can enroll online, download your assignments, email your professors, and check your grades over the Internet anytime, anywhere.

Call New Horizons Career School and let your new future begin today! It's the best move you'll ever make. Keep reading to find out what some of our students are learning at New Horizons Career School.

Perla: Computer Basics

So many businesses use computers today. I'm learning the basics at New Horizons: word processing, spreadsheets, Internet skills, popular software programs, and lots more.

Malik: Appliance Repair

Appliances* are always breaking down. I'm going to earn a living by fixing them. New Horizons is teaching me how to fix appliances such as washing machines, dryers, refrigerators, and microwave ovens. Soon, I will open my own repair shop!

Sol: Pet Grooming

For many people, pets are a part of the family. There is a high demand* for pet grooming* services, so I'm taking a course at New Horizons. I love both dogs and cats, so I'm enjoying this course a lot. I'm learning about pet health and grooming equipment, too.

Josef: Landscaping

I'm finishing my New Horizons course next week. After that, I will work with my hands every day. I can't wait! My class is learning about plant health, soil conditions, and landscape design. I will either work for a greenhouse or start my own business.

---

convenient (adj.): making life easier or more comfortable

appliances (n.): machines that do household work

demand (n.): desire or need for something

pet grooming (comp. n.): cleaning, brushing, and styling animals

LESSON 7: Writing

1 **THINK ABOUT IT.** What kind of personal information do you share with people when you first meet? Talk to a partner and make a list.

2 **BEFORE YOU WRITE.**

WRITING FOCUS: Give specific details

A detail is a fact or opinion that gives more information. When you write, use supporting details to tell more about an idea.

Example:	IDEA	SUPPORTING DETAILS
	I really love animals.	I watch animal shows on TV all the time.
		My favorite animal is the lion.

A. READ this email from a teacher introducing himself to his class. <u>Underline</u> the details in the second paragraph.

---

http://mail.newhorizons.org/michaeldonaldson/239clkvkfi9343sd

From: michaeldonaldson@newhorizons.org
Subject: Accounting 101
Date: September 15, 2009

Dear Students,

Hello, and welcome to Accounting 101. My name is Professor Donaldson, and I will be your instructor for this continuing education course with New Horizons Career School. I'm glad you've decided to take this course.

I have worked in the field of accounting for more than 15 years. At first, I worked as an accountant at Central Dry Cleaners. Then I opened my own accounting business, and many companies hired me to organize their money and bills. In 1998, I began teaching online accounting courses at New Horizons Career School. I love it because it combines three of my favorite things: numbers, computers, and people!

I'm going to tell you a little bit about myself. I have been married for eight years, and I have a wonderful family. In my free time, I have many hobbies. I like to read, go fishing, and play with my kids and our dog.

For your first assignment, please email me about yourself. I'd like to hear about you and why you are taking this course. I know that many of you do not enjoy math, but don't worry. I will help you learn the basics in no time.

I look forward to working with all of you.

Sincerely,

Prof. Michael Donaldson, CPA
New Horizons Career School

B. TALK to a partner. What kinds of details does Professor Donaldson include in his email? Do you think all of these details are okay to share with students? Do you think it's okay for the professor to ask students to tell him the same kind of information?

C. PLAN your writing. Imagine you are writing an email to Professor Donaldson. Before you write, make notes to plan what you will say. Include details for some of your ideas. Pay attention to the verb tenses you use.

Paragraph 1: Introduce yourself and tell why you are taking the class.

_____

_____

_____

_____

Paragraph 2: Give some information about yourself. For example, you can talk about your family, your job (if you have one), your interests, or your hobbies.

_____

_____

_____

_____

Paragraph 3: Give information about your future educational plans.

_____

_____

_____

_____

---

3 WRITE an email to your instructor to introduce yourself. Include a greeting, write sentences that tell the ideas and details from your notes, write a closing, and write your name.

4 AFTER YOU WRITE.

A. EDIT your writing.

1. Did you tell details about yourself and your life?
2. Did you include a greeting and a closing?
3. Did you use verb forms correctly? Check for simple present, present continuous, and future forms.
4. Did you use correct spelling, capitalization, and punctuation?

B. REWRITE your letter with corrections.

> **WRITING FOCUS: Close a letter or email**
>
> When ending an email or letter, people usually write something nice and use a closing.
>
> For example:
>
> _I am looking forward to your class._
>
> _Sincerely,_   ← **closing**
> _(your name)_

Career Connection

1 THINK ABOUT IT. What qualifications or skills do you think are important for a teacher at a daycare center?

2 LISTEN to the conversation between a daycare center administrator and Sally, the program coordinator. Check ✓ *true* or *false*.

	True	False
1. The daycare center held a registration yesterday.	☑	☐
2. A four-year-old child is a toddler.	☐	☑
3. There will be 78 children in the program on Monday.	☑	☐
4. Regina has a lot of experience with three- and four-year-olds.	☐	☑
5. Marcia has a degree in Early Childhood Education.	☑	☐

3 LISTEN to the conversation in Activity 2 again. Complete the chart with the words in the box.

Experience:	2 years	*M* 3 years	*C* 5 years
Education:	*M* Bachelor's degree	*C* Master's degree	*R* still in school
Strengths:	*M* flexible and talented	*C* creative and artistic	*R* organized and patient

Teacher	Experience	Education	Strengths
Regina	2 years		
Marcia			
Cynthia			

4 ROLE PLAY. Imagine that you are a parent bringing your child to this daycare center. You are talking to the program coordinator. What are you going to ask? Use the information in the box. Take turns asking questions with a partner.

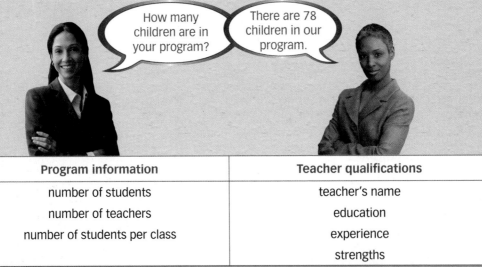

How many children are in your program?

There are 78 children in our program.

Program information	Teacher qualifications
number of students	teacher's name
number of teachers	education
number of students per class	experience
	strengths

5 WHAT ABOUT YOU? Talk with a partner. What are your strengths in your current job? What educational goals do you have? Discuss two or three of your strengths and your educational goals.

Check Your Progress!

Skill	Circle the answers.	Is it correct?
A. Use the simple present and present continuous.	1. Dan **register / registers / is registering** online every semester. 2. **I'm practicing / I practice / I practices** the piano right now. 3. Where **you go / are you going / do you go** on the weekends? 4. **I take / I'm taking / I took** German this semester.	☐ ☐ ☐ ☐

| | | Number Correct | 0 | 1 | 2 | 3 | 4 |

Skill	Circle the answers.	Is it correct?
B. Use *will, be going to*, and the present continuous to express future time.	5. **Will you / Are you going to** help me move this Saturday? 6. **I'm going to / will** meet with an advisor next week. 7. **Are you looking / Will you look** into online courses? 8. It**'s going to rain / 's raining** tomorrow afternoon.	☐ ☐ ☐ ☐

| | | Number Correct | 0 | 1 | 2 | 3 | 4 |

Skill	Circle the answers.	Is it correct?
C. Talk about school matters.	9. The math courses **satisfy / accept** the requirements for his program. 10. Take a **continuing education course / placement test** to find out which English class you should be in. 11. Peter is busy, so he needs **admissions / flexibility** in his schedule. 12. The financial aid doesn't **cover / test out of** her school expenses.	☐ ☐ ☐ ☐

| | | Number Correct | 0 | 1 | 2 | 3 | 4 |

Skill	Circle the answers.	Is it correct?
D. Understand academic requirements.	13. My program is going well. I'm on **credit / track** to graduate in May. 14. May has a lot to do. She'll prioritize her **tasks / credits** this week. 15. Ted needs to **organize / cover** his time so he can study more. 16. Ella will **make / earn** four credits for her English class.	☐ ☐ ☐ ☐

| | | Number Correct | 0 | 1 | 2 | 3 | 4 |

COUNT the number of correct answers above. Fill in the bubbles.

Chart Your Success					
Skill	Need Practice	Okay	Good	Very Good	Excellent!
A. Use the simple present and present continuous.	⓪	①	②	③	④
B. Use *will, be going to*, and the present continuous to express future time.	⓪	①	②	③	④
C. Talk about school matters.	⓪	①	②	③	④
D. Understand academic requirements.	⓪	①	②	③	④

LESSON 1: Grammar and Vocabulary

1 GRAMMAR PICTURE DICTIONARY. What are these people doing at work? Listen and read.

TCD1, 24
SCD6

1 Kristin talked to her boss **before** she **scheduled** the meeting. Then she **followed up** with the team.

2 **As soon as** Andrew **left** his meeting, he **joined** our **conference call**. He **accepted** the assignment after we explained it to him.

3 Samuel and Tyler **met their** deadline. They both **asked** for a day off **after** they completed the **project**.

4 Rachel was sick, so Chris **covered for** her **until** she **got** better.

You have two messages.

5 **After** Natalie **finished** her report, she listened to her **voicemail**. There was a message from her boss.

6 **Before** Andrea **made a presentation** at our meeting this morning, she **pulled together materials** for everyone to see.

2 READ the sentences in Activity 1 with a partner.

3 NOTICE THE GRAMMAR. Circle the words *after, when, as soon as, before,* and *until*. Underline the verb that follows each of these words.

Past Time Clauses with *After, When, As Soon As, Before,* and *Until*

Join time clauses in the past to main clauses in the past to say when events happened. The time clause can come after or before the main clause. If it comes before the main clause, it has a comma.

Main Clause	Time Clause
Kristin followed up with the team	after she talked to her boss.
I listened to my voicemail	when I got to the office.
Did Andrew join the conference call	as soon as he left his other meeting?
Why did he accept the assignment	before he understood it?
Samuel and Tyler didn't ask for a day off	until they met their deadline.

Time Clause	Main Clause
After Kristen talked to her boss,	did she ask for a day off?
When Rachel got sick,	Chris covered for her.
As soon as Natalie listened to her voicemail,	she called her boss.
Before I followed up with the team,	I reviewed our schedule.
Until Andrea pulled together all her materials,	she couldn't make the presentation.

4 COMPLETE. Circle the correct words to complete the sentences.

1. Kathy joined the conference call **until** / **after** she completed her project.

2. I ate breakfast at the restaurant **when** / **before** I arrived at the office.

3. Susan didn't schedule the meeting **before** / **until** her boss finished her conference call.

4. Blake helped me pull together materials for the meeting **before** / **after** it started.

5. The manager helped Grace **as soon as** / **until** he saw her problem.

6. Russ met the deadline **until** / **after** his boss went home.

5 WHAT ABOUT YOU? Write sentences about you. Use the simple past and a time clause. Use *after, as soon as, before, until,* or *when* in your sentences. Then read your sentences to a classmate.

1. I saw my friend Joe *as soon as I arrived at school today.*

2. Yesterday I didn't leave class _____

3. I came to the United States _____

4. I started this English class _____

5. I did my homework _____

6. Last night, I ate dinner _____

vocab : overwhelmed
be burned out
pull together
cover for

LESSON 2: Grammar Practice Plus

8/29

1 **TALK** about the picture. What do you think is going on? How does each person feel?

___3___ Lorenzo   ___4___ Silvia   ___5___ Jenny   ___6___ Donna   ___1___ Luke   ___2___ Thomas

TCD1, 25

2 **LISTEN.** Write the number next to the correct name above.

3 **COMPLETE** the sentences about the people in the picture. Use the words in the box below. Then match each sentence to one on the right.

burned out	helpful	~~overwhelmed~~
creative	organized	punctual

1. Lorenzo is really ____overwhelmed____.
2. Silvia is very _____.
3. Jenny is very _____.
4. Donna is very _____.
5. Luke is very _____.
6. Thomas is very _____.

a. She has a lot of new ideas.
b. He has a lot of work to do.
c. She always arrives at her meetings on time.
d. He is tired of his job.
e. She often takes care of her coworkers.
f. He is careful with his papers and assignments.

4 **WHAT ABOUT YOU?** Describe people you know by using the adjectives from Activity 1. Add a detail to explain.

Example: _My sister is very punctual. She is never late._

| Use feeling words. • Interpret a checklist. • Complete an email.

5 COMPLETE Lorenzo's email to his friend about his new job. Use the simple past tense of the verbs in the box below.

discuss	end	watch	begin	get
answer	tell	want	arrive	listen

http://excellentemployees.net/access/luke_p/inbox/23ldsf

To: Julia.Browne@workernet.com
From: Lorenzo_p@excellentemployees.net
Subject: My first day
Sent: 02/06/08, 12:05 p.m.

Hi Julia,

It's my first day at the new job. It's 12:00 p.m., and I'm feeling a little overwhelmed already!

When I (1)_____ at my new office this morning, I already had six voicemails. Can you believe it? I don't even know six people here yet! I guess I'll meet them soon.

After I (2)_____ to the messages, a guy named Lorenzo (3)_____ me we had a conference call at 9:30 with our office in Atlanta. I (4)_____ to get a cup of coffee before the call (5)_____, but I didn't have time!

As soon as the conference call (6)_____ I had to go to another meeting with the other managers. We certainly have a lot of meetings here.

After that, we (7)_____ a presentation, (8)_____ our schedules, and (9)_____ new assignments. Then I went back to my office and checked my email. I (10)_____ email until my next meeting started at 11:00.

Now I'm back in my office. There are five files on my desk! I think I'll have some lunch first—and a coffee!

Talk to you later,
Lorenzo

6 WRITE. Choose which person in Activity 1 wrote each of the sentences below. Imagine you are one of the people. Starting with his/her sentence, write a longer email, like the one in Activity 5.

1. ___Donna___ We got our new assignment today. It's so exciting!

2. _____ We had three meetings this morning! I just want to go home.

3. _____ I'm ready for my big presentation today. I feel good.

4. _____ A new guy started today. I'm going to introduce him to everyone.

5. _____ When I got to the meeting at 10:00, no one was there.

7 WHAT ABOUT YOU? Tell a partner about your activities yesterday. Use past time clauses.

LESSON 3: Listening and Conversation

1 **LISTEN** to the question. Then listen to the conversation. Listen to the question again. Fill in the correct answer. Replay each item if necessary.

TCD1, 26–31

1. Ⓐ Ⓑ Ⓒ   4. Ⓐ Ⓑ Ⓒ

2. Ⓐ Ⓑ Ⓒ   5. Ⓐ Ⓑ Ⓒ

3. Ⓐ Ⓑ Ⓒ   6. Ⓐ Ⓑ Ⓒ

2 **LISTEN** again. Write what the person says about the time of the activity.

TCD1, 32

1. after I _eat lunch_

2. as soon as I _got to the office_

3. as soon as I _talked to Mrs Jones_

4. until I _finished it_

5. after you _left_

6. before I _go home._

3 **LISTEN** and fill in the schedule for the things Lorenzo did in his busy day.

TCD1, 33

ate lunch	finished the project for Donna	met with my supervisor 10:00
covered for Silvia	had a breakfast meeting	joined a conference call
worked with Thomas 11:00 > 1:00		

8 AM _breakfast meeting_

9 AM _joined a conference call_

10 AM _____

11 AM _____

12 PM _____

1 PM _____

2 PM _____

3 PM _____

4 PM _____

5 PM _____

Pronunciation: Regular Past Tense (-ed) Endings

TCD1, 34

There are three different ways to pronounce -ed endings in the past tense. One way is to make a /t/ sound. Listen to the example and repeat.

Ann **worked** to meet the deadline.   **sounds like** →   Ann work**t** to meet the deadline.

Another way to pronounce –ed endings is by making a final /d/ sound. Listen to the example and repeat.

Ed **joined** the conference call.   **sounds like** →   Ed join**d** the conference call.

The third way to pronounce –ed endings is by saying it as a separate syllable, or /ɪd/. Listen to the example and repeat.

Joe **accepted** the assignment.   **sounds like** →   Joe accept**ɪd** the assignment.

A **PREDICT** the final sound of each -ed ending. Write t, d, or ɪd. Then listen and check.

TCD1, 35
SCD7

1. promised __t__   3. attended _____   5. waited _____

2. scheduled _____   4. covered _____   6. talked _____

TCD1, 36 **B** **LISTEN** again and repeat.

4 LISTEN to the conversation between two coworkers.

TCD1, 37
SCD8

> A: Hi, how's your work coming?
>
> B: Just fine. I've been very busy, but I'm trying to get everything done.
>
> A: Did you <u>call your boss</u>?
>
> B: Yes. I <u>called her as soon as I arrived today</u>.
>
> A: And did you <u>complete the project</u>?
>
> B: No, I didn't. I didn't have time before I left yesterday. I'll work on that <u>this afternoon</u>.

5 PRACTICE the conversation from Activity 4. Speaker A, ask about things to do. Speaker B, answer using the past and future time clauses. Tell what you did do and what you will do. Make three different conversations.

THINGS TO DO	PAST TIME CLAUSE	FUTURE TIME CLAUSE
● *follow up with the team* ● *leave a voicemail with our supervisor* ● *work on the presentation* ● *pull together the materials we need* ● *schedule the meeting* ● *start on that new assignment*	after everyone went home as soon as we finished our conference call before I ate lunch yesterday when I went to the meeting until I met the deadline	after I have lunch as soon as I pull together some more information until I go home today before I go home tonight when I finish what I'm working on now

6 ROLE-PLAY. Choose a situation. With a partner, create your own conversation and practice it. Then act it out for the class. Use one of the responses in the Conversation Strategy box.

Situation 1: You are a manager and you are following up with an employee about an important project.

Situation 2: You are a parent and you want to check on your child's school assignments.

Situation 3: You and a classmate are working on a project together for class.

7 WHAT ABOUT YOU? Write a conversation between you and a family member or coworker. Talk about things you have to do at home.

Conversation Strategy
Positive Responses

That's great.
I'm glad to hear that.
That's very helpful.
Thanks for doing that.
You're so organized.

> I did my work as soon as I got back from lunch.

> I'm glad to hear that. And did you ...?

LESSON 4: Grammar and Vocabulary

TCD1, 38
SCD9

1 **GRAMMAR PICTURE DICTIONARY.** How are Josh and Kara doing at their jobs? Listen and read.

1

Josh has **received positive performance reviews** for the past three years at his company.

2

He has **shown** good **leadership skills**, and he has **managed his time** carefully.

3

He has always **gotten along** well with his coworkers, and he has **developed** good **communication skills**.

4

Last year, Kara attended several **workshops** for management and computer skills, but she hasn't finished all of her training yet.

5

She has also **maintained** her **qualifications** for her job. She has worked hard at the company.

6

She got a management **certification** and received a **promotion** last year.

2 **READ** the sentences from Activity 1 with a partner.

3 **NOTICE THE GRAMMAR.** Circle the verbs in simple past. Underline the verbs in present perfect.

Talk about job performance. • Use simple past. • Use present perfect.

Simple Past and Present Perfect Review

Use the simple past to talk about events or actions that occurred and ended at a specific time in the past.

Simple Past

Adam **attended** several workshops *last year*.
Ed **didn't show** good leadership skills *yesterday*.
Did Mei **receive** a promotion *a month ago*?
Who **was** at the office party *last night*?
Kevin **worked** there *for nine years*.

Simple Past Time Expressions

a month / week / year ago
already
for *(number)* days / weeks / months / years
in 2007 / August
last week / month / year / Monday / summer
yesterday

Use the present perfect to talk about events or actions that:
• occurred at an unspecified time in the past.
• began in the past and continue to the present.

Present Perfect

Adam **has** *already* **attended** several workshops.
Ed **has shown** good leadership skills *so far*.
Has May *ever* **received** a promotion?
Have you **been** to any office parties *yet*?
They **haven't received** any new reports
    since last year.
He **has** *never* **missed** a deadline.

Present Perfect Time Expressions

already
ever *(in questions)*
for a week / a month / six hours / ten years
since Tuesday / last month / year / summer / 2005
so far
yet *(in questions and negatives)*
never

---

4 **COMPLETE.** Chris is writing to his supervisor about his team. Circle the correct form of the verb.

1. Allison **got** / **has gotten** her certification three months ago.

2. Josh **maintained** / **has maintained** his qualifications since he got his promotion.

3. Andrew **attended** / **has attended** five workshops since he started working here.

4. Tamara **didn't get along** / **hasn't gotten along** well with her coworkers since she came back from her vacation.

5. Kent **received** / **has received** a good performance review last week.

6. Alex **didn't develop** / **hasn't developed** better communication skills yet.

5 **WHAT ABOUT YOU?** Write sentences about you. Use time expressions from the chart above and the verbs below.

Example: attend   *I have attended English classes at this school for one year.*
           OR I attended English classes at this school last year.

1. work   3. complete   5. manage
2. study   4. earn   6. receive

LESSON 5: Grammar Practice Plus

Express Similarities with *So, Too, Either,* and *Neither*

We use *so, too, either,* and *neither* to show how two things or situations are the same, or different.

With **so** and **neither**, the verb comes before the subject.
With **too** or **either,** the verb comes after the subject.
Use a comma before **too** and **either.**
For all sentences, use the same verb (or auxiliary verb) that was in the main sentence: *am/is/are, was/were, do/does, did,* or *have/has.*

We also use *but* to express differences. The verb comes after the subject.

Example: Leyla has maintained her qualifications, *but* Hector *hasn't.*

	so/neither + Verb + Subject	Subject + Verb + *too/either*
Mark is always on time,	and **so is** Tom.	and Tom **is**, **too**.
Sam has worked a lot this week,	and **so has** Ed.	and Ed **has**, **too**.
Paul doesn't go to many workshops,	and **neither does** Mary.	and Mary **doesn't, either**.
Ellen hasn't read the report,	and **neither have** I.	and I **haven't, either**.

1 **MATCH** the sentences.

___e___ 1. Steven has worked with his company for 10 years,

___c___ 2. Lisa didn't manage her time well on that project,

___b___ 3. Joanna got along well with the new employee,

___d___ 4. Mark hasn't completed his assignment yet,

___a___ 5. Jane has shown good leadership skills,

a. and Susan has, too.

b. and her supervisor did, too.

c. and neither did her coworker, Isabel.

d. and Shawn hasn't either.

e. and so has his coworker, Cal.

2 **COMPLETE.** Read the training reports to find out which training sessions each employee has attended. Then complete the sentences with the present perfect of *take* and *so, too, either,* or *neither.*

Training Report *Ana Rodriguez*

☑ Computer Skills
☐ Patient Records Training
☑ Benefits and Insurance
☐ Teams that Work

Training Report *Lorenzo Machado*

☐ Computer Skills
☑ Patient Records Training
☑ Benefits and Insurance
☐ Teams that Work

Training Report *Donna Manning*

☑ Computer Skills
☐ Patient Records Training
☐ Benefits and Insurance
☐ Teams that Work

1. Ana ___has taken___ the Computer Skills session, and ___so has___ Donna.

2. Ana ___hasn't taken___ the Patient Records Training yet, and ___neither has___ Donna.

3. Lorenzo ___has taken___ the Benefits and Insurance class, and Ana ___has, too___.

4. Donna ___hasn't taken___ Teams that Work, and Lorenzo and Ana ___haven't either___.

3 **TALK.** Change the sentences in Activity 2 into the simple past with a partner. Use simple past time expressions.

Example: *Ana took the Computer Skills session last month, and so did Donna.*

4 **LISTEN** and read the job evaluation form. Check the qualities that describe Lorenzo.

Area	Exceeds Expectations	Meets Expectations	Below Expectations
Time Management Comments: *manages time nicely*		✓	
Leadership Comments: *Could attend workshop*		✓	
Teamwork Comments: *gets along with others / is helpful.*	✓		
Communication Comments: *great*	✓		
Preparation Comments: *should pull together materials before he needs them*			✓

5 **LISTEN** again. Write comments in the form in Activity 4.

6 **WRITE.** Read about Lorenzo's coworkers. Then compare Lorenzo's performance to theirs by writing sentences with *so, too, either,* or *neither.*

Example: *Silvia has managed her time well, and so has Lorenzo.*

1. Silvia has managed her time well.
2. Thomas has not been very prepared, *and neither has Lorenzo.*
3. Donna has developed good communication skills. *and so has Lorenzo.*
4. Luke has shown good leadership skills. *and Lorenzo has too*
5. Jenny has shown very good teamwork. *and so has Lorenzo.*

Math: Figuring Salary Increases

A **READ.** A salary increase is a raise in pay. It is usually a percentage of the current salary. Read the steps for figuring salary increases.

Step 1: Multiply the percentage of the increase by the current salary.

5% of $20,000 = .05 × 20,000 = $1,000

Step 2: Add the dollar amount of the increase to the current salary.

$1,000 + $20,000 = new salary = $21,000

B **FIGURE** the new salaries with a partner.

1. Angela makes $22,000. She earned a 3% increase. What's her new salary? _____
2. Steven makes $18,000. He will get a 5% increase. What will his new salary be? _____
3. Jeff makes $20,000. He earned a 4% increase. What's his new salary? _____
4. Tania makes $25,000. She got a 6% increase. What's her new salary? _____
5. Max earns $17,000. He will get a 7% increase next year. What will his new salary be? _____

LESSON 6: Reading

1 THINK ABOUT IT. Discuss these questions in a group.

1. What qualities do you need to be successful in the workplace?

2. Have you ever had a conflict with a coworker? How was the situation resolved?

2 BEFORE YOU READ.

A. SCAN. Look at the first paragraph of the article on the next page. Scan and underline the job Marsha and Felix tried to get.

> **READING FOCUS: Scan**
>
> When you scan, you look at a text quickly to find a specific piece of information.

> **READING FOCUS: Use the suffixes -able and -ive to understand meaning.**
>
> The suffix -able forms adjectives from verbs and nouns. These adjectives show ability, possibility, or being appropriate for something.
>
> break ⟶ breakable (able to be broken)
>
> comfort ⟶ comfortable (able to give comfort)
>
> The suffix -ive forms adjectives from verbs. This kind of adjective shows that the noun it describes has a certain quality or is often a certain way.
>
> act ⟶ active (having the quality of acting; often taking action)
>
> communicate ⟶ communicative (having the quality of communicating well)

B. SCAN again. Look at the whole article. Scan for adjectives that end with -able and -ive. Circle them. Underline the nouns and pronouns these adjectives describe.

> **Reading Strategy Summary**
>
> Use prior knowledge.
>
> Scan.
>
> Use the suffixes -able and -ive to understand meaning.

3 READ the article and think about what each word ending in -able or -ive means.

4 AFTER YOU READ.

A. DISCUSS. Work with a partner. Write adjectives from the reading that describe Marsha and Felix. Discuss what each word means. Next to each adjective you write, put a (+) if you think the adjective is a positive quality or a (–) if you think it is a negative quality.

Marsha	Felix

B. TALK with your classmates and compare Felix and Marsha. What qualities do they both have? How are they different? Which candidate would you hire for TV 10 News?

Example: *Felix has worked as a reporter for four years, but Marsha has never been a reporter.*

Marsha or Felix: Who Gets the Job?

Getting a job can be tough. It's important to make a good impression when you interview for a job. Imagine that there are two candidates* for the same job, Marsha and Felix. Both candidates applied for the job of reporter with the local TV 10 News show. After Carol from Human Resources* interviewed the candidates, she wrote these notes:

Marsha	Felix
Marsha - Marsha seems very likeable. She'd have a great "on air" personality because she's quite communicative, too. She seems capable, but some of her job skills are questionable. She has never been a reporter, so we can't be sure that her work will be suitable. When I followed up with her references*, I learned some valuable information. Her last employer did not think Marsha was dependable. Neither did her college professor. I'm not sure she'll be able to meet our deadlines, but she is ready to accept assignments starting immediately. Overall, I think our viewers would really like her youthfulness and enthusiasm, but hiring her could be a risk. Years of work experience: 3	Felix -Felix has worked with a news station before. He has proven that he can complete projects on time. After I saw some of his broadcasts, I knew his work was impressive. However, Felix seemed a bit aggressive to me, so he might not be sensitive enough to interview people well. His last employer described him as reliable and creative, but also said that he asked for a lot of days off. Also, it seems that some coworkers weren't comfortable around him. It sounds like sometimes he can be uncooperative and disagreeable. Overall, I think he would do a good job on camera, but he may be difficult to work with off camera. Years of work experience: 20 (4 years as a reporter).

Carol has a tough decision to make. Both candidates have positive and negative qualities, and neither one is the obvious choice for the job. Reporters need to be outgoing*, capable, and above all, dependable. Good people skills are a must and so is the ability to meet a deadline.

candidate (n.): a person who is trying to get a specific job

human resources (n. phrase): department responsible for employee records and benefits

references (n.): people who can talk about a candidate's job experience

outgoing (adj.): friendly; able to talk easily with other people

LESSON 7: Writing

1 **THINK ABOUT IT.** What is your ideal job? Why would you be good at that job? What would be difficult about the job for you?

2 **BEFORE YOU WRITE.**

A. READ the paragraph below. Juanita is a receptionist. She has asked her boss for a raise, so she must tell why she deserves one. <u>Underline</u> the adjectives that describe her qualities.

◀ ▶ ↺ ✖ http://excellentemployees.net/access/j_gonzales/sent/

To: jh_kwon@excellentemployees.net
From: j_gonzalez@excellentemployees.net
Subject: Request
Sent: 07/22/10, 10:07am

Dear Ms. Kwon,

I'm writing to you today to ask you for a raise in my salary. I have worked here as a receptionist for three years, and am very happy with my job. I am always on time, and I try to use my time as efficiently as possible. I am always sensitive to our clients' needs, and they tell me I am very dependable.

In addition to my regular duties of greeting clients and answering phones, I have also helped many of my coworkers with their projects. It's not part of my normal job, but I enjoy helping them. They have told me several times that they are happy with my work, too.

For example, I helped prepare the materials for the Singapore project last month with Lorenzo, and last year I helped Donna prepare for her advertising presentation. I stayed late and worked many evenings to help with these projects.

I believe that you will agree that I am a capable and valuable part of the team here. I look forward to your response.

Sincerely,

Juanita Gonzalez

B. BRAINSTORM. Make a list of your best personal qualities and skills. Then share your ideas with a partner.

Examples: *always on time, cooperative*

_____   _____

_____   _____

_____   _____

_____   _____

_____   _____

List your best personal skills. • Use persuasive writing.

WRITING FOCUS: Write a persuasive letter

To be persuasive, write about facts that will be important to your reader. Think carefully about what details to include. For example:

Jack Williams has been a very effective mayor. He created a new health clinic, a new library, and a new public transportation system.

When you try to persuade someone, you try to make them decide to do something. Usually, you do this by giving them reasons to do it.

C. **WRITE.** Think about your own job or a job that you would like to have. Reread your list of personal qualities or skills. Which ones would help the most at this job? Write them in the chart, and give a persuasive detail about each one. Add more if needed.

Quality or Skill	Detail
creative	I have designed and planted many gardens.

3 **WRITE.** Imagine that you will ask for a raise or promotion at work, or that you are applying for a job you would like to have. Write a letter that tells why you should get the raise or the promotion or why your personal qualities will be useful at the job. Give persuasive details, and give reasons.

Example: *I'm very creative, and I have cared for many children, so I would be a great daycare teacher.*

4 **AFTER YOU WRITE.**

A. **READ.** Work with a partner. Read each other's letter and find the persuasive words and details. Discuss how you could each make your letters more persuasive.

1. Did you choose the best personal qualities to fit the job you have or want?
2. Can you add details to make your argument stronger?

B. **EDIT** your letter for spelling and grammar errors.

1. Did you use the present perfect correctly?
2. Did you spell *–ive* and *–able* words correctly?
3. Did you use complete sentences?

C. **REWRITE** your letter with corrections.

Career Connection

1 **THINK ABOUT IT.** What are *benefits*? What is an *annual benefit review*? Have you ever had an annual benefit review? What information did you receive?

2 **READ** this employee's annual benefit review from human resources. As you read, circle the dates and percentages in the review.

Human Resources Annual Benefit Review 2008

Date: January 10, 2009

Employee: Delgado, Josef　　　Date of Hire: March 1, 2007

Department: Custodial　　　Title: Janitor I

Health Benefits
Your medical and dental benefits began on June 1, 2007.

Retirement Benefits
You became eligible for* retirement benefits on March 1, 2008. You currently contribute 10% of your pay each month to your retirement fund. We match* 50% of your contributions. You will become 40% vested* in your retirement fund on March 1, 2009.

Vacation Benefits
You used 7 vacation days in August 2008. You must use your remaining 3 vacation days for 2008 before March 1, 2009. After that date, you will lose any vacation days you have left for 2008, and you will begin to use your 10 vacation days for 2009.

VACATION TIME

0–3 years	= 10 vacation days
4–6 years	= 12 vacation days
7–9 years	= 14 vacation days
10+ years	= add 1 day per year

Example: 13 years = 18 days

RETIREMENT VESTING

1 year	= 20% vested
2 years	= 40% vested
3 year	= 60% vested
4 years	= 80% vested
5 years	= 100% vested

---

eligible for (adj.): qualified for

match (v.): contribute an equal amount

vested (adj.): given a legal right to something

3 **TALK WITH A PARTNER.** Answer the questions. Use Josef's benefit review and the information in the charts above to help you.

1. How many vacation days can Josef take before the end of 2009?

2. One year after the date of this review, how many new vacation days will Josef receive?

3. On what date does Josef become 100% vested in his retirement fund?

4 **TALK** with a partner or a group. Josef is applying to be a custodial supervisor at another company. The new job offers a higher salary, but fewer benefits. What benefits do you think he should look for? Why? Should he take the new job if he will lose some of his benefits? What do you think?

5 **WHAT ABOUT YOU?** Work in a group. Discuss the questions.

1. What kinds of benefits are important to you at a job?

2. How much vacation time and sick time do you want?

3. Is a retirement plan important at your job? Why or why not?

Check Your Progress!

Skill	Circle the answers.	Is it correct?
A. Use past time clauses with *after*, *when*, *as soon as*, *before*, **and** *until*.	1. Karen left for work **until** / **after** she ate breakfast. 2. Ed stopped at the coffee shop **before** / **when** he went to the office. 3. I turned off the copier **until** / **as soon as** I saw that it was broken. 4. **Until** / **When** Mike got a car, he had to ride his bike to work.	☐ ☐ ☐ ☐
	Number Correct	0 1 2 3 4
B. Use the simple past and present perfect.	5. Nick **had** / **has had** his performance review yesterday. 6. I **have worked** / **worked** there since July. 7. She **hasn't finished** / **finished** the report yet. 8. Who **was** / **has been** at the meeting this morning?	☐ ☐ ☐ ☐
	Number Correct	0 1 2 3 4
C. Talk about workplace activities.	9. Kim **made** / **scheduled** the meeting before she left for lunch. 10. Did Angela **meet** / **complete** the deadline, or was the report late? 11. Sam **covered for** / **followed up** Mike until he could get to work. 12. Please ask Adam to **join** / **pull together** materials for the meeting.	☐ ☐ ☐ ☐
	Number Correct	0 1 2 3 4
D. Understand terms for professional accomplishments.	13. Jan is nice, and she gets **along** / **about** well with everyone. 14. Ellen received a positive **performance** / **certification** review last year. 15. He has developed good **communicate** / **communication** skills this year. 16. She has **maintained** / **attended** her qualifications for 10 years.	☐ ☐ ☐ ☐
	Number Correct	0 1 2 3 4

COUNT the number of correct answers above. Fill in the bubbles.

Chart Your Success					
Skill	**Need Practice**	**Okay**	**Good**	**Very Good**	**Excellent!**
A. Use past time clauses with *after*, *when*, *as soon as*, *before* **and** *until*.	⓪	①	②	③	④
B. Use the simple past and present perfect.	⓪	①	②	③	④
C. Talk about workplace activities.	⓪	①	②	③	④
D. Understand terms for professional accomplishments.	⓪	①	②	③	④

LESSON 1: Grammar and Vocabulary

1 GRAMMAR PICTURE DICTIONARY. Did Jamie and Lucy have a nice date? Listen and read.

TCD1, 40
SCD10

1 Lucy was waiting patiently for Jamie. **Fortunately**, she (had remembered) to put the **events brochure** in her handbag <u>before</u> she left home.

2 Jamie was late because he had stopped to buy flowers from a **street vendor**.

3 They had planned to go to a **film festival**. But when they arrived at the **box office**, the movie was already sold out.

4 They decided to see the City Symphony's **debut performance**. But by the time they reached the **concert hall**, the performance had already started.

5 **Unfortunately**, Jamie hadn't turned off his cell phone before he sat down in the **auditorium**. The **usher** and audience members were annoyed.

6 Jamie made a dinner **reservation**. By the time they arrived, the **hostess** had already given their table to another couple.

2 READ the sentences in Activity 1 with a partner.

3 NOTICE THE GRAMMAR. (Circle) *had* + the past participle. <u>Underline</u> the words *before, when, by the time,* and *already.*

Past Perfect

You can use the past perfect with the simple past to talk about two events in the past. Use the past perfect to show which event happened first. Use the simple past for the second event.

Subject	*had (not)*	Past Participle		Simple Past Time Clause
I		bought	tickets	*before* I *went* to the film festival.
They	had (not)	made	a reservation	*before* they *went* to the restaurant.
He		eaten	dinner	*when* the pizza *arrived*.

Use *already* or to emphasize that one event happened before another.

> The film had *already* started when we arrived at the theater.

By the time means "some time before, but not after." When the phrase *by the time* is followed by the simple past, the next clause is often in the past perfect.

> *By the time* we arrived at the film festival, the show had already started.

4 **COMPLETE** the sentences with the past perfect form of the verbs in parentheses. Then read the sentences with a partner.

1. Unfortunately, the box office ____had____ already ____closed____ (close) when he reached the theater.

2. Sheila _____ (not hear) the City Symphony play before she attended their debut performance at the concert hall.

3. By the time they reached the auditorium, the usher _____ already _____ (seat) most of the other people.

4. They _____ (call) to confirm their reservation with the hostess before they went to the restaurant.

5. By the time John remembered to buy flowers, the street vendor _____ already _____ (leave) the corner.

6. Jill was not happy when she reached the post office. She _____ (forget) to bring the letters.

7. They didn't serve any dinner at the party. Fortunately, James _____ (buy) a hotdog from a street vendor before he arrived!

8. Meg was sure she _____ (put) the events brochure in her bag, but when she looked for it, it was gone.

5 **WHAT ABOUT YOU?** What did you do for fun last week? Tell a partner. Had you done the activity before? Practice asking your partner.

LESSON 2: Grammar Practice Plus

1 **TALK** about the picture. What are the people doing? Use the words in the vocabulary box below. What do you think happened before each of these things?

> The man and woman had already bought their tickets before they arrived.

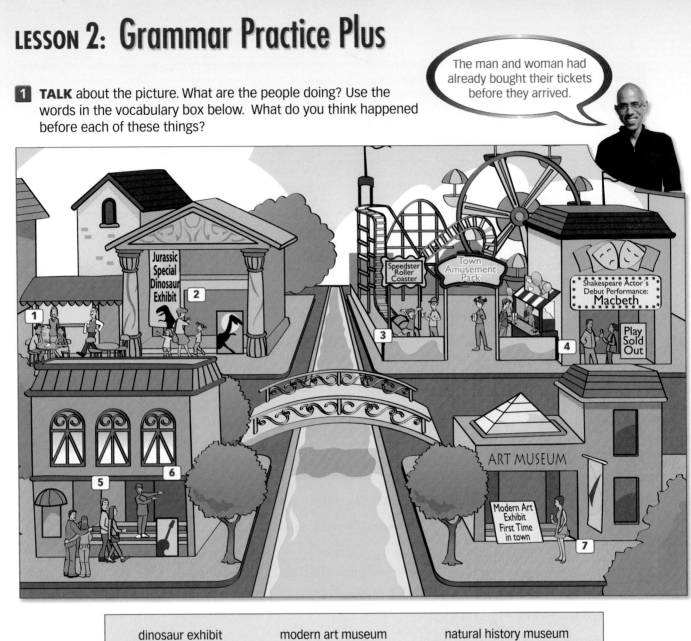

dinosaur exhibit	modern art museum	natural history museum
theater	concert hall	sidewalk café	amusement park

2 **LISTEN** to the statements about the people in Activity 1 and write the number next to the names below.

TCD1, 41

_____ Andy and Amy

_____ Jane

_____ Mark and Jill

_____ Tom and Tammy

_____ Tony (the usher)

_____ Uma and Rajiv

_____ Joey

> Use *never* with the past perfect to talk about an event that had **not** happened before another event in the past.
>
> The City Symphony had **never** performed here **before last night**.
>
> You can end a sentence with the adverb *before* and omit the rest of the phrase. The meaning does not change.
>
> The City Symphony had **never** performed here **before**.

3 **TALK** with a partner about the people in the picture. Find three things you think had never happened before.

Example: *Rajiv and Uma had never been on a date before.*

(9/12)

4 READ. Henry won $1,000 and a trip to his favorite city. He took the trip last weekend. He checked into a luxury hotel last Friday night. On Saturday night, he wrote about how he had spent his day. Read his journal and <u>underline</u> the things he did for the first time.

	Morning		Afternoon		Evening/Night
6 A.M.		**NOON**	I ordered tickets online. Best seat!	**6 P.M.**	I rented a limousine for the first time!
7 A.M.		**1 P.M.**	I had lunch at a sidewalk café, then bought ice cream from a street vendor.	**7 P.M.**	I ate at the new restaurant! Great food!
8 A.M.		**2 P.M.**	I visited the Natural History Museum for the first time!	**8 P.M.**	I arrived at the concert hall and the usher took me to my seat.
9 A.M.	I slept late.	**3 P.M.**	I made a dinner reservation at a new restaurant.	**9 P.M.**	I saw my first symphony concert!
10 A.M.	I ordered breakfast from the hotel restaurant.	**4 P.M.**	I went shopping and bought a new MP3 player and some CDs.	**10 P.M.**	
11 A.M.	I read the events brochure and found a symphony concert.	**5 P.M.**	I relaxed in the park and listened to a new classical music CD!	**11 P.M.**	The driver drove me back to the hotel.

5 WRITE five sentences about what Henry did. Look at the schedule in Activity 4.

1. What had Henry done by 5:00 P.M.?

   By 5:00 p.m., Henry had already ordered tickets online, had eaten lunch . . .

2. What had he done by 11 A.M.?

3. What had he done by 7 P.M.?

4. What had he done by 9 P.M.?

5. What had he never done before?

6 WHAT ABOUT YOU? Tell a partner which things you had or hadn't done before you took this English course.

1. study with this group of classmates

2. take a class with this teacher

3. study grammar

4. take an English class

5. _____

9/12

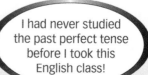

I had never studied the past perfect tense before I took this English class!

LESSON 3: Listening and Conversation

1 LISTEN to the conversation. Then listen to a question. Fill in the correct answer. Replay each item if necessary.

TCD1, 42–47

1. (A) (B) (C)   4. (A) (B) (C)

2. (A) (B) (C)   5. (A) (B) (C)

3. (A) (B) (C)   6. (A) (B) (C)

2 LISTEN. Look at a TV schedule from the newspaper. Then listen to a couple talk about what TV shows to watch tonight. Fill in the times that you hear.

TCD1, 48

Saturday Night TV Schedule		
Channel 2	*Win Big Money!*	_____ P.M.
Channel 3	*Crime Scene Detectives*	_____ P.M.
Channel 4	*Fun Times with Mr. Doozy*	_____ P.M.
Channel 4	*History of the American West*	_____ P.M.
Channel 5	*Sleepover House*	_10_ P.M.

3 LISTEN to the couple continue their conversation. Read the movie listing and fill in the missing information.

TCD1, 49

At the Movies		
Town Theater Film Festival		
Theater 1	*Jaws*	_____ P.M.
Theater 2	*The Terminator*	_____ P.M.
Theater 3	_____	8:10 P.M.
Theater 4	_____	8:15 P.M.
Theater 5	*The Lion King*	_____ P.M.

4 LISTEN to the conversation again. Read the statements and check ☑ *True* or *False*.

	True	False
1. The man really loves movies about fish and sharks.	☐	☐
2. The man enjoys action films.	☐	☐
3. The woman doesn't want to watch an early movie.	☐	☐
4. The woman had already seen *You've Got Mail*.	☐	☐
5. By the time they saw the movie listing, *The Lion King* had already ended.	☐	☐

5 WHAT ABOUT YOU? Use the information in the box to write sentences about things you had never seen or places you had never been to as a child. Use *by the time* to write about things you had seen or places you had been to before a certain age. Then talk with a partner.

Examples: *I'd never seen a horror movie before I was in middle school.*

I had been to a lot of amusement parks by the time I was nine.

horror movie	dinosaur exhibit	symphony performance
TV game show	cartoons	natural history museum
expensive restaurant	reality TV show	amusement park

TCD1, 50
SCD11

6 **LISTEN** to the conversation. Then practice with a partner.

> A: Did you go to the <u>film festival</u> yesterday?
>
> B: No. By the time I got there, it had already sold out.
>
> A: <u>Oh, that's too bad</u>. So, then what did you do?
>
> B: I went to <u>the modern art exhibit at the museum</u>.
>
> A: Wow! You did?
>
> B: Yes. I'd never seen such <u>incredible paintings</u> before.
>
> A: Oh, that's great.

7 **PRACTICE** the conversation from Activity 6 with a partner. Use the information in the chart.

Planned activity	Expression to show surprise or sympathy	Where you went	What you saw
1. concert	Oh, I can't believe it.	the dinosaur exhibit at the Natural History Museum	huge dinosaurs
2. Shakespeare play	What a waste of time.	The Space Museum	amazing exhibits
3. dance performance	Oh, that's a shame.	the new amusement park	huge roller coasters

TCD1, 51 **Pronunciation:** Compound Nouns vs. Noun Phrases

A compound noun is a phrase made up of more than one word. The phrase acts like a single noun. Most compound nouns usually have stress on the first word.

In regular adjective + noun phrases which are *not* compound nouns, the stress falls on the second word in the phrase. Sometimes this stress is important to understand the meaning. Look at the examples. Then listen and repeat.

> He wrote on the **white** board. (a board in a classroom)
>
> He nailed the sign onto a white **board**. (a flat piece of wood that is white)

TCD1, 52
SCD12 **A** **LISTEN** for the stressed words in the sentences. Circle the letter of the sentence you hear.

1. a. She was at the **green**house.   b. She was at the green **house**.
2. a. They'd gone to the **White** House.   b. They'd gone to the white **house**.
3. a. Did he get his **hair**cut?   b. Did he get his hair **cut**?

TCD1, 53 **B** **LISTEN** again and repeat.

LESSON 4: Grammar and Vocabulary

1 **GRAMMAR PICTURE DICTIONARY.** Look at the pictures of some surprising events. Then read and listen to the conversations.

TCD1, 54
SCD13

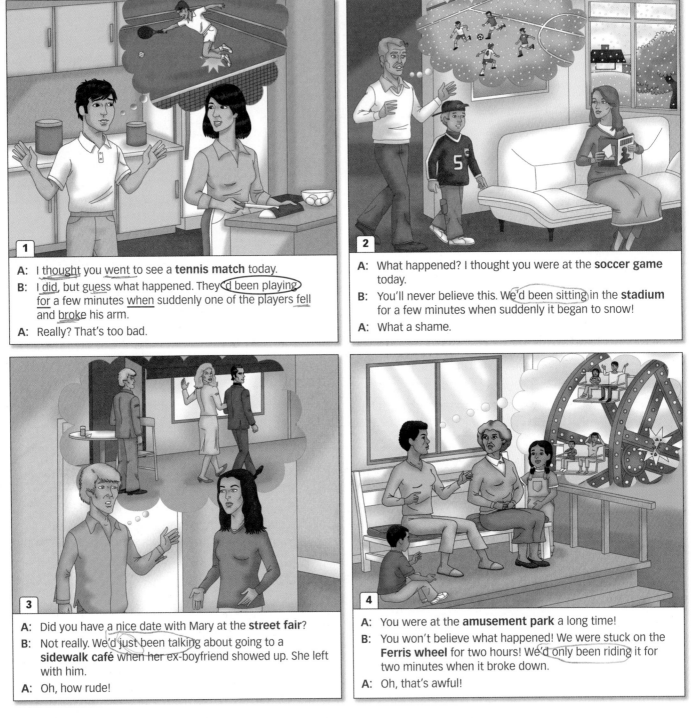

1

A: I thought you went to see a **tennis match** today.
B: I did, but guess what happened. They'd been playing for a few minutes when suddenly one of the players fell and broke his arm.
A: Really? That's too bad.

2

A: What happened? I thought you were at the **soccer game** today.
B: You'll never believe this. We'd been sitting in the **stadium** for a few minutes when suddenly it began to snow!
A: What a shame.

3

A: Did you have a nice date with Mary at the **street fair**?
B: Not really. We'd just been talking about going to a **sidewalk café** when her ex-boyfriend showed up. She left with him.
A: Oh, how rude!

4

A: You were at the **amusement park** a long time!
B: You won't believe what happened! We were stuck on the **Ferris wheel** for two hours! We'd only been riding it for two minutes when it broke down.
A: Oh, that's awful!

2 **PRACTICE** the conversations from Activity 1 with a partner.

3 **NOTICE THE GRAMMAR.** Circle the past perfect continuous verb forms in the conversations above. Underline the words *when* and *for*.

Past Perfect Continuous

The past perfect continuous describes an action that had been in progress before another event happened. We often use *for* to talk about how long the first event had been happening.

	Past Perfect Continuous Statement			Time Clause (optional)
Subject	*had*	***been* + Verb + *ing***	*for* + time	***when* + Subject + Simple Past**
I	had	been jogging	for an hour	*when* it started to rain.
They	had	been talking	for a while	*when* Tom showed up.

In addition to *when*, time expressions using *by the time*, *until*, and *by* are also common with the past perfect continuous..

By the time they arrived with the keys, we **had been waiting** in the cold for over 30 minutes.

Scott became a professional tennis player in 2005. *Until then,* he **had been working** at an amusement park near Chicago.

Of course Mike was tired when you got here! He'**d** already **been working** for six hours *by then*.

> The past continuous is often used instead of the past perfect continuous, especially when the order of events is clear to the listener. *I was standing in line when it started to rain.*

4 COMPLETE the conversations. Use the past perfect continuous with the verbs in parentheses.

1. *A:* Did you try that new Italian restaurant last night?

   B: Well, we went there, but we didn't eat there. When we finally got our menus, we ___had been sitting___ (sit) at our table for over twenty minutes. So we decided to go somewhere else.

2. *A:* How was the meeting with the new boss?

   B: Good and bad. I didn't realize until after we left that I _____ (call) her the wrong name all evening.

3. A: Where did you find the cats? I spent all afternoon looking for them!

   B: So did I. Then I discovered that they _____ (sleep) under my bed the whole day.

4. *A:* Eric had to come home early from his big trip to Europe. He broke his leg in a bicycle accident.

   B: Oh no! I know he _____ (look) forward to it for such a long time!

5. *A:* You lost your new necklace? How?

   B: I was at the amusement park. By the time I realized it was gone, I _____ (walk) around for two hours already. I never found it.

6. *A:* How did your date with Sara go?

   B: Not so good. We went out for dinner, but by the time she got to the cafe, I _____ (drink) coffee for almost an hour. I was too full to eat anything!

5 PRACTICE the conversations in Activity 4 with a partner. Partner A, use expressions in the Conversation Strategy box to respond Partner B.

Conversation Strategy

Expressing Surprise or Sympathy

Oh, that's too bad.	Wow, I can't believe it.
Oh, that's terrible.	What a shame.
How rude!	What a waste of time.
How strange!	

LESSON 5: Grammar Practice Plus

1 TALK. What are these people doing? Tell a partner. Use the words in the vocabulary box below.

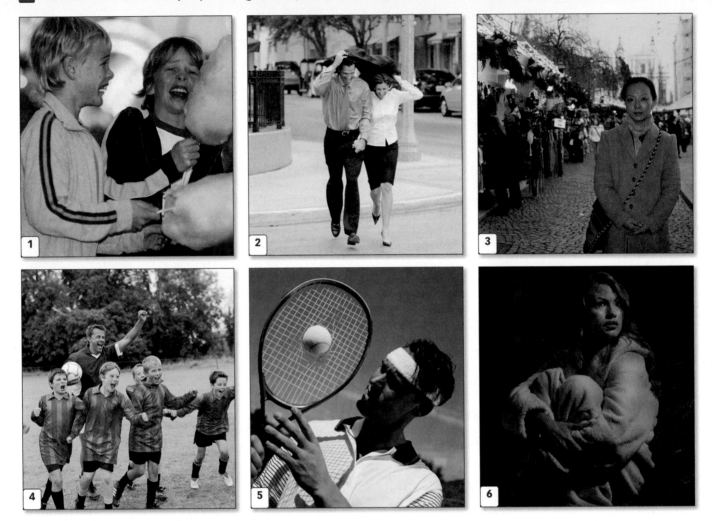

2 LISTEN to the conversations about the people in Activity 1. Write the number of the picture next to the correct question.

TCD1, 55

a. _____ Why was Holly so upset?

b. _1_ Why were the boys so sick?

c. _____ Why was Hugo so frustrated?

d. _____ Why was the soccer team so happy?

e. _____ Why was Marcie so scared?

f. _____ Why was Suzie so disappointed?

amusement park	scary movie
cotton candy	sidewalk café
ex-boyfriend	storm
power	street fair
racket	tennis match
roller coaster	

3 WRITE. Listen again to the conversations in Activity 2. Write the answers to the questions. Tell a partner your answers.

Example: *Holly was upset because she ran into her ex-boyfriend.*

| Use *so* + adjective. • Read a description from a TV magazine. • Calculate sales tax.

4 **WRITE.** Read the descriptions from a TV magazine. Then answer the questions using the past perfect continuous.

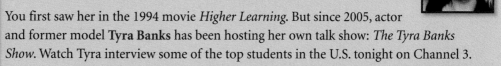

If you're old enough to remember **Johnny Depp** from his days in the lead role in the TV series *21 Jumpstreet* (1987–1990), you might also know that his first movie role was in *The Nightmare on Elm Street* (1984). Watch the film tonight on the Movies of Yesterday channel.

You first saw her in the 1994 movie *Higher Learning*. But since 2005, actor and former model **Tyra Banks** has been hosting her own talk show: *The Tyra Banks Show*. Watch Tyra interview some of the top students in the U.S. tonight on Channel 3.

Long before he directed movies like *Letters from Iwo Jima* (2006) and *Million Dollar Baby* (2004), **Clint Eastwood** was famous for acting in western and action films. Watch him tonight in his first big film, *A Fistful of Dollars* (1964).

1. How long had Johnny Depp been appearing in movies before he played in a TV show?

   _____

2. How long had Tyra Banks been acting before she started her own talk show?

   _____

3. How long had Clint Eastwood been starring in films before he directed *Million Dollar Baby*?

   _____

5 **TALK** with a partner. Tell your partner your answers to the questions in Activity 4.

Math: Calculating Sales Tax

Sales tax is a small fee paid to the government for certain items you buy. To calculate sales tax, multiply the total amount by the percentage. For example, 7% tax on $15.00 is $15.00 × .07 = $1.05.

A **READ** the situation below.

Lisa had $100 to take her family to the movies. She bought tickets for three adults, two senior citizens, and two children. There was no tax on movie tickets. She bought four bags of popcorn, seven sodas, and four boxes of candy. She paid 7% tax on refreshments.

B **ANSWER** the questions.

1. How much did she spend on tickets? _____

2. How much did she pay for refreshments? _____

3. How much tax did she pay for refreshments? _____

4. How much money did she have left? _____

MOVIE TICKETS	
Adults: $11.00	Senior citizens: $8.00
Children: $6.00	

REFRESHMENTS	
Bag of Popcorn: $3.00	Soda: $2.00
Box of Candy: $2.50	

LESSON 6: Reading

1 **THINK ABOUT IT.** Do you know of any politicians who were once in the field of entertainment? Who do you know? Talk with a partner or in a group.

2 **BEFORE YOU READ.** Preview the article. Do you recognize the man in the photographs? What do you know about him?

3 **READ** the article. As you read, circle the dates. Underline the words *before, after, when, by,* and *by the time.*

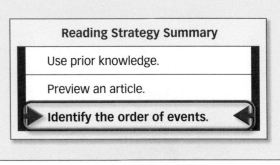

Reading Strategy Summary

| Use prior knowledge. |
| Preview an article. |
| ▶ **Identify the order of events.** ◀ |

READING FOCUS: Identify the order of events

As you read, you can use dates and verb forms to help you identify the order of events. Signal words such as *then, before, by, since, when, by the time,* and *after* help you identify the order of events.

4 **AFTER YOU READ.**

A. SEQUENCE the events. Put the events of Arnold Schwarzenegger's life in order. Number them 1–10.

- _2_ won the Mr. Universe competition
- _9_ starred in comedy films
- _1_ began lifting weights
- _3_ moved to the United States
- _8_ starred in action films
- _4_ learned English
- _10_ became governor
- _7_ married Maria Shriver
- _5_ received his college degree
- _6_ became a U.S. citizen

B. VOCABULARY. Find and draw a rectangle around the vocabulary words in the article. Read the sentences that include the words, and the sentences before and after them to help you understand the meaning of the words. Then use the words to complete the sentences below.

| bodybuilding | elected | futuristic | competitions | emissions | versatility |

1. Arnold Schwarzenegger had participated in ___bodybuilding___ competitions since he was a teenager.
2. Gas _emissions_ from cars and trucks are dangerous for the environment.
3. It is important for an actor to play different roles and show _versatility_.
4. The American people _elected_ Ronald Reagan as their president in 1980 and 1984.
5. Many people watch singing or dancing _competitions_ on television and vote for their favorite performer.
6. Some amusement parks have a _futuristic_ theme—the exhibits make you feel like you are living in the future.

5 **TALK** with a partner. Use the events in Activity 4A and the words in the Reading Focus box to talk about Arnold Schwarzenegger's life.

A Man of Many Talents

You might not recognize this man as a politician. He might be more familiar as an actor. Before Arnold Schwarzenegger became the 38th Governor of California, he had had two other exciting careers.

Arnold Schwarzenegger was born in Austria in 1947. As a child, Arnold was very athletic. In fact, he began lifting weights as a teenager. He worked hard at bodybuilding, and by the age of 20, he
5 had become the youngest man to win the Mr. Universe title*. He moved to the United States in 1968. When he first arrived in the U.S., he didn't speak much English. But he studied hard and learned English well enough to attend college.
10 By the time he became a U.S. citizen in 1983, he had already received a degree from the University of Wisconsin (1979). In 1986, he married Maria Shriver, a famous journalist* and a niece of former President John F. Kennedy.

15 After he stopped entering bodybuilding competitions, Arnold Schwarzenegger became an actor and a big Hollywood star. Early in his career, he starred in films such as *Hercules in New York* (1970), *Conan: The Barbarian* (1982)
20 and futuristic action movies like *The Terminator* (1984). He later showed his versatility by appearing

in several comedies, including *Twins* (1988) and
25 *Kindergarten Cop* (1990). He last appeared in a film in 2005, *The Kid and I.*

Schwarzenegger had been interested in politics for many years before the people of California elected him governor in 2003 and again in 2007.
30 He believed that he could do a lot for California, especially for the environment. By 2006, Governor Schwarzenegger had already helped reduce California's greenhouse gas emissions* and had started other programs to clean up the
35 environment.

Governor Schwarzenegger set goals and achieved them. He is a man of many talents. He may be one of the most famous and successful immigrants in the United States.

title (n.): name given to the winner of a sports competition

journalist (n.): a person who writes news reports for newspapers, magazines, radio, TV, or the Internet

greenhouse gas emissions (n. phrase): the release of harmful pollution into the air that becomes trapped in the Earth's atmosphere

LESSON 7: Writing

1 **THINK ABOUT IT.** Have you ever gone back to visit your hometown or your childhood friends? What was the same? What was different?

2 **BEFORE YOU WRITE.**

A. TALK. Look at the picture and talk with a partner. Where are the people? What do you think they are talking about?

 B. LISTEN to the conversation between two friends at a school reunion. Take notes in the T-charts below.

TCD1, 56

Ten-year reunion at Smithtown High School

Chim Doc	
Then	**Now**
Lived in Smithtown	Lives in Miami

Juanita	
Then	**Now**

 C. WHAT ABOUT YOU? Fill in the T-chart with notes about yourself. Write about important events or activities in your life now, and in the past. Talk with a partner about your information.

Then	Now

D. COMPLETE Chim Doc's timeline. Then write a timeline for yourself.

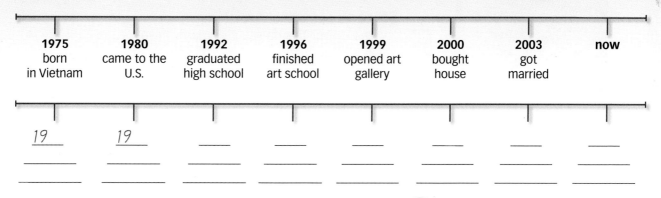

1975	1980	1992	1996	1999	2000	2003	now
born in Vietnam	came to the U.S.	graduated high school	finished art school	opened art gallery	bought house	got married	

19___   19___   ___   ___   ___   ___   ___   ___

E. READ Chim Doc's short autobiography in the Reunion Newsletter. Circle the ages and dates.

Chim Doc: I came to the U.S. when I was five. I've loved art since I was very small. I had always known I wanted to be a painter and to own a gallery where I could exhibit my work.

I applied to an art program when I was in high school, and got accepted. By the time I was 25, I had already had my first art show and had opened my own gallery. I got married in 2003, and I have two wonderful children—Hoang and Nhung. Today I own galleries in New York, Miami, and Los Angeles.

WRITING FOCUS: Include personal details
A narrative essay or an autobiography (a description a person writes about his or her own life) should specify details about a person's life. Include dates, places, and events to enrich your story and inform your reader.

3 WRITE a short autobiography to include in a class reunion newsletter from your high school.

1. What was your country like when you were a child?
2. Where had your family been living before you moved to the U.S. or to your current town?
3. What had you done by the time you were a teenager? By the time you graduated from school?
4. What were your interests or activities as a student? What do you enjoy doing now?
5. List three things you had already accomplished before you got married or before you started to study English at this school.

4 AFTER YOU WRITE.

A. EDIT. Read your partner's autobiography. Ask yourself the questions below.

1. Is there anything you don't understand?
2. Did your partner mention specific events from the past?
3. Did your partner mention what he or she is doing now?
4. Did your partner use dates and times correctly to make it clear when things happened?
5. Did your partner use the past perfect and the past perfect continuous correctly?

B. DISCUSS the corrections with your partner.

C. REWRITE your autobiography with corrections.

Career Connection

MD

1 **LOOK** at the photo. What job responsibilities do security guards have?

2 **LISTEN** to the conversation between Marcel, a security guard at a museum, and Mr. Hanif, his manager. Check ☑ *True* or *False*.

TCD1, 57

	True	False
1. Marcel works in a natural history museum.	☐	☐
2. When Mr. Hanif contacted Marcel, Marcel had been helping patrons find an exhibit.	☐	☐
3. Marcel's co-worker Horace had put the warning signs back up before he finished his shift.	☐	☐
4. The guards put up barricades to keep visitors safe.	☐	☐

3 **TALK.** *To take the initiative* means to think of ideas for making something better without being asked to do it. How did Marcel take the initiative after talking to Mr. Hanif? Circle the things Marcel decided to do. Then tell a partner.

give directions to patrons	turn off the alarm system	put signs up
read Horace's report	reset the alarm system	secure the barricades

4 **READ** about Horace's security report and talk with a partner. What had Horace already taken care of before he left? What hadn't Horace done before he left?

Security Report

Security Guard: _Horace McGee_   Date: _11/9/09_   Time: _4:46 P.M._

Comments:

Visitors on the third floor were in a restricted area. The T-Rex dinosaur display fell down. There was no damage to the exhibit or injuries to patrons. The warning signs are on the floor. Room temperature control is not working.

Security Checklist:

- ☐ Barricades and ropes in place
- ☑ Stairwells clean
- ☑ Emergency exits secure
- ☑ Restricted areas checked
- ☐ Alarm system activated
- ☑ Alarm system shut down
- ☐ Warning signs in place and secure
- ☐ Temperature control set

---

5 **WHAT ABOUT YOU?** What are some ways you can take the initiative at work or at home? What ideas do you have about making positive changes? Discuss your ideas with a partner.

Check Your Progress!

9/14

Skill	Circle the answers.	Is it correct?
A. Use the past perfect.	1. I had found the ticket before Ed **knew / known / know** it was gone. 2. Had you **see / saw / seen** him before you went to the theater? 3. No, I **had / hadn't / hasn't**. 4. We hadn't found our seats before the film **starts / start / started**.	☐ ☐ ☐ ☐
	Number Correct	0 1 2 3 4
B. Use the past perfect continuous.	5. They had been **talking / talk / talks** when the movie started. 6. Ann had been watching TV when I **call / called / calling**. 7. We had been **stand / standing / stood** when the play started. 8. I had not been **listen / listening / listened** when he asked the question.	☐ ☐ ☐ ☐
	Number Correct	0 1 2 3 4
C. Talk about entertainment.	9. We got our tickets from the **box office / street vendor**. 10. The **usher / events brochure** has a list of interesting things to do. 11. They saw a performance at the new **reservation / concert hall**. 12. I love watching movies. Let's go to the film **festival / fair**.	☐ ☐ ☐ ☐
	Number Correct	0 1 2 3 4
D. Understand terms used to discuss leisure activities.	13. The soccer game was in the **auditorium / stadium** today. 14. We're going to the amusement **park / exhibit** tomorrow. 15. Do you want to watch the tennis **racket / match** with us? 16. We bought lunch at a **sidewalk café / debut performance**.	☐ ☐ ☐ ☐
	Number Correct	0 1 2 3 4

COUNT the number of correct answers above. Fill in the bubbles.

Chart Your Success					
Skill	Need Practice	Okay	Good	Very Good	Excellent!
A. Use the past perfect.	⓪	①	②	③	④
B. Use the past perfect continuous.	⓪	①	②	③	④
C. Talk about entertainment.	⓪	①	②	③	④
D. Understand terms used to discuss leisure activities.	⓪	①	②	③	④

LESSON 1: Grammar and Vocabulary

1 GRAMMAR PICTURE DICTIONARY. What problems are people having with banking and personal finances? Listen and read.

TCD2, 2
SCD14

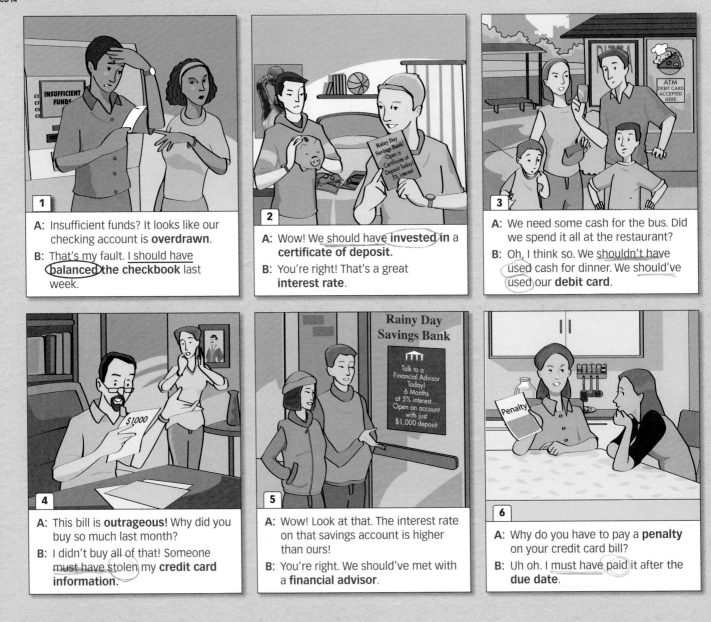

1
A: Insufficient funds? It looks like our checking account is **overdrawn**.
B: That's my fault. I should have balanced the checkbook last week.

2
A: Wow! We should have **invested in** a **certificate of deposit**.
B: You're right! That's a great **interest rate**.

3
A: We need some cash for the bus. Did we spend it all at the restaurant?
B: Oh, I think so. We shouldn't have used cash for dinner. We should've used our **debit card**.

4
A: This bill is **outrageous!** Why did you buy so much last month?
B: I didn't buy all of that! Someone must have stolen my **credit card information**.

5
A: Wow! Look at that. The interest rate on that savings account is higher than ours!
B: You're right. We should've met with a **financial advisor**.

6
A: Why do you have to pay a **penalty** on your credit card bill?
B: Uh oh. I must have paid it after the **due date**.

2 PRACTICE the conversations in Activity 1 with a partner.

3 NOTICE THE GRAMMAR. Underline *should (not) have* and *must (not) have*. Circle the past participles.

Past Modals: *Should (not) / Must (not)* + *have* + the Past Participle

Use a modal + *have* + past participle to express regret, give advice, and express certainty about things in the past.

Past Regret and Advice

Use *should / should not* + *have* + past participle to give better solutions (advice) or when you want to express a wish that the event had happened differently (regret).

Subject	Modal (not)	*have* + Past Participle	
I	should	have saved	more money. Now I'm broke.
You	shouldn't	have paid	your bill late. Now you have to pay a penalty.

Past Certainty

Use *must have* + the past participle to say you are sure or very certain that a past action happened or didn't happen.

Subject	Modal (not)	*have* + Past Participle	
Someone	must	have stolen	my credit card!
He / She	must not	have paid	the bill by the due date.

---

4 **MATCH** the statement on the left with the correct expression on the right. Then read the statements with a partner.

_f_ **1.** They received a notice for insufficient funds on their monthly statement. They . . .

a. should have opened a high-interest certificate of deposit instead.

_____ **2.** I had to pay a penalty on my account this month. I . . .

b. should have used our debit card to pay for our movie tickets.

_____ **3.** We didn't have any cash left for the bus. We . . .

c. should not have charged so much.

_____ **4.** They didn't get a good interest rate on their new savings account. They . . .

d. must not have paid my bill by the payment due date.

_____ **5.** Your credit card statement is very high. You . . .

e. must have stolen his credit card information.

_____ **6.** Ron got a bill for purchases he didn't make. Someone . . .

f. must have overdrawn their checking account.

5 **TALK** with a partner. Take turns reading the sentences, and giving answers using *should (not) have* or *must (not) have*.

1. I had to pay a penalty on my credit card bill.

2. My credit card statement was very high.

3. I didn't get a good interest rate on my savings account.

4. I didn't have enough cash for dinner last night.

6 **WHAT ABOUT YOU?** Have you ever made a mistake with your money or your finances? What should you have done differently? Write three sentences.

Example: *I spent too much money on my new car. I should have bought a used car.*

LESSON 2: Grammar Practice Plus

1 **TALK** with a partner about the picture. What were the people doing at the bank last Friday? Use the words in the box below.

credit card fraud

credit report

deposit slip

insufficient funds

mortgage loan

teller

withdrawal

2 **LISTEN** and write the correct number next to each name.

_____ Paolo   _____ Tamir   _____ Millie   _____ Bart   _____ Juan and Rosa   _____ Winnona   _____ Sarah

3 **TALK** about what happened at the bank. Use the verb and noun phrase in parentheses to make a new sentence with *should (not) have* or *must (not) have*.

1. Millie tried to cash a personal check, but she couldn't. (forget / ID)

2. Tamir needed to make a business withdrawal. (use / different withdrawal slip)

3. Sarah thought someone had committed credit card fraud. (speak with / a bank officer)

4. Bart wanted to make a deposit to his checking account.
   (wait in line / business accounts window)

5. Juan and Rosa asked the financial advisor about getting
   a mortgage loan. (request / credit report)

6. Paolo got a receipt for insufficient funds from the ATM.
   (balance / checking account)

> She must have forgotten her ID.

> She should not have forgotten her ID.

56 | Discuss banking problems. • Give advice for financial problems.

4 WRITE sentences about the bank customers in Activity 1. Answer the questions with *should (not) have* or *must (not) have.*

1. What should Millie have done?

   She should have brought her ID.

2. What shouldn't Tamir have done?

3. What must have happened to Sarah's credit card information?

4. What should Bart have done differently?

5. What must Juan and Rosa not have done before they talked to the financial advisor?

6. What should Paolo have done before he went to the ATM?

7 What must the security guard have done when Winnona shouted?

5 READ the online banking email message. Then talk with a partner. Have you, or has anyone else you know ever received a message like this?

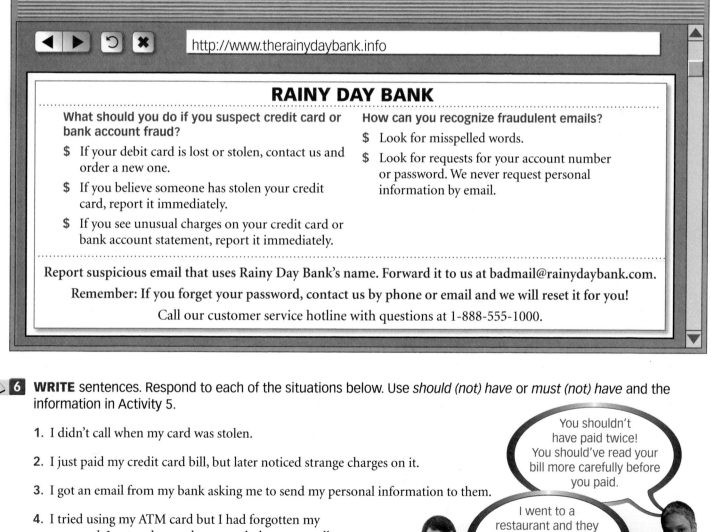

http://www.therainydaybank.info

RAINY DAY BANK

What should you do if you suspect credit card or bank account fraud?

$ If your debit card is lost or stolen, contact us and order a new one.

$ If you believe someone has stolen your credit card, report it immediately.

$ If you see unusual charges on your credit card or bank account statement, report it immediately.

How can you recognize fraudulent emails?

$ Look for misspelled words.

$ Look for requests for your account number or password. We never request personal information by email.

Report suspicious email that uses Rainy Day Bank's name. Forward it to us at badmail@rainydaybank.com.

Remember: If you forget your password, contact us by phone or email and we will reset it for you!

Call our customer service hotline with questions at 1-888-555-1000.

6 WRITE sentences. Respond to each of the situations below. Use *should (not) have* or *must (not) have* and the information in Activity 5.

1. I didn't call when my card was stolen.

2. I just paid my credit card bill, but later noticed strange charges on it.

3. I got an email from my bank asking me to send my personal information to them.

4. I tried using my ATM card but I had forgotten my password. I entered several passwords, but eventually the ATM took my card!

You shouldn't have paid twice! You should've read your bill more carefully before you paid.

I went to a restaurant and they charged me twice for my dinner. I didn't notice until I got home.

7 WHAT ABOUT YOU? Tell a partner about a problem you have had with money (with a bank, a bill, a check, etc.). Then take turns giving each other advice. What should/shouldn't your partner have done?

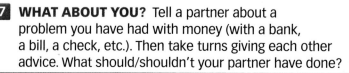

LESSON 3: Listening and Conversation

1 **LISTEN** to the conversation. Then listen to a question. Fill in the correct answer. Replay each item if necessary.

TCD2, 4–9

1. Ⓐ   Ⓑ   Ⓒ   4. Ⓐ   Ⓑ   Ⓒ

2. Ⓐ   Ⓑ   Ⓒ   5. Ⓐ   Ⓑ   Ⓒ

3. Ⓐ   Ⓑ   Ⓒ   6. Ⓐ   Ⓑ   Ⓒ

2 **LISTEN** to the conversation. Where are the two people? What are they talking about?

TCD2, 10

3 **LISTEN** again to the conversation. Write answers to the questions. Then discuss your answers with a partner.

1. How much is the interest rate for the savings account? _____

2. What is the interest rate on a certificate of deposit (CD)? _____

3. What does the woman decide to do? Why? _____

_____

4. Do you think it's better to have a savings account, a CD, or both? _____

_____

Math: Calculating Interest Earned

A **READ** about interest.

Interest is money earned in a savings account, a CD (certificate of deposit), or another type of investment. When you invest in a savings account or a CD, look for a high interest rate. You can open CDs for four months, six months, a year, or 18 months. The principal is the amount of money you start with and invest.

Principal x Interest Rate x Time = Interest Earned

Example: $1,000 (Principal) x 0.04 (4% Rate) x 1 (Time is 1 year) = $40 Interest

B **CALCULATE** interest earned.

1. If you open a one-year CD with $500 at 5% interest, how much interest will you earn after one year? _____

2. If you open a one-year CD with $2,000 at 4% interest, how much interest will you earn after one year? _____

---

4 **LISTEN** to the conversation. Then practice with a partner.

A: Hi. I'm calling about my credit card statement.

B: Sure. Could I have your name and account number please?

A: I'm Jack Johnston. My account number is 9876-5432. Why is there a $40 penalty on my statement?

B: Oh. I see that on your account. You should have made a payment by the due date.

A: I must have forgotten it. What should I do?

B: You should make an online payment today.

A: Okay. Good idea. Thanks.

5 **TALK** with a partner. Make new conversations with the words in the chart. Use Activity 4 as a model.

Statement type	Statement notice	*Should have*	Advice
1. savings account	$20 maintenance fee	checked your balance	a deposit
2. checking account	charge for insufficient funds	made a deposit	a transfer from another account

6 **READ** about Simone's day. What should Simone have done differently? What should Simone not have done? Ask and answer questions with a partner.

What happened to Simone's credit card?

She must have left it at the supermarket. Someone must have stolen it!

Simone is often forgetful. She doesn't always pay her bills by the due date and she doesn't always look at her statements. Last month, she had to pay a $40 penalty. When Simone got her credit card statement today, she saw something unusual. There was a charge for $400 to East-West Auto. But Simone doesn't own a car! Simone didn't know what to do. Simone looked in her wallet but she couldn't find her credit card. The last place Simone had used her credit card was at the supermarket last week. She remembered that she paid for groceries with the credit card, because she had forgotten her debit card. She searched all over the house, but her credit card was not there. She tried to look at her account statement online. But she was so nervous she couldn't remember her password. Today wasn't a good day for Simone.

7 **ROLE-PLAY.** Simone needs advice. Use the information in the story to form questions. Use the information in the box to respond to the advice.

Simone: I think someone stole my credit card.

Friend: You should contact your credit card company right away.

Simone: I'll do that, thanks.

Conversation Strategy

Responding to Advice

I'll do that, thanks.

That's a great idea.

I never thought of that.

That's good advice, thanks.

That's an excellent suggestion.

LESSON 4: Grammar and Vocabulary

1 **GRAMMAR PICTURE DICTIONARY.** Listen to the conversations about money and banking.

TCD2, 12
SCD16

A: I should **shred** all of my bills and unwanted **credit card offers,** shouldn't I?

B: Yes. It's one way to prevent **identity theft.** Thieves can steal your personal information from documents in the garbage.

A: We forgot to make our **mortgage payment** this month, didn't we? I can't enjoy myself if I'm thinking about our house payment.

B: No, we didn't forget. I scheduled an **automated payment** on the bank's website.

A: If you have a good **credit score,** you have a better chance to get a loan. You've requested your **credit report,** haven't you?

B: Yes, I have. I just got it in the mail yesterday.

A: More video games? You haven't been following our **monthly budget,** have you?

B: Yes, I have! Those were on sale. I haven't gone over our **spending allowance** at all.

2 **PRACTICE** the conversations in Activity 1 with a partner.

3 **NOTICE THE GRAMMAR.** Underline the verb in the main part of each question. Then circle the two words at the end of each question.

Tag Questions

To emphasize an idea, or to check or confirm your understanding of something, put a tag question at the end of the statement.
When the statement is **affirmative**, the tag is **negative**.
When the statement is **negative**, the tag is **affirmative**.

> **Be Careful!**
> With the subject pronoun *I*, we use *am* in the affirmative tag, but we use *are* in the negative tag. For example:
> I'm not funny, **am** I?
> I'm funny, **aren't** I?

	Statement + Question Tag	Affirmative	Negative
Simple Present	**It has** a great interest rate, **doesn't it**?	Yes, it does.	No, it doesn't
	You like that bank, **don't you**?	Yes, I do.	No, I don't.
	My credit score isn't too low, **is it**?	Yes, it is.	No, it isn't.
Simple Past	**She made** the mortgage payment, **didn't she**?	Yes, she did.	No, she didn't.
	Paul didn't mail the check, **did he**?	Yes, he did.	No, he didn't.
Present Perfect	**They've been** here before, **haven't they**?	Yes, they have	No, they haven't.
	He hasn't seen the budget, **has he**?	Yes, he has.	No, he hasn't.
Modals	**Lisa should balance** her checkbook, **shouldn't she**?	Yes, she should.	No, she shouldn't.
	I shouldn't send my account number, **should I**?	Yes, you should.	No, you shouldn't.

---

4 MATCH the tag question with the statement.

_____ 1. You shredded those unwanted credit card offers,   **a.** shouldn't I?

_____ 2. We haven't gone over our monthly budget,   **b.** didn't you?

_____ 3 I should watch my spending allowance,   **c.** will they?

_____ 4. The automated payment has already gone through,   **d.** have we?

_____ 5. The credit card companies won't put that on our credit report,   **e.** hasn't it?

5 WHAT ABOUT YOU? Complete the sentences below with the missing tag questions. Then ask a partner the questions.

1. You read your credit report every year, ___*don't you*___?

2. You paid your bills last month, _____?

3. You have a credit card, _____?

4. You have never paid a penalty on a bill, _____?

5. You will follow your monthly budget next month, _____?

You read your credit report every year, don't you?

No, I don't.

LESSON 5: Grammar Practice Plus

9/26

Pronunciation: Intonation in Tag Questions

When intonation falls for the tag question, the speaker is expressing certainty (is sure). When intonation rises for the tag question, the speaker is expressing uncertainty (is not sure). Listen to these examples.

This is a great interest rate, isn't it? ⟶ (sure)

This is a great interest rate, isn't it? ⟋ (not sure)

TCD2, 14
SCD17 **A** **LISTEN** to each statement. Check ☑ whether the speaker is *sure* or *not sure*.

	sure	not sure
1. We didn't make the mortgage payment on time, did we?	☐	☐
2. You saw the notice for insufficient funds, didn't you?	☐	☐
3. We won't go over our budget, will we?	☐	☐
4. My credit score should be higher, shouldn't it?	☐	☐
5. They charge a penalty for withdrawing money from your CD early, don't they?	☐	☐
6. You've never experienced identity theft, have you?	☐	☐

TCD2, 15 **B** **LISTEN** again and repeat.

1 **COMPLETE** the conversations with the correct tag.

1. NANCY: You didn't pay the Internet bill with the credit card, ___did you___?

   IAN: No, I didn't. I used the automated payment from our checking account.

2. IAN: We need to cut back on our entertainment expenses, ___don't we___?

   NANCY: Yes. Maybe we shouldn't have gone to the movies so often.

3. IAN: I haven't been doing a good job with the budget lately, ___have I___?

   NANCY: Oh, yes, ___you have___. You've been managing it very well.

4. NANCY: We've gone over our $50 spending allowance for gas, ___haven't we___?

   IAN: I'm not sure. We should check our credit card statement.

5. NANCY: They charge a penalty for withdrawing money from a CD early, ___don't they___?

   IAN: I think so. We'd better transfer money from our savings if we want to balance our budget.

2 **LISTEN** to the conversations in Activity 1 and check your answers.

TCD2, 16

3 **LISTEN** again. Check ☑ whether the first speaker is *sure* or *not sure*.

sure	not sure		sure	not sure
1. ☐	☐	4.	☐	☐
2. ☐	☐	5.	☐	☐
3. ☐	☐			

4 **LISTEN** to Ian and Nancy talk about their March budget. Fill in the amounts that you hear in the March column. Together, they have a total income of $3,500 and their budget is $3,000.

TCD2, 17

Monthly Expenses	Budget	March	April
Car payment and gas expenses	$300		
Cable TV bill	$65	$65	$65
Entertainment (films, music, dining out)	$150		
Food	$250		$300
Internet	$35	$35	$35
Mortgage payment	$1,700	$1,700	$1,700
Phone bill	$100		$125
Utilities (electricity)	$200	$200	$175
Miscellaneous (clothes, computer, etc.)	$200	$220	
Total	$3,000	$3,335	

5 **READ** Ian and Nancy's credit card statement below. Use information in the statement to complete the budget chart in Activity 4 for April.

Account number: 5678-9999	Nancy and Ian Peterson	Period ending: April 30	Payment due date: May 17
Credit limit: $5,000.00	New balance: $2,740.00	Available credit: $2,260.00	Min. payment due: $150.00

		Purchase date	Activity since last statement	Amount
Previous balance (+)	$1,400.00	4/2	Gas-Stop Station	$ 85.00
Purchases (+)	$1,325.00	4/3	Late fee	$ 40.00
Payments (-)	60.00	4/5	Payment – THANK YOU	$ -60.00
Late fee (+)	40.00	4/6	Chip Computer Store	$ 785.00
Finance charges (+)	35.00	4/10	Gianni's Restaurant	$ 130.00
NEW BALANCE (+)	$2,740.00	4/12	Coco's Clothes Shop	$ 250.00
		4/20	Mega Music & Video Store	$ 45.00
		4/28	Sunshine Movie Theater	$ 30.00

6 **WRITE** short conversations about what Nancy and Ian spent in March and April. Then role-play the conversations with a partner.

They spent more than their budget on food in March, didn't they?

Yes, they did.

7 **WRITE** advice for Ian and Nancy about what they should have done differently to stay within their budget.

8 **WHAT ABOUT YOU?** Who manages the finances in your family? Do you have a monthly budget? Why or why not? Talk with a partner.

LESSON 6: Reading

9/25

1 THINK ABOUT IT.

A. READ this short questionnaire. Check ☑ *Yes* or *No*.

	Yes	No
1. Do you have more than three credit cards?	☐	☐
2. Have you ever applied for a loan?	☐	☐
3. Have you ever tried to buy a car, house, or condominium?	☐	☐
4. Are you concerned about identity theft?	☐	☐

B. TALK to a partner. Discuss your answers to the questionnaire.

2 BEFORE YOU READ.
Preview the title and the subheadings. What do you think this article is about?

3 READ
the article about credit reports. As you read, find and ⟨circle⟩ these words: *denies, database, debts, monitor.*

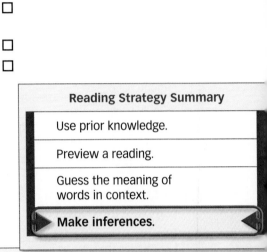

Reading Strategy Summary

Use prior knowledge.
Preview a reading.
Guess the meaning of words in context.
Make inferences.

4 AFTER YOU READ.

A. VOCABULARY. Read the sentence and ⟨circle⟩ the letter with the closest meaning. Guess the meaning of the word from the context.

1. A company **denies** you a credit card or a loan if you haven't paid your bills on time.
   a. turns down   b. permits   c. offers

2. Credit card companies collect information about your credit and keep it in a large **database**.
   a. warehouse   b. computer file   c. cabinet

3. When people spend too much, they sometimes have a lot of **debts** to pay.
   a. credits   b. interest   c. bills

4. Many credit card companies **monitor** your account and inform you if they see unusual activity.
   a. watch   b. report   c. ignore

B. MAKE INFERENCES about the information in the reading. Check ☑ if the statement is *True* or *False*.

> **READING FOCUS: Make inferences**
>
> When a writer does not state information directly, the reader has to figure out the meaning by studying the vocabulary and other information. This is called making an inference.

	True	False
1. Employers can request to see your credit report.	☐	☐
2. If you don't have a good credit rating, it can be difficult to get car insurance.	☐	☐
3. Credit card companies never inform you about unusual activity on your account.	☐	☐
4. Credit bureaus get some information about you from the government.	☐	☐

How's Your Credit?

9/25

Have you ever wanted to buy a house, but could not get a loan? Have you applied for a credit card, but the company denied you credit? You probably should have looked at your credit report.

What Is a Credit Report?

If you want to buy a home or a car, or pay for college, you usually have to take out a loan. If you want to make large purchases without paying cash, a credit card is usually the best way to pay. However,
5 to get a credit card or a loan, you must apply for them. Companies need to have information about you before they will give you credit. A company denies you a credit card or a loan if you have been delinquent on your account. *Delinquent* means you
10 must have been late paying your credit card, a loan, or a mortgage payment. This information appears on your credit report.

When you apply for a credit card or a loan, most lending companies get a copy of your credit report.
15 The credit report contains important information about your credit activity. It is a list of all your credit cards, your personal or college loans, how much you owe, and how often you make your payments. It also contains your full name, address, social security
20 number, and other personal information. It also shows if you pay your bills and taxes on time.

A consumer-reporting agency (CRA) is a company that collects information about your credit activities. They store this information in a large database. They
25 also charge a fee to give out this information to other companies—banks, credit card companies, landlords, or future employers. The most common type of CRA is called a *credit bureau.*

I should have paid my credit card bills on time!

What Is a Credit Score?

30 Your credit score comes from your credit report. Credit card companies calculate your credit score based on how well you manage your finances. A good credit score can help you achieve your financial goals. A poor score could prevent you from getting a
35 loan, buying a house or car, getting a job, renting an apartment or house, or getting insurance.

It is important to pay attention to your credit history. You should always make your mortgage, loan, and other payments on time, and keep your
40 debts to a minimum. If you have many late and missed payments, this will result in a poor credit history and credit score. A good credit history will give you a good credit score.

A credit report can also protect you against identity theft and credit card fraud. Many companies
45 will monitor your account and inform you if they see unusual activity or charges for more than you usually spend. Your credit history information stays on your credit report for seven years.

50 You can receive one free credit report per year from any of the three major credit reporting agencies in the U.S.—Equifax, Experian, and TransUnion.

LESSON 7: Writing

HD

1 **THINK ABOUT IT.** What should you do if you find incorrect information on your credit card bill? Do you think this affects your credit report?

2 **BEFORE YOU WRITE.**

A. READ about what to do if you see unusual charges on your credit card or if you think someone has stolen your credit card information. What information should you give your credit card company in a letter? <u>Underline</u> the information.

How to Dispute a Charge on Your Credit Card

1. **NOTIFY YOUR CREDIT CARD COMPANY.**
Contact your credit card company within 60 days of the date they sent the bill. In your letter, include your credit card number, the date of the bill with the disputed or incorrect charge, a description of the charge, and your reasons for the dispute.

2. **MAIL THE LETTER USING CERTIFIED MAIL.**
Use "return receipt requested," and send it to the address for billing inquiries. Include a check to pay for the current amount due. Do NOT pay the

disputed charge. Pay the bill on time or you will have to pay a late payment fee.

3. **THE CREDIT CARD COMPANY WILL INVESTIGATE THE CHARGES.** If the credit card company finds the seller or store has charged you incorrectly, or someone else took your information and charged your card, you will not have to pay the charge.

B. LISTEN to John call the Access credit card company about his statement. Why is he calling? Check ☑ the answer.

TCD2, 18

☐ He wants to pay his bill.

☐ He sees a mistake on his statement.

☐ He wants to cancel his credit card.

☐ He wants another credit card.

C. READ John's letter to the credit card company. Two sentences have unimportant information. They are not needed. Cross them out.

NO

December 5, 2009
John Green
27 East Second Street
Apt. 5B
Midville, CA 90456

TO: Access Credit Card Company

        Billing Inquiry Department

Dear Sir or Madam:

I am writing because I received my credit card statement for November and it includes a charge that I didn't make. My account number is 365 922 076. I have two other credit cards, too.

The incorrect charge is dated November 17th. I remember that I was working that day. The statement says that I made a purchase at Wash-Co Appliance for $300. I have never bought anything at Wash-Co Appliance. I think someone else must have used my credit card information, or maybe the store made a mistake.

Would you please take this charge off my statement? Thank you.

Sincerely,

John Green

John Green

555-1234

johngreen@speednet.com

Access Credit Card Company

ACCOUNT NUMBER: 365 922 076
STATEMENT DATE: November 24, 2009
Current Charges:

Date	Description	Amount
10/30	Corner Gas Station	47.00
11/08	Buy-Fresh Market	15.23
11/10	Midville Stationary	9.89
11/17	Wash-Co Appliances	300.00
11/21	Corner Gas Station	22.00
11/24	Buy-Fresh Market	33.64

---

3 WRITE. Imagine that you received a credit card statement. There is a charge for $250 at Amy's Golden Travel Agency. Write a letter to the credit card company to dispute the charge. Include the following information.

1. State the problem clearly and describe the charge.

2. Explain what you want the credit card company to do.

4 AFTER YOU WRITE.

A. CHECK YOUR WORK.

1. Does the letter state your purpose clearly?

2. Did you include all the necessary information?

3. Did you include any information that the company doesn't need?

4. Did you check your grammar, spelling, and punctuation?

B. REWRITE your letter with corrections.

WRITING FOCUS: Write a business letter

When you write a letter to a company, follow these guidelines.

- Include a heading with the date, your name, and your address.

- If possible, write the letter to a specific person by name. If you don't have a person's name, use *To Whom It May Concern* or *Dear Sir* or *Dear Madam*.

- Start by telling why you are writing. This is called *stating your purpose*. Use *I am writing because …*

- Keep the letter short. Include only the important facts.

- Close with *Sincerely,* and sign your name. Print your name below your signature. You may want to include your phone number and email address.

Career Connection

1 **THINK ABOUT IT.** How do hotels improve their guests' stay at the hotel? What are some ways that hotel staff can get information about their customer service and make improvements?

2 **READ** this memo addressed to the front desk staff at a hotel. As you read, circle these vocabulary words. Then match each word with its definition.

1. unattended
2. prevented
3. implementing
4. security measures
5. encrypting
6. motto

____ **a.** unmonitored
____ **b.** ways of keeping things safe
____ **c.** slogan; marketing phrase
____ **d.** hiding information electronically
____ **e.** putting into action
____ **f.** kept something from happening

> **confirm** (v.): check to make sure
>
> **feedback survey** (n. phrase): questions to get customers' opinions about service

---

MEMO

To:	Front Desk Staff, GoodNight Hotel
From:	Management
Date:	March 15, 2008
Re:	New Credit Card Reservations System

Recently, one of our guests was the victim of credit card identity theft. Apparently someone saw Mr. Waters's credit card information on the front desk, and used it. Mr. Waters complained that we should have kept his information more secure. He pointed out that staff should not have left guests' records unattended on the front desk. We could have prevented this situation.

In response, we are implementing new security measures for credit card reservations:

- Employees should no longer use the current registration system. Enter all transactions electronically into our new password-protected Online Reservation System. This system prevents identity theft by encrypting each customer's information.
- When taking a customer's credit card or debit card number by phone, you should never repeat the number out loud. Instead, ask the customer to repeat the number and confirm* that it is correct.

Tomorrow we will hold training classes for the new Online Reservation System. We will also introduce our new feedback survey*. At GoodNight Hotel, we want our customers to sleep peacefully. That's why our motto is *A GoodNight to All!*

---

3 **TALK** with a partner or in a group. How will the GoodNight Hotel improve security? Do you think these new security measures will prevent future identity theft? Why or why not?

4 **WRITE.** Hotels and other service-related businesses often ask customers to fill out a feedback survey about their experience. Write two complaints that guests might have at a hotel and two possible recommendations. Then talk with a partner and compare your charts.

Guest's Complaint	Guest's Recommendation
The heater doesn't work.	You should give me a different room.

5 **WHAT ABOUT YOU?** What are some problems you have had at hotels or restaurants? Did the staff do anything to correct the problem? What should they have done differently? Talk with a partner.

Check Your Progress!

9/28 ✓

Skill	Circle the answers.	Is it correct?
A. Use perfect modals.	1. You should've **use / used** your debit card. 2. The bank charged a late fee. I **must / should** not have paid on time. 3. We should **have opened / had opened** a savings account. 4. I should not have **gave / given** him my credit card information.	☐ ☐ ☐ ☐
	Number Correct	0 1 2 3 4
B. Use tag questions.	5. You have a credit card, **do / don't** you? 6. This is your bank, **wasn't / isn't** it? 7. She'll save more money, **will / won't** she? 8. We didn't get a good interest rate, **did / didn't** we?	☐ ☐ ☐ ☐
	Number Correct	0 1 2 3 4
C. Talk about banking and personal finances.	9. I'd better balance my **debit card / checkbook**. 10. What's the **interest rate / payment due date**? Don't pay late!. 11. Do you own a certificate of **deposit / credit card information**? 12. If you pay late, you'll get a **credit / penalty**.	☐ ☐ ☐ ☐
	Number Correct	0 1 2 3 4
D. Understand credit and loan terms.	13. How can I prevent **identity theft / a credit report**? 14. You shouldn't go over your **credit score / spending allowance**. 15. We need to make our **credit card offers / mortgage payment**. 16. You should schedule **automated payments / monthly budgets**.	☐ ☐ ☐ ☐
	Number Correct	0 1 2 3 4

COUNT the number of correct answers above. Fill in the bubbles.

Chart Your Success

Skill	Need Practice	Okay	Good	Very Good	Excellent!
A. Use perfect modals.	⓪	①	②	③	④
B. Use tag questions.	⓪	①	②	③	④
C. Talk about banking and personal finances.	⓪	①	②	③	④
D. Understand credit and loan terms.	⓪	①	②	③	④

LESSON 1: Grammar and Vocabulary

1 GRAMMAR PICTURE DICTIONARY. There are three branches in the United States federal government: executive, legislative (Congress), and judicial. Listen and read about federal, state, and city government in the U.S.

TCD2, 19
SCD18

1

The president is a member of the executive branch and is advised (by) a group called the Cabinet.

2

New **laws** are written and **approved** by the legislative branch. This branch is made up of 100 **senators** and 435 **congressmen** and **congresswomen**.

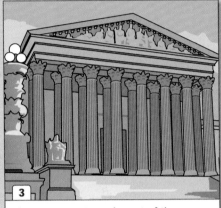

3

The Supreme Court is part of the judicial branch. It is the highest **court** in the country. Laws are explained and important decisions are made by this branch.

4

The leaders of state governments are called **governors**. They are elected by the people of their state.

5

Mayors are responsible for city government. They are elected by the people of their city.

6

United States **citizens** are given certain rights, such as the right to vote. Citizens have the right to vote at age 18.

2 READ the sentences in Activity 1 with a partner.

3 NOTICE THE GRAMMAR.

A. <u>UNDERLINE</u> *is/are* + past participle in each sentence above. (Circle) the word *by*.

B. **READ** the words and phrases that come after *by*. Check ☑ what type of information is included after *by*.

☐ who or what does the action
☐ where the action happens
☐ how the action happens

Active and Passive Voices (Simple Present and Simple Past)

Sentences in the active voice focus on the noun that does the action of the verb. Sentences in the passive voice focus on the noun that receives the action of the verb. Use the passive voice when you want to focus on the receiver of the action.

Active Voice

Subject	Active Verb	Object
Ted Lam	advises	the mayor.
The president	doesn't write	laws.
The governor	approved	the budget.
The mayor	didn't give	a speech.

Passive Voice

Subject	Passive Verb		by + Agent
	be	Past Participle	
The mayor	is	advised	by Ted Lam.
Laws	aren't	written	by the president.
The budgets	were	approved	by the governor.
A speech	wasn't	given	by the mayor.

In passive sentences, you can use *by* before the person or people who did the action (the agent). If you don't know who the agent is, or it's not important to mention the agent, don't use *by* + agent. For example:

The article about the governor was written by a local reporter.

A president is elected every four years.

---

4 **READ** the sentences. Write *A* for active sentences and *P* for passive sentences.

_A_ **1.** Bill Clinton served as president for eight years.

_P_ **2.** Federal laws are written by Congress.

_P_ **3.** Cameras are not allowed in the courtroom of the Supreme Court.

_A_ **4.** The vice president's speech included many important issues.

_P_ **5.** Two new laws were approved by the senators.

_P_ **6.** Senators are elected every six years.

5 **REWRITE** each sentence in the passive form. Use *by* + agent if that information is known, and if it is important to mention.

1. The United States elected a new president this year.

A new president was elected this year.

2. Senators make important decisions every day.

3. People sent many letters to the governor.

4. The people didn't invite the congressman to speak at the meeting.

5. Someone wrote a long article about the mayor.

6. The mayor asked citizens to help clean up the parks.

6 **WHAT ABOUT YOU?** Complete the sentences. Use the verbs below, or your own ideas. Then talk with a partner.

invited to	hired by	visited by	introduced to	taken to

1. Last year, I was _____.

2. Recently, my family was _____.

LESSON 2: Grammar Practice Plus

1 TALK about the picture. What community services do you see?

 2 LISTEN to the sentences. Then write the number of the correct sentence next to each verb.

TCD2, 20

_____ sponsor	_____ provide	_____ knock over
_____ hand out	_/_ collect	_____ give (a speech)

3 COMPLETE the article with the passive voice of the verbs in parentheses. Use the past form.

Over 200 families came out to celebrate the grand opening of Mission Park last Sunday.
The party (1)_____ *was not sponsored* _____ (not sponsor) by the city. Instead, it
(2)_____ (pay for) by the Mission Public Safety Department. The event
(3)_____ (organize) by representatives from both the police and fire departments.

Children, parents, singles, and seniors (4)_____ (welcome) by community service
employees who were there to offer equipment, information, and advice related to public safety and services.
Over 100 bike helmets (5)_____ (provide) to children by local police officers. Two
hundred people (6)_____ (give) free blood pressure tests. One hundred first-aid kits
(7)_____ (hand out). A speech (8)_____ (give) by the mayor.
The event was fun and informative for everyone who attended.

4 WRITE eight new sentences about the picture in Activity 1: four affirmative and four negative. Use the passive voice in simple past. You can use the verbs and nouns in the box or other words you know. Then share your sentences with a partner.

Example: *The dog wasn't caught by an animal control officer.*

catch / dog	offer / tutoring
clean / park	provide / blood pressure checks
drive / van	serve / refreshments
eat / cookies	give / speech

5 TALK with a partner. Read the names of the community organizations below. Write the kinds of things you think each community organization provides. Share your answers with a partner.

1. Public Safety Department _*police and fire, emergency*_
   *medical services, animal control, and 911*

2. Public Works Department _____
   _____

3. Legal Services Department _____
   _____

4. Senior Services Department _____
   _____

5. Community Center _____
   _____

6. Free Health Clinic _____
   _____

> I think the Public Safety Department provides police and fire, emergency medical, animal control, and 911 services.

LESSON 3: Listening and Conversation

Pronunciation: Content Word Stress
TCD2, 21

Sentences have content words and function words. *Content* words include nouns, verbs, adjectives, adverbs, and negatives. *Function* words include articles, short prepositions, conjunctions, auxiliary verbs, and some pronouns.

Content words are usually stressed, or emphasized, and function words are usually unstressed. Listen to the examples. Notice the stress on the content words.

The **senator** was **taken** to the **hotel** by his **driver**.

The **photographer** was **not allowed** in the **courtroom**.

The **state budget wasn't approved** by the **Senate**.

A **UNDERLINE** the content words to predict the stress patterns in the following sentences. Then listen and check.
TCD2, 22
SCD19

1. The congresswoman was elected two years ago.
2. Senior citizens are given seats at the front of the room.
3. The votes were counted electronically.
4. The governor's speech was not shown on TV.

B **LISTEN** again and repeat.
TCD2, 23

---

1 **LISTEN** to the conversation. Then listen to the question. Fill in the correct answer. Replay each item if necessary.
TCD2, 24–29

1. (A) (B) (C)   3. (A) (B) (C)   5. (A) (B) (C)
2. (A) (B) (C)   4. (A) (B) (C)   6. (A) (B) (C)

2 **LISTEN.** Read the sentences and check ☑ *True* or *False*.
TCD2, 30

	True	False
1. The caller saw a car hit a sign.	☐	☐
2. The caller was inside her house when the accident happened.	☐	☐
3. No one was injured in the accident.	☐	☐
4. The caller talked to the driver of the car.	☐	☐
5. The accident was seen by three other people.	☐	☐

3 **LISTEN** again. Then use the cues below to write passive sentences. Some sentences should be affirmative and some should be negative. Include *by* + agent when the agent is included in the cue.
TCD2, 30

1. A stop sign _____was hit by a car._____ (hit / car)

2. The stop sign _____ (knock over)

3. The driver _____ (injure)

4. The caller _____ (injure)

5. The accident _____ (see / three other people)

10/90 ✓

4 **LISTEN** to the conversation. Then practice with a partner.

TCD2, 31
SCD20

A: Lakeside Legal Aid Services. How may I help you?

B: Hello. I'm having a problem with my landlord. My apartment was robbed last week and the window was broken. My landlord refuses to pay for a new window.

A: I see. This is a tenant's rights issue. Would you like to set up an appointment?

B: That would be great.

A: How about Monday at 9:00 A.M.?

B: That's fine. Thank you.

5 **COMPLETE.** Read the information from the website. Then complete the chart below with the correct service.

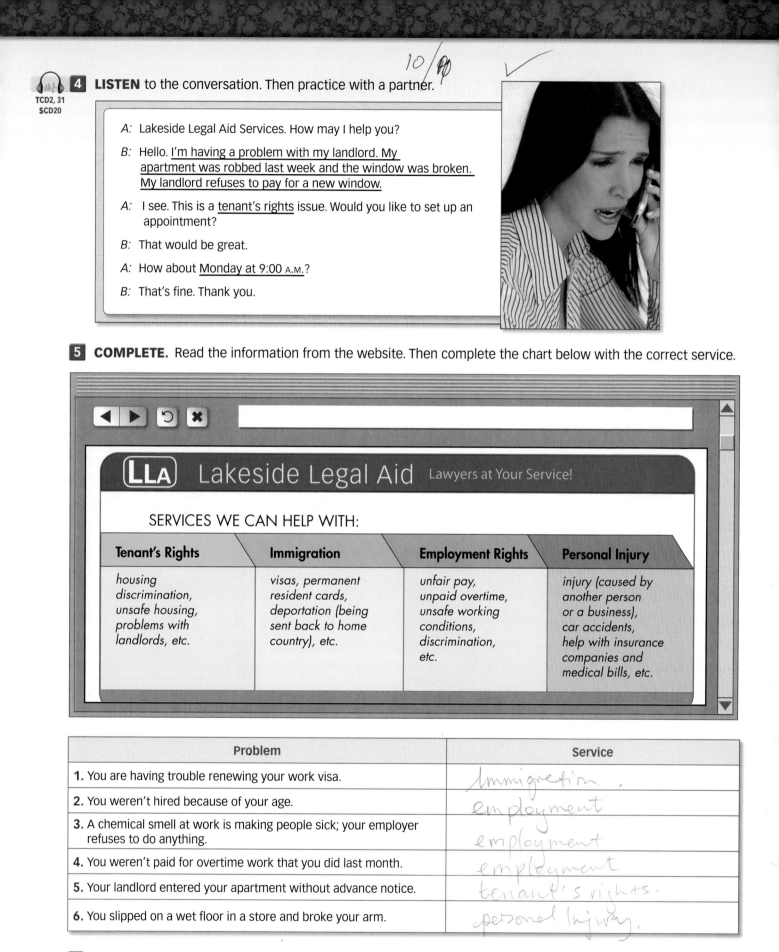

LLA Lakeside Legal Aid Lawyers at Your Service!

SERVICES WE CAN HELP WITH:

Tenant's Rights	Immigration	Employment Rights	Personal Injury
housing discrimination, unsafe housing, problems with landlords, etc.	visas, permanent resident cards, deportation (being sent back to home country), etc.	unfair pay, unpaid overtime, unsafe working conditions, discrimination, etc.	injury (caused by another person or a business), car accidents, help with insurance companies and medical bills, etc.

Problem	Service
1. You are having trouble renewing your work visa.	Immigration
2. You weren't hired because of your age.	employment
3. A chemical smell at work is making people sick; your employer refuses to do anything.	employment
4. You weren't paid for overtime work that you did last month.	employment
5. Your landlord entered your apartment without advance notice.	tenant's rights
6. You slipped on a wet floor in a store and broke your arm.	personal injury

6 **ROLE-PLAY.** Use the information in the chart in Activity 5 to practice the conversation from Activity 4 with a partner. Make up appointment times.

LESSON 4: Grammar and Vocabulary

1 GRAMMAR PICTURE DICTIONARY. What kinds of legal issues are the people talking about? Listen and read.

T CD2, 32
SCD21

1

A: Why was the man stopped by the police?

B: He was **accused of** stealing a computer.

2

"I need a lawyer."

A: Are people required to answer police officers' questions when they are **arrested**?

B: No, they don't have to say anything. They can ask for a lawyer.

3

A: Was an **attorney** provided for him?

B: Yes, he couldn't afford a lawyer, so the judge provided one.

JURY SUMMONS

YOU ARE REQUIRED

TO REPORT FOR

JURY DUTY

DURING THE WEEK

OF AUGUST **14-18**.

PLEASE CALL:

818-555-6549

4

A: Is everyone in the United States required to **serve on** a **jury**?

B: Any U.S. citizen can be called to **report** for jury duty.

5

"I have to leave for college on Friday"

A: Why aren't you required to serve on the jury?

B: Because the **trial** is going to start on Friday, and I have to leave for college next week.

6

A: Was the **defendant** found **guilty**?

B: No, he wasn't. The jury decided he was **innocent**.

2 PRACTICE the conversations from Activity 1 with a partner.

3 NOTICE THE GRAMMAR. Circle the form of *be* and the past participle in each **question** above. Underline the subject. Which word order below is correct?

a. *be*, (optional question word), subject, past participle

b. (optional question word), *be*, past participle, subject

c. (optional question word), *be*, subject, past participle

Talk about crime. • Use *yes/no* and information questions in the passive voice.

Yes/No and Information Questions in the Passive Voice

Yes/No Questions

be	Subject	Past Participle		(by + Agent)
Was	the defendant	found	guilty?	
Are	attorneys	provided	to some defendants	by the court?

Information Questions

Question Word	be	Subject	Past Participle		(by + Agent)
What	was	the jury	asked	to do?	
Where	is	the defendant	taken	after the trial?	
When	were	you	chosen	to serve on the jury?	
Why	wasn't	the man	found	guilty	by the jury?
How	are	the decisions	made?		

4 **WRITE** passive *yes/no* and information questions using the cues below. Include *by* + agent when that information is available.

Present

1. (Elizabeth / require / serve on a jury) _Is Elizabeth required to serve on a jury?_

2. (where / people / take / after they're arrested)_____

3. (attorneys / provide / by the court)_____

4. (what / defendant / accuse / of)_____

5. (how / the information / give)_____

Past

6. (Jay Abrams / find / guilty) _Was Jay Abrams found guilty?_

7. (when / they / call / to report for jury duty)_____

8. (why / Mark / accuse / by the store owner)_____

9. (how / people / choose / for the jury_____

10. (why / we / not tell / about the trial)_____

5 **WRITE** three passive voice questions asking for personal information. Use the verbs in the box or other verbs. Then ask and answer questions with a partner.

employ	invite	make	give	spell

1. _____

_____

2. _____

_____

3. _____

_____

> How is your last name spelled?

LESSON 5: Grammar Practice Plus

1 TALK. Write answers to the questions below. Then ask and answer the questions with a partner.

1. Who has to pay income taxes? _____

2. By what date of each year are taxes due? _____

3. Where can you find tax booklets? _____

4. What information do you need in order to do your taxes? _____

2 READ the information about taxes. <u>Underline</u> each of the following words once: *file, income tax, tax return, federal tax, state tax, W-2 form, wages, withheld.* After you read, check your answers to the questions in Activity 1.

Tax FAQs (Frequently Asked Questions)

Who is required to file income taxes? All citizens, residents, and non-residents need to file tax returns if they receive more than a certain amount of money during the year. This money can come from jobs, interest from savings accounts, and unemployment pay.

To find out if you made enough money to file taxes, go to tax websites or check tax booklets. For federal taxes (Internal Revenue Service or IRS), go to <u>www.irs.gov</u>. To find the tax website for your state, go to an Internet search engine and type the name of your state and "taxes." In most states, you have to file both federal and state taxes.

When are taxes due? Taxes are due on April 15 of each year.

Where can I get tax booklets? If you filed taxes last year, you will receive your tax booklets in the mail. If your booklets are not mailed to you, you can get federal booklets at <u>www.irs.gov</u>. Some forms and booklets are provided by public libraries and post offices.

What information do I need to file my taxes? You need W-2 forms, 1099 forms, and any other forms that show your wages (how much money you made during the year). These forms also show how much money was withheld as income tax. These forms are mailed to you by your employer and usually arrive at the end of January.

Where can I get help? Call your local IRS office and ask for the Taxpayer Education Coordinator to get information about free help with your taxes. To find the phone number for your local IRS office, go to <u>www.irs.gov</u> and click on "Contact IRS."

---

3 MATCH each word below with its definition.

1. __*d*__ W-2 form
2. _____ withhold (taxes)
3. _____ income tax
4. _____ state tax
5. _____ federal tax
6. _____ tax return
7. _____ wages
8. _____ file

a. the form a taxpayer completes to calculate annual (yearly) taxes

b. all the money an employee pays the government for the money he or she earned

c. the money that an employee earns

d. a document showing a person's total wages and withheld taxes

e. the portion (part) of a person's income tax that is paid to the state government

f. the portion of a person's income tax that is paid to the federal government

g. submit a document formally

h. keep a portion of a person's income for taxes

4 **READ** the W-2 form. What were Carlos's wages last year? Circle the amount.

a Employee's social security number				
		OMB No. 1545-0008	Safe, accurate, FAST! Use **e-file**	Visit the IRS website at *www.irs.gov/efile.*

b Employer identification number (EIN) **77-0545077**		1 Wages, tips, other compensation **16890.24**	2 Federal income tax withheld
c Employer's name, address, and ZIP code **Sunshine Catering** **1400 West Bay View St.** **South San Francisco, CA** _____		3 Social security wages **16890.24**	4 Social security tax withheld **1036.16**
		5 Medicare wages and tips **16890.24**	6 Medicare tax withheld **243.92**
		7 Social security tips	8 Allocated tips
d Control number **000145 LTY**		9 Advance EIC payment	10 Dependent care benefits
e Employee's first name and initial **Carlos** Last name **Tejada** Suff.		11 Nonqualified plans	12a See instructions for box 12 **D 2000.00**
		13 Statutory employee ☐ Retirement plan ☐ Third-party sick pay ☐	12b
f Employee's address and ZIP code _____ **South Ocean Drive** **Oakland, CA** _____		14 Other	12c
			12d

15 State Employer's state ID number **CA**	16 State wages, tips, etc. **16,890.24**	17 State income tax **444.40**	18 Local wages, tips, etc.	19 Local income tax	20 Locality name

Form **W-2**   **Wage and Tax Statement**   Department of the Treasury—Internal Revenue Service

---

5 **LISTEN.** Fill in the missing information in the W-2 form above.

TCD2, 33

6 **WRITE** questions using the past passive voice. Then answer the questions with a partner.

1. money / withhold / for local income tax / ?
   Was money withheld for local income tax?
2. Carlos / assign / a Social Security number / ?
3. how much money / withhold / by the state / ?
4. where / Carlos / employ / ?
5. how much money / withhold / by the federal government / ?

Math: Calculating Refunds and Taxes Owed

Every year, U.S. workers file taxes to find out if they owe more money to the government or if they will receive a refund. Fill in the blank with information from the W-2 form in Activity 3. Then calculate how much money Carlos will get back, or how much he owes.

  a. Federal income tax due   _____$2,154_____

  b. Federal income tax withheld   _____

If line b is more than line a, subtract line a from line b. This is his *refund amount*.
If line a is more than line b, subtract line b from line a. This is the *amount he owes*.

Circle one and write the amount: (**Refund / Amount he owes**): _____

---

7 **WHAT ABOUT YOU?** Ask and answer the questions below with a partner.

1. Do you file income taxes every year?
2. Do you prepare your own tax forms or are they prepared by someone else?
3. Did you receive a refund the last time you filed taxes, or did you owe more taxes?
4. When do you usually complete your tax forms?

LESSON 6: Reading

1 **THINK ABOUT IT.** Write the names of three American holidays. Are these holidays celebrated to remember a person? An event? Which ones have you celebrated before? What did you do to celebrate the holiday?

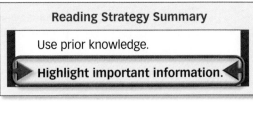

Reading Strategy Summary

Use prior knowledge.

▶ **Highlight important information.** ◀

2 **BEFORE YOU READ.**

A. **READ** the encyclopedia entry on the next page quickly. Which two holidays are discussed in detail? What do you already know about these holidays?

B. **DISCUSS** the highlighted information. Read only the highlighted words. Then read the whole paragraph. Why do you think each part is highlighted? Why are some parts not highlighted? Discuss with a partner.

READING FOCUS: Highlight important information

As you read, use a marker to highlight information that you will want to find again easily. Some things you might want to highlight are names, dates, places, and key facts or events. Be careful not to highlight *too* many things—just pick the most important ones.

Labor Day Parade

People in the United States celebrate Labor Day on the first Monday in September. In 1884, the Knights of Labor, a workers' organization, held a large parade in New York City to honor the working class. The parade was held on the first Monday in September. The Knights agreed to hold all future parades on the same day, which they named Labor Day. In 1894, Congress passed a law recognizing Labor Day as an official national holiday. Today, it is seen not only as a celebration of the working class, but even more so as the unofficial end of the summer season. It is celebrated with parades, barbecues, and fireworks.

3 **READ** the encyclopedia entry on the next page. Highlight (or <u>underline</u>) the key facts in each paragraph.

4 **AFTER YOU READ.**

A. **ANSWER** the questions. Then discuss your answers with a partner.

1. How many days are federal holidays?
2. What happens to offices and banks on a federal holiday?
3. Describe one New Year's tradition.
4. Why was Martin Luther King Jr. honored with a holiday?
5. What was the speech "I Have a Dream" about?
6. How do people celebrate Martin Luther King Jr. Day?

B. **READ** the information you highlighted again. Did it help you answer the questions? Compare with a partner. Did you highlight the same information? Did you miss anything? Did you highlight too many things?

Federal Holidays in the United States

Every year, 10 national holidays are recognized by the United States federal* government. On these days, government employees do not work and all federal offices are closed. Banks, the stock market, and the
5 post office are also closed.

New Year's Day marks the beginning of the new year. Traditions include having parties, counting down to midnight on New Year's Eve, making lists of New Year's resolutions*, and remembering the
10 year that has passed. One famous celebration of New Year's Eve happens in Times Square in New York City. Thousands of people gather there to welcome the New Year together. In addition, new laws often take effect* on January 1.

15 Martin Luther King Jr. Day celebrates the life of Dr. Martin Luther King Jr. King was born in Atlanta, Georgia, in 1929. He was trained as a Baptist

minister, and he became an activist* and a leader of the civil rights movement*. At the 1963 March on
20 Washington, he gave his famous speech, "I Have a Dream." In the speech, King asked for people of all races to live in peace*. King received the Nobel Peace Prize in 1964. He was the youngest person ever to win this honor. King was killed in 1968. Later, a bill
25 was introduced by Congress to honor his memory. The bill was signed into law by President Reagan, and the holiday was observed for the first time in 1986. Martin Luther King Jr. Day is celebrated differently across the United States. In many cities, citizens
30 have peace parades or candlelight marches at night. Churches may hold special services. Schools often put on plays or have exhibits about King's life. Martin Luther King Day is also a popular day to hold special community events such as service projects, volunteer
35 programs, and fundraisers*.

Federal Holidays

New Year's Day: January 1
Martin Luther King Jr. Day: 3rd Monday in January
Presidents Day: 3rd Monday in February
Memorial Day: last Monday in May
Independence Day: July 4
Labor Day: 1st Monday in September
Columbus Day: 2nd Monday in October
Veterans Day: November 11
Thanksgiving Day: 4th Thursday in November
Christmas Day: December 25

federal (adj.): of the national government

resolutions (n.): promises to do something

take effect (idiom): to begin

activist (n.): a person who is active to help a cause

civil rights movement (n.): movement in the United States beginning in the 1960s for the rights of African American citizens

peace (n.): lack of fighting and arguments

fundraisers (n.): events that raise money

Tip

An **encyclopedia** is a collection of information on a wide variety of topics. The topics are organized in alphabetical order. An encyclopedia can be one large book, a set of several books, or a website. You can find encyclopedias in libraries or online.

LESSON 7: Writing

1 **THINK ABOUT IT.** When you write a paragraph or essay, do you go back to look for ways you could make it better? What do you look for? What changes do you make? Do you ask anyone else to help you?

2 **BEFORE YOU WRITE.**

WRITING FOCUS: Revise your writing

After we write a paragraph or essay, we often go back and revise it. When we revise, we make sure a reader can understand what we want to say.

Ask yourself these questions when you revise:

1. Is my topic stated clearly?
2. Is there any information that is not about the topic?
3. Is the information in the right order?
4. Do I need to add any information?

A. READ the paragraph that a student wrote about the history of Memorial Day. Is it easy to understand?

> There are ten federal holidays. People celebrate
>
> Memorial Day in many ways. Memorial Day is an
>
> important federal holiday. After World War I, the
>
> holiday was changed to include all people who died
>
> in military service or Wars. It was begun to honor soldiers who died
>
> in the American Civil War. The Civil War lasted from 1861 to 1865.
>
> People have parades and visit cemeteries to put flowers on graves on
>
> Memorial Day. They have picnics and family reunions, too. In my family,
>
> we like to have a picnic on Labor Day.

B. **DISCUSS** the questions with a partner. Make notes on the paragraph in Activity 2A as you discuss each question.

1. What is the topic sentence of the paragraph? Circle it. Is the topic sentence in the correct place? If not, draw an arrow from the topic sentence to the place it should be moved.

2. Is there any information that is not about the topic? If so, cross it out.

3. Is the information in the right order? Usually, information should be given in the order it happened.

4. Can you think of any important information that is missing? What should be added?

3 **WRITE.**

A. **REWRITE.** Look at the revisions you made to the paragraph on the previous page. Rewrite the paragraph. Include all of the changes that you made.

_____

_____

_____

_____

_____

_____

_____

_____

_____

_____

_____

_____

_____

_____

_____

_____

_____

_____

B. **WRITE** about a holiday that is special to you. Use books or the Internet to research the holiday. Write two paragraphs about the holiday. In the first paragraph, write about the history. In the second paragraph, write about how the holiday is celebrated.

4 **AFTER YOU WRITE.**

A. **REVISE** your paragraphs. Ask yourself the questions in the Writing Focus box on page 82.

B. **EDIT.** Check your work.

1. Does every sentence have a subject and a verb?

2. Is the spelling correct? Check the words in a dictionary if you are not sure.

3. Is the punctuation correct? Check commas, apostrophes, and periods.

4. Did you use the passive correctly?

C. **REWRITE** your paragraphs with corrections.

D. **DISCUSS.** Exchange papers with a partner. What interesting information did you learn from your partner's paragraphs? Discuss with your partner.

Career Connection

1 **THINK ABOUT IT.** Look at the photo. What kind of workplace is this? Who are the people?

2 **LISTEN** to the presentation. The general manager at a manufacturing plant is introducing the new chief supervisor to the workers. Check ☑ True or False.

TCD2, 34
SCDx

	True	False
1. Dylan Anderson is the new chief supervisor.	☐	☐
2. Ms. Rivers was hired by Mr. Anderson.	☐	☐
3. Shift supervisors oversee the operations on the floor.	☐	☐
4. Some workers will report to a new shift supervisor.	☐	☐
5. The maintenance team will be supervised by Alexis Moran.	☐	☐
6. No one has met his or her new shift supervisor yet.	☐	☐

3 **TALK** with a partner or in a group. Discuss the following questions.

1. What kinds of good things can happen when a new manager comes to a company? What kinds of problems can happen?

2. Is it better to promote someone from inside a company, or to bring in someone from outside the company? Give reasons for your opinions.

4 **WRITE** a conversation about the people in the picture. Who is the manager? How do you know? Write about what you think they are saying. Then read your conversation with a partner.

5 **WHAT ABOUT YOU?** Would you like to work in a big company with many levels of workers (such as the manufacturing plant in Activity 2), or do you prefer a small company where everyone knows each other well? Why? Discuss with a partner.

Check Your Progress!

Skill	Circle the answers.	Is it correct?
A. Use the active and passive voices.	1. Every four years, a new president **elected / elects / is elected**. 2. Mayors **are chosen / choose / are chose** by the people of their cities. 3. The car **wasn't driven / weren't driven / wasn't drive** by the police officer. 4. Helmets **gave / were given / was given** to the children.	☐ ☐ ☐ ☐
	Number Correct	0 1 2 3 4
B. Ask *Yes/No* and information questions in the passive voice.	5. What was the defendant **ask / asked / asks** to do? 6. How was the story **wrote / written / write**? 7. Are photographers **allowed / allow / allows** in the courtroom? 8. Were the men **accuses / accuse / accused** of the crime?	☐ ☐ ☐ ☐
	Number Correct	0 1 2 3 4
C. Talk about the U.S. government.	9. New **rights / laws** are written by the legislative branch. 10. **Mayors / Governors** are elected by the people of their city. 11. The Supreme Court is the highest **senator / court** in the U.S. 12. The **citizens / cabinet members** advise the president.	☐ ☐ ☐ ☐
	Number Correct	0 1 2 3 4
D. Understand terms of the legal system.	13. Why was he **accused / arrested** of the crime? 14. I was called to **serve on / report to** jury duty. 15. The **jury / defendant** was found guilty. 16. The **attorney / trial** lasted two weeks.	☐ ☐ ☐ ☐
	Number Correct	0 1 2 3 4

COUNT the number of correct answers above. Fill in the bubbles.

Chart Your Success

Skill	Need Practice	Okay	Good	Very Good	Excellent!
A. Use the active and passive voices.	⓪	①	②	③	④
B. Ask *Yes/No* and information questions in the passive voice.	⓪	①	②	③	④
C. Talk about the U.S. government.	⓪	①	②	③	④
D. Understand terms of the legal system.	⓪	①	②	③	④

LESSON 1: Grammar and Vocabulary

1 GRAMMAR PICTURE DICTIONARY. What problems do these people have? Listen and read.

TCD2, 35
SCD22

1 The phone is **dead**. Do you have a cell phone? I need to call the phone company.

2 I keep **losing my Internet connection**. I need to find a new Internet service provider.

3 The electricity is **out** again! We had a **power outage** last Friday, too.

4 The **signal** on my cell phone is **weak**. I can't make a phone call. Do you have a strong signal?

5 I need to call the cable company. There's an **error** on my bill.

6 We have a **gas leak**. We have to call the gas company right away.

2 READ the sentences in Activity 1 with a partner.

3 NOTICE THE GRAMMAR. Work with a partner. Underline *the*, and circle *a* and *an* in the sentences above. What parts of speech come after *the, a,* and *an*? Why is *an* used instead of *a* before the word *error*?

Articles

Indefinite articles *a*, *an*, and *some* are used to talk about general or not specific things. The definite article *the* is used to talk about specific things or things already known by the listener or reader.

Indefinite Articles

Use indefinite articles to make general statements.

A gas leak is very dangerous.

Use indefinite articles when you are not thinking of an exact person, place, or thing.

I need *a new battery* for my phone.
The repairman dropped *some tools* in the driveway.

Use *a* or *an* with singular count nouns. Use *a* before consonant sounds, and *an* before vowel sounds.

a gas leak   a weak signal   an error   an estimate

Use *some* or no article with plural count nouns and with noncount nouns.

(some) tools   (some) phones   (some) gas   (some) money

Definite Articles

Use the definite article *the* when you are discussing a specific person, place, or thing.

Did you call *the repairman* again?
The men on *the street* are checking *the power lines*.

Use *the* when a noun is talked about for the second time.

They found a leak in the furnace last week. *The leak* had been there for a long time.

Use *the* with superlative adjectives.

June wants *the best* cell phone she can buy.

---

4 **MATCH** each sentence or conversation with the correct rule.

_b_ **1.** I need to call **the** gas company because we have a gas leak.

____ **2.** **A** flashlight can be very useful when there is a power outage.

____ **3.** I can't call anyone. My home phone is dead and my cell phone has **a** weak signal!

____ **4.** Sarah thought she had **the** worst cable service because she kept losing her connection.

____ **5.** Ted found an error on his phone bill. **The** error was corrected by the phone company.

a. A noun is talked about for the second time.

b. The speaker is talking about a specific person, place, or thing.

c. Superlative adjectives are used.

d. It is a general statement.

e. The speaker is not thinking of an exact person, place, or thing.

5 **WHAT ABOUT YOU?** Have you ever had a problem with utilities in your home? What was the problem? What did you do? Write sentences. Then talk with a partner.

1. _____

_____

2. _____

> My oven didn't work. I called a repairman.

3. _____

_____

LESSON 2: Grammar Practice Plus

1 **TALK** about the picture. Who are the people? What are they talking about?

2 **LISTEN** to the sentences about the picture. Write the number next to the correct word.

TCD2, 36

| | peeling | | broken | | cracked | | dripping | | stained |

3 **COMPLETE.** Read each sentence. Complete the sentences with the words in Activity 2.

Dad: The paint is ____peeling____. But the biggest problem is the sink.

Water is ____dripping____ onto the floor.

Mom: The carpet is ____stained____. Somebody spilled some coffee on it. Also, the

kitchen wall is ____cracked____. Look at this big line in the middle of the wall.

Dad: And the doorknob is ____broken____! This is the worst apartment I've ever seen.

Son: But it's the cheapest apartment I could find!

A and an with adjectives. • Calculate an estimate for work time.

A and *An* with Adjectives

When an article comes before an adjective + singular count noun, pay attention to the sound at the beginning of the adjective. Use *a* with adjectives that start with consonant sounds. Use *an* with adjectives that start with vowel sounds.

a house   *but*   **an o**ld house

an apartment   *but*   **a b**ig apartment

4   **COMPLETE** the sentences with *a, an, some,* or *the*.

1. There is _____*an*_____ ugly stain on _____*the*_____ bedroom wall. Can you clean it for me?

2. There is _____ little mouse in _____ apartment. Are there a lot of mice in _____ building?   *a the the*

3. How much is _____ security deposit for _____ larger apartment across the hall?   *The the*

4. Can I have _____ paper towels? I want to clean _____ kitchen counter.   *some the*

5. I need _____ advice. I can't decide which kind of apartment to look for. Do you think I should *some a an* find _____ new apartment or _____ old apartment?

6. I know _____ excellent plumber. He can fix _____ leaking pipes in your apartment. I'll give *an the the* you _____ phone number.

7. _____ oven doesn't work. Will your landlord buy you _____ new oven?   *the a*

8. When my oven broke, my landlord bought me _____ oven the next day.   *an*

5   **WHAT ABOUT YOU?** Are there any problems with your home that you would like to fix or change? Talk with a partner.

> The paint on my bathroom walls is very old. I want to paint the bathroom. I also want to get a new sink.

10/10.

Math: Calculating an Estimate for Work

Marco is a painter. He's preparing an estimate for the cost to paint a customer's house. His rate is $350 per day for labor (work). He thinks he will need six days to paint the house. He will buy nine cans of paint ($42 each) and six brushes ($12 each) for the job. How much is the estimate?

rate _____ **× days** _____ = $ _____

paint _____ **+ brushes** _____ = $ _____

ESTIMATE = $ _____

LESSON 3: Listening and Conversation

TCD2, 37 🎧 **Pronunciation:** The Articles *The, A,* and *An*

Articles are usually not stressed. The *e* in *the* sounds like ə when it is followed by a word that begins with a consonant sound. The ə sound is called the *schwa* sound. *The* is usually pronounced with a long *e* when it is followed by a word that begins with a vowel sound.

TCD2, 38
SCD23 **A** **LISTEN** to the examples. Then repeat.

the complaint	**sounds like →**	thə complaint
the Internet		thee Internet

The article *a* sounds like ə. The *a* in *an* also sounds like ə and the *n* is linked to the first letter of the next word.

TCD2, 39
SCD24 **B** **LISTEN** to the examples. Then repeat.

a policy	**sounds like →**	ə policy
an agreement		ə nagreement

C **PRACTICE** saying the phrases below.

1. an office
2. the policy
3. the other apartment
4. a complaint
5. a big apartment
6. the issue

🎧 **1** **LISTEN** to the conversation. Then listen to the question. Fill in the correct answer. Replay each item if necessary.

TCD2, 40–45

1. Ⓐ Ⓑ Ⓒ   4. Ⓐ Ⓑ Ⓒ
2. Ⓐ Ⓑ Ⓒ   5. Ⓐ Ⓑ Ⓒ
3. Ⓐ Ⓑ Ⓒ   6. Ⓐ Ⓑ Ⓒ

🎧 **2** **LISTEN** again. Circle the incorrect charges on the phone bill below.

TCD2, 46

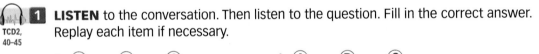

Call	Date	Time	Number	Location	Min.	Charges
1	3/3	4:02 P.M.	212-555-0084	New York, NY	30	$ 2.40
2	3/5	7:47 A.M.	214-555-3657	Dallas, TX	15	$ .90
3	3/8	3:22 P.M.	818-555-6904	Los Angeles, CA	22	$ 1.76
4	3/14	8:07 A.M.	619-555-4983	San Diego, CA	6	$ .48
5	3/16	9:55 P.M.	619-555-4983	San Diego, CA	30	$ 1.80

TCD2, 47
SCD25

3 **LISTEN** to the conversation. Then practice with a partner.

A: Good morning. Union Gas and Electric. How can I help you?

B: <u>I'm calling because there are</u> two errors on my bill. My name is Anna Jong. My account number is 894427B.

A: I'm sorry about that, Ms. Jong. Can you tell me what the errors are?

B: Yes. First, you charged me for gas, but I don't have any gas in my apartment.

A: I see. And what is the second error?

B: There is a charge for a late payment, but I paid my bill on time last month.

A: All right. Please hold for a moment while I check your bill. Ms. Jong, I've corrected the errors on your bill. We'll send you an updated bill this week.

B: Thank you for your help.

4 **PRACTICE** the conversation from Activity 3 with a partner. Use the expressions in the Conversation Strategy box.

Conversation Strategy
Stating the reason for a phone call
I'm calling because there is/are…
The reason I'm calling is…
I'm calling to ask/find out…

✓ 10/11

5 **ROLE-PLAY.** Discuss the errors in the phone bills below. Write a conversation with a partner. Take turns being a customer and a representative from the phone company.

Call	Date	Time	Number	Location	Min.	Amount
1	5/10	7:17 A.M.	510-555-1733	Oakland, CA	10	.80
2	5/10	7:47 A.M.	214-555-4482	Dallas, TX	11	.88
3	5/18	3:45 P.M.	206-555-4590	Seattle, WA	4	.36
4	5/22	5:33 P.M.	619-555-7346	San Diego, CA	18	1.62
5	5/27	7:25 P.M.	510-555-0084	Oakland, CA	9	.81

don't know anyone in Dallas

was out of town

Call	Date	Time	Number	Location	Min.	Amount
1	8/4	9:19 P.M.	386-555-7811	Live Oak, FL	3	.24
2	8/9	8:22 A.M.	831-555-7045	Seaside, CA	15	1.20
3	8/11	5:00 P.M.	305-555-5933	Miami, FL	7	.63
4	8/11	7:30 A.M.	407-555-8162	Orlando, FL	45	3.60
5	8/16	6:45 P.M.	305-555-9064	Miami, FL	12	1.08

wasn't home

didn't make this call

LESSON 4: Grammar and Vocabulary

1 **GRAMMAR PICTURE DICTIONARY.** What do people want to know about an apartment? Listen and read.

TCD2, 48
SCD26

1

A: I don't know why I didn't get the apartment. Maybe I'm too old.

B: Landlords can't **discriminate against** people because of their age.

2

A: My landlord comes into my apartment without my permission. Do you know if that's illegal?

B: Yes, it definitely is! He can't come in without your **consent**.

3

A: Can you tell me how I can **file a complaint** against my landlord?

B: Yes, you can start by filling out this form.

4

A: Could you tell me what your pet **policy** is?

B: Yes. We allow cats and small dogs only.

5

A: Before you rent the apartment, check to see whether it's in good **condition**.

B: I checked it yesterday. It's clean, and nothing is broken or damaged.

6

A: I want to move, but I signed a one-year lease. Do you know how I can **break my lease**?

B: No, I don't. You should call the legal aid office for advice.

2 **PRACTICE** the conversations from Activity 1 with a partner.

3 **NOTICE THE GRAMMAR.** Circle *if, whether,* and *wh-*question words in the sentences above. Then underline the sentences where these words appear.

Embedded Questions with *If, Whether,* and Other Question Words

> If the main clause begins like a question, use a question mark. *Do you know whether they allow pets?*

An embedded question is a question within a sentence. You can use an embedded question to ask for information politely or to say that you don't know something. Questions can be embedded (included in) a statement or a question.

Direct Questions	Sentences with Embedded Questions				
	Main Clause	Question Word	Subject	Verb	
Did they give their consent?	I wonder	if	they	gave	their consent.
Should I call a lawyer?	I'd like to know	whether	I	should call	a lawyer.
Who is the landlord?	I'm not sure	who	the landlord	is.	
What is the policy?	I don't know	what	the policy	is.	
Where did the landlord go?	Do you know	where	the landlord	went?	
How can I file a complaint?	Can you tell me	how	I	can file	a complaint?

4 **REWRITE** each question as a sentence (ending with a period) containing an embedded question.

1. Is the house in good condition?

   I don't know if the house is in good condition.

2. What is the lateness policy?

   _____

3. Where can I file a complaint?

   _____

4. Why did they discriminate against Tom?

   _____

5. Did he give his consent?

   _____

6. How can I break my lease?

   _____

5 **WRITE** each of your sentences in Activity 4 as a question containing an embedded question.

Example: *Do you know if the house is in good condition?*

6 **WHAT ABOUT YOU?** Think of three questions to ask your partner. Use embedded questions.

> Can you tell me how long you've lived in your apartment?

LESSON 5: Grammar Practice Plus

1 **READ** the advice column. <u>Underline</u> the two embedded questions.

Advice for Renters by *Jean Lake*

Dear Jean,

I just found a great apartment. It's larger than my <u>current</u> apartment, and it's $200 cheaper. The problem is that I want to move in right away. Can you tell me when I have to tell my landlord that I want to move out? I've been in my apartment for two years.

Sincerely,
<u>Anxious to Move</u>

Dear Anxious,

Congratulations on finding a great apartment. You usually have to give your landlord 30 days <u>notice</u> before you move out. But check your <u>lease</u> to make sure.

Good luck,
Jean

Dear Jean,

I <u>sublet</u> my apartment to a friend of mine while I was out of town for three months. When I came back, my landlord said it was <u>illegal</u> for me to <u>sublet</u>, and now he's going to <u>evict</u> me. My lease doesn't say that I can't **sublet**. Do you know what I can do to keep my apartment?

Best regards,
Evicted in Evanston

Dear Evicted,

The first thing you should do is call a legal <u>aid</u> office for advice. Someone at the office will be able to help you work with your landlord.

Good luck,
Jean

2 **MATCH** the words from the advice column to their definitions.

1. _____ current
2. _____ notice
3. _____ sublet
4. _____ evict

a. to force someone out of their home legally
b. at the present time; now
c. to charge someone else money to live in your rented apartment when you are not there
d. an announcement about something that will happen at a particular time in the future

3 **WRITE** each sentence in the correct order.

1. to my landlord / when / do you know / that I'm moving out / I have to give notice / ?

   Do you know when I have to give notice to my landlord that I'm moving out?

2. can you / the tenants' rights organization / the current phone number for / tell me / ?

3. what / do if my / I'm not sure / I have to / landlord evicts me / .

4. should call / with my landlord / do you know / a problem / who I / if I have / ?

5. I wonder / to the meeting / are coming / if the other tenants / .

6. whether / I don't know / sublet my apartment / I can / .

4 **WRITE** each of your sentences in Activity 3 as a direct question.

   Example: *When do I have to give notice to my landlord that I'm moving out?*

5 **LISTEN** to the radio program. Look at the list of problems below. Check ☑ the problems that you hear. Then listen again, and write the suggested solution.

TCD2, 49

✔	Problem	Solution
	1. The landlord discriminated against someone because of his age.	
✓	**2.** Another tenant in the building makes a mess in the laundry room — spills laundry soap and doesn't clean it up.	
	3. The tenant can't sleep because her upstairs neighbor plays loud music late at night.	
✓	**4.** The landlord is going to evict a tenant for late payment, but the rent check was only two days late.	
✓	**5.** The tenant asked the landlord to get rid of cockroaches (bugs) in her apartment, but he hasn't done it yet.	

6 **TALK** with a partner. Think of other possible solutions for the problems in Activity 5 that you didn't hear on the radio program. Write your ideas with the other solutions in the chart above.

7 **ROLE-PLAY.** Look at the list of problems in Activity 5. Role-play with a partner. Take turns being the caller and the radio program host.

A: Thanks for calling. What's the problem?

B: My landlord didn't let someone move into our building because of the person's age. Do you know who I can talk to about that?

8 **WHAT ABOUT YOU?** Have you ever had a problem with a landlord, an apartment manager, or a neighbor? What happened? Talk with a partner.

My neighbor's dog barks all night! I don't know if I should tell my landlord about it, or talk to my neighbor.

LESSON 6: Reading

1 **THINK ABOUT IT.** Have you ever rented an apartment? Did you have to sign a lease? What were the rules in the lease? Did you have any problems with the apartment? What happened? Who fixed the problem?

2 **BEFORE YOU READ.** Preview the rental agreement on the next page. Read each word in boldface. What do you think each section will be about?

Reading Strategy Summary
Use prior knowledge.
Preview the text.
Use resources.

READING FOCUS: Use resources

When you read legal texts, you will find many words you do not know. Use a dictionary or the Internet to look up new words. In addition, some community organizations offer services to help you understand legal documents.

3 **READ** the rental agreement on the next page. Put a check ☑ next to two sections that you want to learn more about.

4 **AFTER YOU READ.**

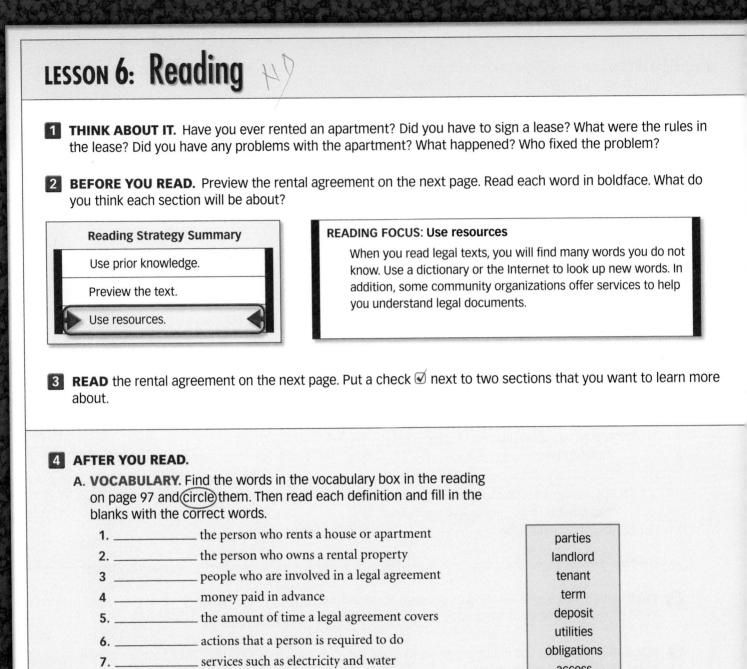

A. VOCABULARY. Find the words in the vocabulary box in the reading on page 97 and ⟨circle⟩ them. Then read each definition and fill in the blanks with the correct words.

1. _____ the person who rents a house or apartment
2. _____ the person who owns a rental property
3. _____ people who are involved in a legal agreement
4. _____ money paid in advance
5. _____ the amount of time a legal agreement covers
6. _____ actions that a person is required to do
7. _____ services such as electricity and water
8. _____ to enter a property

parties
landlord
tenant
term
deposit
utilities
obligations
access

B. REREAD the two sections that you put a checkmark ☑ next to. ⟨Circle⟩ any words that you don't know. Reread each sentence, then guess the meaning of each word. Next, use a dictionary or the internet to look up the new words. Were your guesses correct?

C. TALK with a partner. Answer the questions.

1. How many people may live in the property?
2. What is the term of the lease?
3. After the term ends, how does the agreement change?
4. What is the penalty for paying rent late?
5. Will the tenant receive a refund of the security deposit at the end of the lease? Why or why not?
6. What utilities does the landlord pay for?
7. Who is responsible for keeping appliances in good repair?
8. Can the tenant open a business on the property?

Rental Agreement

Parties: This agreement is between <u>Mark Wilson</u>, Landlord, and <u>Richard Rashan</u>, Tenant. No other Tenants may be permitted to occupy the property. Subletting is prohibited* except as approved in advance in writing by the Landlord.

Property: The Landlord agrees to lease the following property to Tenant: <u>2301 West 1st Avenue, Anytown, USA.</u>

Term*: This rental agreement is for a term of <u>12 months, beginning September 1, 2008, and ending August 31, 2009</u>. After completion of the term, Tenant may continue to rent the property on a month-to-month basis, during which either party may terminate the agreement. Written notice must be provided 30 days in advance to the other party.

Rent: The monthly rental rate shall be <u>$500 per month</u>, due and payable by check or money-order on the 1st day of the month. A late charge of $10 per day will apply to each payment received after due date.

Deposit: Tenant agrees to pay <u>$1,000</u> to Landlord (first and last months' rent) and a security deposit of <u>$300</u> at the time this lease is signed. Within three weeks after the tenant moves out, the security deposit will be refunded to Tenant, less any fees necessary for cleaning and repair of the property due to the negligence* of the Tenant.

Utilities: Tenant shall pay all utilities, including water, electricity, and gas supply.

Tenant's obligations: Tenant shall: (1) Maintain the property in a clean, undamaged, and unaltered* condition; (2) follow all rules and notices; (3) be responsible for any damage caused to the property with the exception of usual wear and tear; (4) dispose of trash in provided containers; (5) not conduct business or commercial activities on the property.

Landlord's obligations: Landlord shall: (1) Maintain the property in good repair, including: electrical, plumbing, and heating systems; appliances; (2) keep common areas of complex clean and safe; (3) control infestation of insects, except where caused by Tenant.

Access: Landlord has the right to access the property after giving 48 hours advance notice. Landlord does not need to give advance notice before entering in case of emergency.

prohibited (adj.): not allowed; not permitted

term (n.): length of time for lease

negligence (n.): lack of care forwsomething or someone

unaltered (adj.): not changed

LESSON 7: Writing

1 **THINK ABOUT IT.** Have you ever written a letter of complaint? What was the letter about? What happened after you wrote the letter? If you haven't ever written a letter of complaint, have you ever wanted to? Why?

2 **BEFORE YOU WRITE.**

A. **SCAN** the letter below. What is the main problem?

> **WRITING FOCUS: Give examples**
> Giving specific examples can help you to explain a situation or a problem. Examples can also persuade your reader that your opinion is right. When you write about a problem or your opinion, be sure to include specific examples.

B. **READ** this letter to an advice column. Circle the examples.

Dear Home Guy,

  Six months ago, I signed a one-year apartment lease. Now my landlord wants to break our lease because he wants his daughter to move into the apartment. According to the lease, he can't ask me to move out early unless I damage the apartment, or I don't pay my rent. I haven't caused any damage and I pay my rent on time. Now, he is being a terrible landlord because I won't move. The toilet leaks and he won't fix it. He has entered my apartment three times without my consent and with no notice. Do you know if that's legal? Can you tell me what I should do? I'm not sure who to talk to about this problem.

Signed,
Frustrated in Phoenix

C. **WRITE.** Imagine you are having a serious problem with your apartment or house. Answer these questions and make notes about the problem.

1. What is the problem?
2. Who or what is causing the problem?
3. Give two or three examples of the problem.
4. Who should fix the problem?
5. How can the problem be fixed?

D. **DISCUSS** your problem with a partner. Can you add more details to your notes?

3 WRITE. Using your notes, write a letter about a housing problem to an advice columnist at a local newspaper. Be sure to sign your letter with a creative anonymous name (like *Frustrated in Phoenix*)!

Dear _____ ,

4 AFTER YOU WRITE.

A. **DISCUSS.** Exchange letters with your partner. Read your partner's letter. Then talk with your partner and answer his or her letter.

B. **EDIT.** Check your letter. Ask yourself these questions.

1. Did you explain the problem clearly?
2. Did you include specific examples?
3. Did you use articles *(a, an, the)* correctly?
4. Did you use embedded questions correctly?

 C. **REWRITE** your letter with corrections.

D. **ROLE-PLAY.** Choose one of the letters that you and your partner wrote. With your partner, role-play the situation for the class. For example, if the problem is between you and a neighbor, act out a scene in which you ask the neighbor to fix the problem.

Career Connection

1 **THINK ABOUT IT.** In what kinds of situations do you write email, talk on the phone, send a text message, or speak face-to-face with people as part of your job? What are the advantages of each way of communicating? Are there situations in which one or more of these ways do not work well? Explain.

2 **READ** the series of email messages between Jack, a building contractor, and Carl, the foreman at a construction site. What are the two things that Carl misunderstood in Jack's first message?

On 8/31/2007 at 08:35, Jack Lamond wrote:

```
Carl,

I just spoke with the architect regarding the schedule. He said there's been
a change of plans. We need to fax it before we can ask the site engineers to
start laying the foundation. Please let the site engineers know.
Jack
```

On 8/31/2007 at 08:39, you replied:

```
Jack,

I'm waiting here by the fax machine, but nothing has come through yet. I told the
site engineers that new plans are coming, and to stop drilling for now. Are you sure
you have the right fax number? It's 860-555-1300.
Carl
```

On 8/31/2007 at 09:16, Jack Lamond wrote:

```
Carl,

I'm sorry! I meant "fix," not "fax." The change is to the schedule, not to the
building plans. Please tell the site engineers to get back to work. I'll call
you later, after we fix the schedule.
Jack
```

New reply:

```
Jack,

Got it! Thanks for letting me know. If you need to contact me later, send me a text
message. I'll be on the site, and won't be able to hear the phone if it rings.
Carl
```

---

3 **MATCH** the word from the reading in Activity 2 with its definition.

a. architect   b. plans   c. foundation   d. site engineer   e. drilling

__a__ **1.** person who creates the plans for a building

____ **4.** drawings of a building

____ **2.** a person who follows plans to build something

____ **5.** below ground, the base of a building

____ **3.** making a hole with a machine

4 **WRITE** answers to the questions. Then discuss your answers with a partner.

1. What does Jack want Carl to do?

2. Why does Carl send Jack his fax number?

3. What does *change of plans* mean?

4. Why does Carl want Jack to send him a text message?

5 **WHAT ABOUT YOU?** Have you had an experience when there was a misunderstanding in email or on the phone, but you did not ask for clarification? What happened? Talk to a partner.

Check Your Progress!

Skill	Circle the answers.	Is it correct?
A. Use definite and indefinite articles.	1. I need **the** / **a** new cell phone. This one is too big. 2. If you have **a** / **the** gas leak, you should get out of the house quickly. 3. This is **a** / **the** biggest gas bill I've ever received. 4. I found an error on my bill. **An** / **The** error is on the third page.	☐ ☐ ☐ ☐

		Number Correct	0	1	2	3	4

Skill	Circle the answers.	Is it correct?
B. Use embedded questions with *if*, *whether*, and other question words.	5. I wonder **if** / **did** they signed the lease. 6. Do you know **who is the landlord** / **who the landlord is**? 7. Can you tell me **what is the rent** / **what the rent is**? 8. I'd like to know **whether I should** / **should I** file a complaint.	☐ ☐ ☐ ☐

		Number Correct	0	1	2	3	4

Skill	Circle the answers.	Is it correct?
C. Talk about house problems.	9. I lost my Internet **connection** / **signal** again! 10. We had a power **leak** / **outage** last night. 11. I can't hear you. My cell phone signal is too **weak** / **strong**. 12. Call the phone company. There's an error on the **charge** / **bill**.	☐ ☐ ☐ ☐

		Number Correct	0	1	2	3	4

Skill	Circle the answers.	Is it correct?
D. Understand language about renting.	13. Employers can't discriminate **on** / **against** women. 14. The apartment is new. It's in great **condition** / **consent**. 15. I want to file a **lease** / **complaint** against my landlord. 16. I want to get a dog. What is your pet **policy** / **permission**?	☐ ☐ ☐ ☐

		Number Correct	0	1	2	3	4

COUNT the number of correct answers above. Fill in the bubbles.

Chart Your Success					
Skill	Need Practice	Okay	Good	Very Good	Excellent!
A. Use definite and indefinite articles.	⓪	①	②	③	④
B. Use embedded questions with *if*, *whether*, and other question words	⓪	①	②	③	④
C. Talk about house problems.	⓪	①	②	③	④
D. Understand language about renting.	⓪	①	②	③	④

LESSON 1: Grammar and Vocabulary

1 GRAMMAR PICTURE DICTIONARY. What stories are in the news? Listen and read.

TCD3, 2
SCD27

1

A: Did you hear about the man who **donated** money to our community center?

B: Yes, I did. He's a great **role model** for children. They want to be like him.

2

A: Did you hear about the five-car **collision** that happened on the freeway?

B: No, I didn't. When did it happen?

3

A: Did you hear about the **demonstration** that was held outside City Hall today?

B: Yes. The **demonstrators** want the mayor to make the city safer.

4

A: How is the firefighter who **rescued** the little boy?

B: He's in the hospital, but he's okay.

5

A: Did you talk to the officers who are **investigating** the robbery?

B: Yes, I did. I was a witness, so I described the person that **committed the crime**.

6

A: I read there might be a flu **epidemic** this winter. A lot of people might get sick.

B: I read that, too. Fortunately, people who are over 65 can get free flu vaccinations.

2 PRACTICE the conversations in Activity 1 with a partner.

3 NOTICE THE GRAMMAR. Underline the pronouns *who* and *that* in the sentences above. Then check ☑ the correct lines below.

	Used for People	Used for Places and Things
1. who	_____	_____
2. that	_____	_____

Adjective Clauses with Relative Pronouns as Subjects

An adjective clause comes after a noun and gives additional information about the noun.

An adjective clause has its own subject and verb. The subject of an adjective clause can be a relative pronoun: *who* or *that*. An adjective clause always comes immediately after the noun it describes. When the noun is the subject of the main clause, the adjective clause comes *inside* the main clause.

Main Clause	Adjective Clause		Main Clause
Subject	Relative Pronoun	Verb (+ Object)	Verb (+ Object)
The **man**	who/that	robbed the store	was convicted.
The **car**	that	caused the collision	was red.

When the noun is the object of the main clause, the adjective clause comes *after* the main clause.

Main Clause		Adjective Clause	
Subject + Verb	Object	Relative Pronoun	Verb (+ Object)
I saw	the **man**	who/that	robbed the store.
The man drove	the **car**	that	caused the collision.

> The relative pronoun *which* is also used to refer to nouns. However, *that* is much more common.

4 **READ** each sentence and <u>underline</u> the adjective clause. (Circle) the relative pronoun *who* or *that*. Then draw an arrow from the relative pronoun to the noun that it refers to.

1. Did you hear about the man (who) <u>rescued the girl from the river</u>?

2. I read about an epidemic that is happening in South America.

3. Politicians who are honest and hardworking are good role models for citizens.

4. The woman who donated money to the hospital was a patient there two years ago.

5. The police officer that investigated the crime got a promotion.

5 **WRITE** sentences in your notebook. Put the words in the correct order.

1. who works / police station downtown / I met a woman / at the / .

   I met a woman who works at the police station downtown.

2. who committed / the crime / the men / were punished / .

3. that happened / in the traffic jam / were you / after the collision / stuck / ?

4. positive role models / musicians / healthy lifestyles / who have / are / for children / .

5. hear about / did you / that rescued his sister / the little boy / from a burning house / ?

6 **WHAT ABOUT YOU?** Complete the sentences below. Then talk with a partner.

> I read about a man who escaped a fire.

1. I read about a person who _____.

2. I heard about a _____ that

   _____.

LESSON 2: Grammar Practice Plus

1 **VOCABULARY.** Read the definitions. Then complete the sentences with the correct forms of the words.

> **evidence:** facts or signs that help prove how something happened
>
> **suspect:** someone who might have committed a crime
>
> **theory:** an idea or possible explanation of how something might have happened
>
> **identify:** to point out, recognize, or give the name of a person

1. The robber was ___identified___ by a security guard who saw him go in the back door.

2. My _____ that our barbecue grill was stolen by the neighbor might be true! I think I saw it in his backyard!

3. Did the police find any _____ that proves Alex committed the crime?

4. The police have four _____. They may be the thieves who stole the diamonds from the jewelry store.

2 **READ** the sentences. Circle the words that correctly complete each sentence.

1. Mark is the man **that live / who lives** next door.

2. Scientists have evidence **who proves / that proves** the bones are 600 years old.

3. Did Carol identify the man **who rescues / who rescued** her cat?

4. Did you hear that a man **who works / that work** in my office is a suspect?

5. The police officers **who are / who is** investigating the crime have a new theory.

3 **WRITE.** Combine each pair of sentences to make one sentence.

1. John thanked the firefighter. The firefighter helped him.

   ___John thanked the firefighter who helped him.___

2. The police are looking at the evidence. The evidence was in the apartment.

   _____

3. A woman has a theory about the missing tests. The woman is in my class.

   _____

4. The witness saw everything. The witness identified a suspect.

   _____

5. A woman donated a million dollars to her university. The woman graduated 30 years ago.

   _____

6. The witnesses identified the suspect. The witnesses were inside the bank during the robbery.

   _____

7. A reporter interviewed several witnesses. The reporter wrote a story about the crime.

   _____

🎧 TCD3, 3 **4** **TALK** about the picture. Then listen and write the correct number next to each name.

What's the evidence?

_____ Robin Gale　　_____ Officer King　　_____ Lee West　　_____ Tina Ruiz　　_____ Officer Dill　　_____ Tom Lee

5 **COMPLETE** the article with the adjective clauses in the box below.

that led to the park	who stole the steaks
who were in the butcher shop	who arrived at the scene
that were behind the window	that was walking by

SURFSIDE - There was a robbery at Lee's Butcher Shop on First Street yesterday afternoon. The thief stole some steaks

(1) _____ . The officers (2) _____a

few minutes after it happened began investigating immediately. People (3) _____

when the steaks were stolen didn't see anything. One woman (4) _____ said

she saw the person (5) _____ , but she was not able to describe him. The

police followed some paw prints (6) _____ and found the thieves. Two dogs

were hiding behind a tree eating the stolen steaks. When Mr. Lee found out who robbed his store, he laughed and said,

"Well, those dogs have good taste!"

LESSON 3: Listening and Conversation

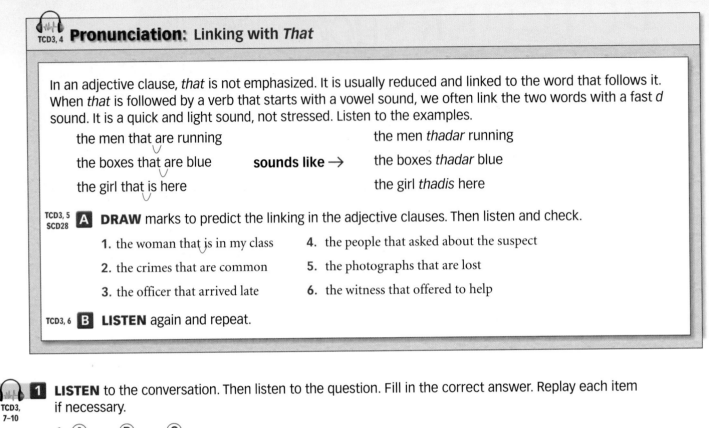

TCD3, 4 **Pronunciation:** Linking with *That*

In an adjective clause, *that* is not emphasized. It is usually reduced and linked to the word that follows it. When *that* is followed by a verb that starts with a vowel sound, we often link the two words with a fast *d* sound. It is a quick and light sound, not stressed. Listen to the examples.

the men that are running   the men *thadar* running

the boxes that are blue   **sounds like →**   the boxes *thadar* blue

the girl that is here   the girl *thadis* here

TCD3, 5 SCD28 **A** **DRAW** marks to predict the linking in the adjective clauses. Then listen and check.

1. the woman that is in my class
2. the crimes that are common
3. the officer that arrived late
4. the people that asked about the suspect
5. the photographs that are lost
6. the witness that offered to help

TCD3, 6 **B** **LISTEN** again and repeat.

TCD3, 7–10 **1** **LISTEN** to the conversation. Then listen to the question. Fill in the correct answer. Replay each item if necessary.

1. Ⓐ   Ⓑ   Ⓒ
2. Ⓐ   Ⓑ   Ⓒ
3. Ⓐ   Ⓑ   Ⓒ
4. Ⓐ   Ⓑ   Ⓒ

TCD3, 11 **2** **LISTEN** to the conversations again. Write the number of each conversation next to the correct headline.

_____ **a.** Demonstration Still Going Strong after Two Weeks

_____ **b.** Man Finds Surprising Treasure in Home

_____ **c.** Hundreds Line Up for Free Vaccinations

_____ **d.** Crash Stops Traffic for Five Hours on Monday

TCD3, 12 **3** **LISTEN** to the conversation. Then read the sentences and check ☑ *True* or *False*.

	True	False
1. The story that they are talking about is from the TV news.	☐	☐
2. A couple that met at an airport gift shop got married.	☐	☐
3. The man and woman got married soon after they first met.	☐	☐
4. Thirty years later, they got divorced.	☐	☐
5. The man and woman saw each other at a restaurant at the airport.	☐	☐

4 **LISTEN** to the conversation.

A: Did you hear about the woman who was lost in the woods for over two weeks?

B: No, I didn't. How did she get lost?

A: She went hiking by herself and stayed out too late. It got really dark and she couldn't find her way back to the parking lot.

B: How did she survive in the woods for so long?

A: She ate wild berries and slept inside an old tree to stay warm.

B: <u>Are you serious</u>?

A: <u>Absolutely</u>! She's okay now. A man who was hiking with his kids found her last weekend.

5 **PRACTICE** the conversation from Activity 4 with a partner. Use the expressions below.

Conversation Strategy	
Responding to news	
A: Are you serious?	B: Absolutely!
A: I can't believe it!	B: It's true!
A: No way!	B: It's in the news!
A: Really?	B: Yeah!
A: You're kidding!	B: No, I'm serious.

6 **TALK** with a partner. Make up a conversation about the news story below. Student A, read the news story below. <u>Underline</u> the interesting points. Then tell your partner about the story. Student B, ask your partner questions about the story.

Dog Pulls Owner Out of River

SAN CARLOS - Last night, a dog named Ollie saved his owner, Jose Gonzalez, from drowning. The man and his dog had been canoeing on a river that is near Gonzalez's home. Suddenly, the canoe hit a rock and tipped over. Both the man and his dog fell in the water. Gonzalez doesn't know how to swim and was unable to get back into the canoe. Ollie held onto Gonzalez's jacket with his teeth. The dog swam to shore and dragged Gonzalez onto the sand. A witness, Janice Dunn, saw what happened and called 911.

"I'm so thankful to the two who saved my life—Ollie and Janice," Gonzalez says. Dunn adds, "Ollie is the real hero. He's an amazing dog."

LESSON 4: Grammar and Vocabulary

1 GRAMMAR PICTURE DICTIONARY. What kinds of news items are the people talking about? Listen and read.

1

A: Can I borrow your newspaper? Where's the story that you told me about?
B: Here you go. It's on the **front page**.

2

A: Look at the **headline** for today's **top story**. This looks interesting.
B: Oh, that's the story about the woman who the hikers rescued.

3

A: Do you read the advice **column** that Carly Baker writes?
B: Yes, I do. She's my favorite **columnist**.

4

A: Here's a great **human-interest** story in the **local** section. A three-year-old boy can play the violin.
B: That's the boy who Karen told me about! He lives next door to her.

5

A: Have you ever found a good job in the **classified ads**?
B: Yeah. The job that I had three years ago was from a classified ad.

6

A: What's the **website address** for the **blog** that you write?
B: The **URL** is www.edwardzblog.com.

2 PRACTICE the conversations in Activity 1 with a partner.

3 NOTICE THE GRAMMAR

A. CIRCLE the relative pronoun in each adjective clause above. <u>Underline</u> the subject and verb that come after each relative pronoun.

B. **READ** the adjective clauses in the grammar chart on page 103. Find each relative pronoun and look at the word after it. What part of speech is the word after the relative pronoun?

108 | Use adjective clauses and object relative pronouns. • Talk about news media.

Adjective Clauses with Relative Pronouns as Objects

A relative pronoun, *who*, *whom*, or *that*, can serve as the object of an adjective clause. When it is the object, it comes before the subject of the adjective clause. *Who* and *whom* refer only to people. *Whom* is more formal and is not as common as *who*. *That* refers to things and people.

Main Clause	Adjective Clause			Main Clause
	Relative Pronoun	Subject	Verb	
The **columnist**	who(m)/that	Lisa	met	was British.
The **story**	that	I	heard	isn't true.

Main Clause		Adjective Clause		
		Relative Pronoun	Subject	Verb
She's	the **columnist**	who(m)/that	Lisa	met.
That's	the **story**	that	I	heard.

When the relative pronoun is the *object* of the adjective clause, it can be omitted.
Correct ✔: She's the columnist **whom** Lisa met.
Correct ✔: She's the columnist Lisa met.

4 WRITE. Combine each pair of sentences to make one sentence. Include an adjective clause with a relative pronoun as the object.

1. This is the human-interest story. I told you about it.

   This is the human-interest story that I told you about

2. The column was entertaining. Janice wrote it.

   _____

3. The photo was in the local section. I was looking for the photo.

   _____

4. The doctor writes a medical blog. I met her.

   _____

5. The URL for the blog is www.drlisablog.com. Lisa writes it.

   _____

5 READ. Put parentheses around the relative pronouns in the sentences you wrote in Activity 4. Read the sentences with a partner. First read them with the relative pronoun, then read them without the relative pronoun.

6 WHAT ABOUT YOU? Complete the sentences with your own ideas.

1. The newspaper that I usually read is _____.

2. The city that I was born in is _____.

3. The person who I spend the most time with is _____.

4. The TV shows that I like to watch are _____.

LESSON 5: Grammar Practice Plus

1 **COMPLETE** the article. Write the correct relative pronoun in each sentence below. Then (circle) the subject relative pronouns.

Childhood obesity is an important issue (1) _____*that*_____ is currently affecting many children. Some even call it an epidemic. According to researchers, about 15 percent of children (2) _____ live in the United States and more than 20 percent of Australian children are dangerously overweight.

There are several factors (3) _____ may be responsible for this problem. First, many of these children eat fast food or junk food instead of nutritious meals (4) _____ are prepared at home. The food (5) _____ they eat is full of fat and sugar and doesn't contain the vitamins and nutrients (6) _____ they need.

Second, children (7) _____ spend all their time in front of a television, a computer, or a video game don't get enough exercise. They don't do activities (8) _____ burn calories, such as playing sports or simply playing outside. If children don't burn off the calories (9) _____ they consume, they gain weight.

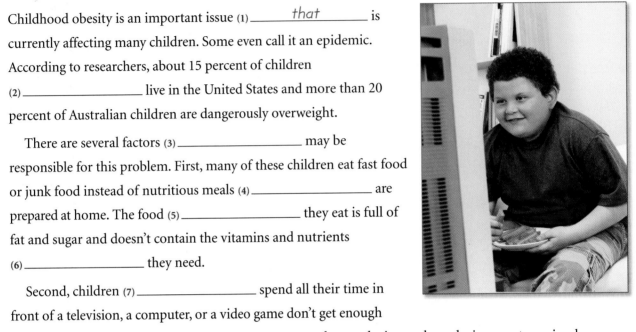

2 **WRITE.** Combine each pair of sentences to make one sentence. If a relative pronoun is the object of the relative clause, put it in parentheses to show that it can be omitted.

1. Many activities are fun and good exercise. Children do them outdoors.
   Many activities (that) children do outdoors are fun and good exercise.

2. Many parents pack nutritious lunches for their children. Parents worry about what their kids eat at school.
   _____

3. Children spend more time online. They have computers in their bedrooms.
   _____

4. Health groups provide programs. The programs teach children how to choose nutritious foods.
   _____

5. Junk food is full of fat and sugar. Children buy it at school.
   _____

6. Video games keep children indoors. Children play them.
   _____

7. Playing outside is an activity. Children can do it to stay healthy.
   _____

Math: Reading Bar Graphs

Look at the bar graph about childhood obesity in the United States. Then answer the questions with a partner.

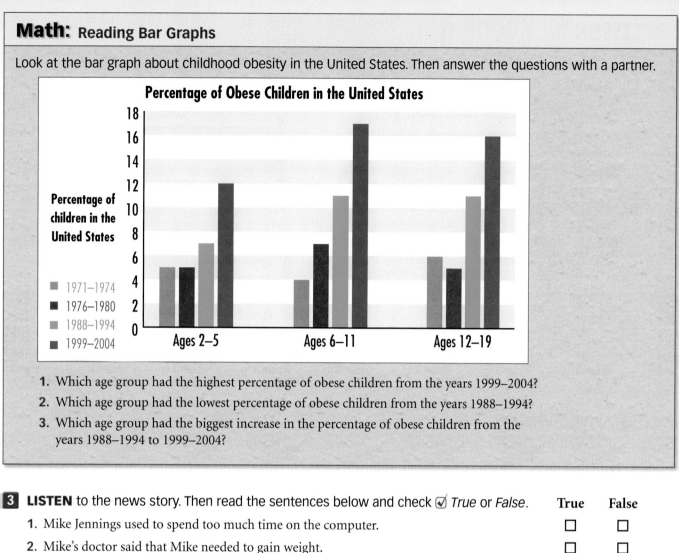

Percentage of Obese Children in the United States

Percentage of children in the United States

- 1971–1974
- 1976–1980
- 1988–1994
- 1999–2004

Ages 2–5   Ages 6–11   Ages 12–19

1. Which age group had the highest percentage of obese children from the years 1999–2004?
2. Which age group had the lowest percentage of obese children from the years 1988–1994?
3. Which age group had the biggest increase in the percentage of obese children from the years 1988–1994 to 1999–2004?

---

3 **LISTEN** to the news story. Then read the sentences below and check ☑ *True* or *False*.

TCD3, 15

	True	False
1. Mike Jennings used to spend too much time on the computer.	☐	☐
2. Mike's doctor said that Mike needed to gain weight.	☐	☐
3. Mike has never read a blog before.	☐	☐
4. Mike couldn't find any blogs about health.	☐	☐
5. Mike lost weight when he started to exercise.	☐	☐
6. Mike's doctor doesn't think reading blogs is a good idea.	☐	☐
7. Blogs can be a good source of information and support.	☐	☐

4 **WHAT ABOUT YOU?** Think of an idea for your own blog and ideas you would like to share on it. Use the phrases below to write your sentences. Then share your ideas with a partner.

I'd like people who . . . to read my blog.	I'd like to share information that helps people . . .

Your topic: _____

Ideas you want to share:

1. _____
2. _____
3. _____

LESSON 6: Reading

1 **THINK ABOUT IT.** Do you like to shop at big corporate stores or small privately owned stores? Why? With a partner, list the names of several large corporate stores and several small independent stores that you know. Discuss the benefits of shopping at both kinds of stores.

2 **BEFORE YOU READ.** Read the title of the newspaper article on the next page. What do you already know about "big business"? Can you give an example of a "big business"? Skim the text by reading the first sentence of each paragraph. What is the article about?

3 **READ** the article. <u>Underline</u> the details that answer *who*, *what*, *where*, *when*, *why*, and *how*.

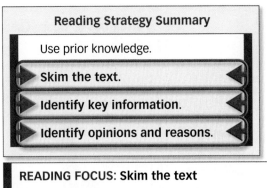

Reading Strategy Summary

Use prior knowledge.

Skim the text.

Identify key information.

Identify opinions and reasons.

READING FOCUS: Skim the text

Skim by reading the title and the first sentence in each paragraph.

READING FOCUS: Identify key information

As you read, look for details that answer the questions *who*, *what*, *where*, *when*, *why*, and *how*. Underlining the details will help you understand the reading.

4 **AFTER YOU READ.**

A. DISCUSS the questions with a partner. Look at what you underlined in the article on page 113.

    1. Which park downtown is in danger?

    2. What does BigMart want to do downtown?

    3. Who thinks that a BigMart will bring many jobs to the area?

    4. Why do people from Shadyside Manor support BigMart?

    5. Who leads the opposition to BigMart? What reasons does he give for his opinion?

    6. How can citizens give their opinion about this situation?

B. COMPLETE the chart with the names of people in the article and the reasons for their opinions.

READING FOCUS: Identify opinions and reasons

When reading an opinion about a topic, look for the reasons that support the person's opinion. A reason will answer the question, *Why do you think that?*

Opinion: BigMart will be good for downtown.	Opinion: BigMart will not be good for downtown.
Reasons	Reasons
Kathy Jones-more jobs	

Davidson Park in danger as big business* moves in

Downtown has changed a lot over the years, but some things have always remained the same. Davidson Park is one of the things that hasn't changed. For years, residents and visitors have
5 enjoyed this quiet, green space in the middle of the city. But Davidson Park may soon be gone if BigMart wins its bid* to build a new store there.

Supporters* of BigMart want a new store that will bring more visitors—and money—to
10 downtown. One resident who asked not to be named said, "Downtown is old and run down right now. BigMart will help clean it up. More visitors will want to come then, and all the businesses will get more customers."

15 Kathy Jones is a single mother of three who lives downtown. She said, "BigMart will bring lots of jobs downtown. There are so few jobs here now. I can't work at a job that is in the suburbs. I don't have a car, and the bus that goes to the suburbs
20 takes two hours. If BigMart opens downtown, I can get a good job there."

Miles Morris likes the idea of a BigMart, too. He lives at Shadyside Manor, a downtown retirement community* that is home to nearly 300 senior
25 citizens. "It's hard for us to leave downtown," said Morris. "Yes, there is a BigMart just five miles away, but many of us who live here can't drive. Right now, there are no good stores downtown. We don't need little gift shops, cafes, and art stores.
30 We need food, clothing, and medicine. BigMart has the things we need, and we could walk there."

Opponents* of BigMart have their own opinions. Jonas Wilson is the man who is leading the opposition. As the leader of Boycott Big Business,
35 a group that supports small businesses, Wilson

A father and daughter enjoy Davidson Park.

is well known downtown. "Building a BigMart downtown would be a big mistake," he said. "We may get more shoppers, but they'll all go to BigMart instead of to the small shops. Those
40 shops have been here since our town began, and we should support them. BigMart will take away their customers, and the shops will have to close."

Lacey Briggs works at Town Bank, across the street from Davidson Park. "Losing the park would
45 be a shame," she said. "Many of us who work downtown eat our lunch in the park. There are also many children who play there every day. Davidson is the only park we have downtown. We should fight to keep it!"

50 Denny Peters has lived downtown for more than 70 years and is strongly opposed to a new BigMart. "We love the old buildings and the history here. BigMart is a big, ugly monster that would ruin the charm of this neighborhood. What's next? Fast-food
55 restaurants and drive-through coffee shops? We don't want those here."

Concerned citizens can give their opinion at the next town council meeting on Friday at 7:00 P.M.

big business (n.): large companies that have a lot of economic power

bid (n.): a business proposal or plan

supporters (n.): people who think something is a good idea

retirement community (n.): a building or several buildings where many retired people live

opponents (n.): people who think something is a bad idea

LESSON 7: Writing

1 **THINK ABOUT IT.** List three recent news stories in the newspaper or on television that were interesting to you.

1. _____

2. _____

3. _____

2 **BEFORE YOU WRITE.**

A. **WRITE** ideas. Look at the stories you listed in Activity 1. Which one do you have the strongest opinion about? Write your opinion about the story you chose.

_____

_____

_____

_____

_____

> **WRITING FOCUS: Express and support an opinion**
>
> An opinion is something you think or believe. When you write an opinion paragraph, state your opinion clearly in your topic sentence. Then give your reasons. Reasons can include facts, feelings, or details that support your opinion. Reasons are the supporting details of your paragraph.
>
> For example:
>
> - I really like our new mayor. She is an excellent speaker who has sensible ideas.
> - Building a subway in our city is a bad idea. The tax increase that would pay for the subway is too expensive for most people.

B. **READ** the paragraph that a parent wrote about a news story. Find the sentence that tells the parent's opinion. Circle it.

> In my opinion, our school district should not make students pay to play sports this year. Sports that used to be free will now cost $200 for each student. Kids who can't afford to pay won't be allowed to play, and that isn't fair. Also, we pay taxes for our school's sports program, so kids shouldn't need to pay even more money. Finally, we might lose some of our best student athletes if their parents don't have the extra money. A program that charges such a high fee is wrong! We need a sports program that works for everyone.

C. **READ** again. What reasons does the parent give for the opinion? Find three reasons. <u>Underline</u> them.

D. WRITE your ideas about a current issue in the news. Fill in the chart below with complete sentences. Use adjective clauses with *who* and *that*. Follow these steps.

1. Write a sentence or two that introduces the topic in the Opinion box. State your opinion clearly.

2. In each Reason box, write a reason for your opinion. Your reasons may be facts, feelings, or details.

Opinion
Reason 1
Reason 2
Reason 3

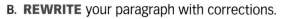 **3** **WRITE** a paragraph about the issue you chose. Use the information in the chart above. Add details and supporting information.

4 **AFTER YOU WRITE.**

A. **EDIT** your work. Ask yourself these questions.

   1. Did I state my opinion clearly?
   2. Did I give reasons—facts, feelings, and details—to support my opinion?
   3. Did I use adjective clauses?
   4. Did I use correct spelling, capitalization, and punctuation?

B. **REWRITE** your paragraph with corrections.

C. **DISCUSS** these questions with a partner.

   1. Do you think everyone agrees with you on the issue you wrote about?
   2. What opinions might other people have?

Career Connection

1 THINK ABOUT IT. Look at the photo. What food safety rules do you think restaurant employees have to follow?

TCD3, 16

2 LISTEN to the presentation. A trainer is talking to a group of employees in a restaurant. Check ☑ *True* or *False*.

	True	False
1. Restaurants can be shut down if they don't follow health codes.	☐	☐
2. Handling food can spread bacteria.	☐	☐
3. Unwashed vegetables and fruits can contain bacteria.	☐	☐
4. E. coli and salmonella are the same type of bacteria.	☐	☐
5. All food preparation staff must wear hairnets.	☐	☐

3 COMPLETE the sentences with the correct vocabulary word from the presentation.

contagious	food poisoning	outbreak	plastic gloves	thoroughly	temperatures

1. People could get _____ from eating uncooked meat or unwashed vegetables.

2. Food servers who don't wash their hands _____ might spread bacteria.

3. E. coli and salmonella bacteria are _____ and can spread easily from person to person.

4. Food must be well cooked and stored at the correct _____.

5. All food preparation staff must wear _____ while handling food.

6. An E. coli or salmonella _____ can happen if restaurant employees don't follow health codes.

4 WRITE three things that employees must do to protect themselves and customers from food poisoning.

5 TALK with a partner or in a group. What could happen if employees do not follow the health codes? Can you think of other places in the community where health or food safety codes are important to follow?

6 WHAT ABOUT YOU? Have you heard any news stories about illnesses caused by foods in local fast-food restaurants? Have you ever been sick from something that you ate? Describe what happened.

Check Your Progress!

Skill	Circle the answers.	Is it correct?
A. Use adjective clauses with relative pronouns as subjects.	**1.** Did you hear about the man **who live** / **who lives** in my building? **2.** He committed the robbery **who was** / **that was** on the news. **3.** That's the officer **that arrests** / **that arrested** the man. **4.** Did you see the car **that caused** / **who caused** the accident?	☐ ☐ ☐ ☐

		Number Correct	0	1	2	3	4

Skill	Circle the answers.	Is it correct?
B. Use adjective clauses with relative pronouns as objects.	**5.** The story **that I read** / **who I read** was too long. **6.** She's the woman **I told you about** / **I told you about her**. **7.** That's the story **she wrote** / **who she wrote**. **8.** The doctor that **we know him** / **we know** works at the hospital.	☐ ☐ ☐ ☐

		Number Correct	0	1	2	3	4

Skill	Circle the answers.	Is it correct?
C. Talk about news and current events.	**9.** Did you hear about the **collision** / **epidemic** on the freeway? **10.** The police are **investigating** / **donating** the robbery. **11.** They aren't sure who **committed** / **rescued** the crime. **12.** I like him. He's a positive **demonstrator** / **role model** for children.	☐ ☐ ☐ ☐

		Number Correct	0	1	2	3	4

Skill	Circle the answers.	Is it correct?
D. Understand news media terms.	**13.** I found a new car in the **classified** / **human-interest** ads. **14.** What is the **blog** / **URL** for your website? **15.** The most important news story is called the **top** / **blog** story. **16.** Ted Sanders writes a **column** / **columnist** about film and music.	☐ ☐ ☐ ☐

		Number Correct	0	1	2	3	4

COUNT the number of correct answers. Fill in the bubbles.

Chart Your Success					
Skill	Need Practice	Okay	Good	Very Good	Excellent!
A. Use adjective clauses with relative pronouns as subjects.	⓪	①	②	③	④
B. Use adjective clauses with relative pronouns as objects.	⓪	①	②	③	④
C. Talk about news and current events.	⓪	①	②	③	④
D. Understand news media terms.	⓪	①	②	③	④

LESSON 1: Grammar and Vocabulary

1 **GRAMMAR PICTURE DICTIONARY.** What is happening with the weather? How do the people feel about it? Listen and read.

TCD3, 17
SCD31

1

A: I didn't hear the **forecast**. Is there a **severe thunderstorm warning** today?

B: I don't know. But I'm <u>nervous about</u> (driving) in **torrential rain**.

A: So am I. We'd better take the train instead.

2

A: The **air quality** is really terrible! There isn't a **smog advisory** today, is there?

B: I don't know. But I'm concerned about running outdoors.

A: So am I. Maybe we should exercise at the gym instead.

3

A: Uh-oh! We just had another power outage!

B: Right. I'm not surprised because there's an **extreme heat alert** today.

A: I'm worried about keeping our food cold.

4

A: Wow! What a strong **gust of wind**!

B: I know. The National Weather Service **issued** a **tornado warning**. They're serious about taking **precautions**.

A: Let's get out of here and find shelter right away!

2 **PRACTICE** the conversations from Activity 1 with a partner.

3 **NOTICE THE GRAMMAR.** <u>Underline</u> adjective + preposition combinations. (Circle) the gerunds (verb + *ing*) that follow them.

Gerunds as Objects of Prepositions

Form a gerund with the base verb + -ing. A gerund can follow be + adjective + preposition.

Subject	be	Adjective + Preposition	Gerund + Phrase
I	am not	nervous about	**driving** in the torrential rain.
She	was	serious about	**finding** shelter.
They	are	concerned about	**having** a blackout.
Sara	was	afraid of	**getting** lost in the storm.
The managers	were	interested in	**knowing** more.

Be careful! We cannot use infinitives instead of gerunds in this kind of sentence.
Correct ✔: I'm nervous about driving.
Incorrect ✗: I'm nervous about to drive.

4 COMPLETE the sentences with the correct forms of the words in parentheses. Use the present or past form of *be*.

1. George ___was nervous about driving___
   (be / nervous about / drive) during the tornado advisory yesterday.

2. The man _____
   (be / serious about / take) precautions during the smog advisory.

3. Sue _____
   (not be / concerned about / exercise) in the torrential rain.
   She always wears her rain hat and a rain coat.

4. The children _____
   (not be / worried about / play) soccer during a thunderstorm
   warning, but the school officials cancelled the game.

5. I _____
   (be / excited about / play) tennis until I heard about the extreme
   heat alert.

6. They _____
   (be / nervous about / have) a power outage in the city.

Tip

The National Weather Service uses different levels of notifications to tell people about bad weather.

Notification	Level of danger
advisory	dangerous
watch	
alert *or* warning	
emergency	extremely dangerous

5 WHAT ABOUT YOU? Answer the questions below with your own information. Complete the sentences. Then talk about them with a partner.

1. I'm worried about _____.

2. I'm concerned about _____.

3. I'm responsible for _____.

4. I'm interested in _____.

LESSON 2: Grammar Practice Plus

→ w/ P220 → Students Read in group.

1 **LISTEN** to the statements and look at the map. Write the number in the box next to the area where the situation is happening.

TCD3, 18

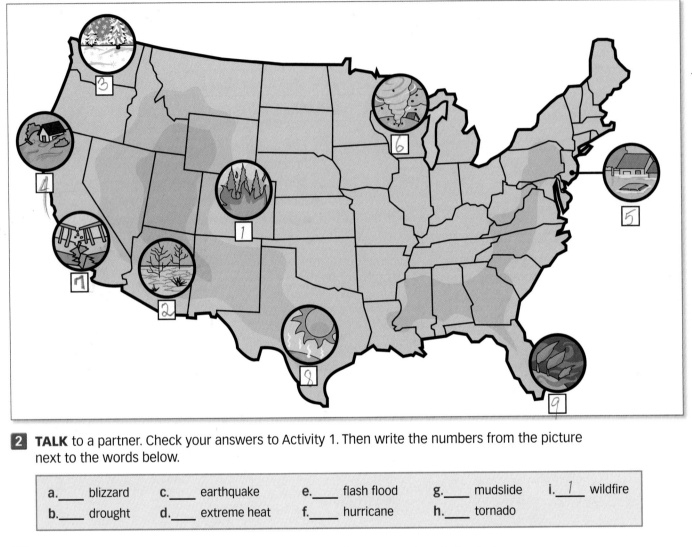

2 **TALK** to a partner. Check your answers to Activity 1. Then write the numbers from the picture next to the words below.

a.____ blizzard	c.____ earthquake	e.____ flash flood	g.____ mudslide	i. _1_ wildfire
b.____ drought	d.____ extreme heat	f.____ hurricane	h.____ tornado	

3 **WRITE** each word from the box in Activity 2 next to the correct description below.

flash flood **a.** sudden high levels of water

_____ **b.** heavy snow storm with low visibility

_____ **c.** torrential rain and wind gusts

_____ **d.** wet earth that falls down a hill

_____ **e.** very high temperatures

_____ **f.** no rain for a long time

_____ **g.** a fire that is very difficult to control

_____ **h.** ground shaking

_____ **i.** extremely strong and spinning winds

4 **WRITE.** How do people feel about each area in Activity 1? Use *be* with the adjectives + prepositions in the box, and the vocabulary from Activity 3.

Example: *In the Southwest, people are cautious about using water. There's a drought.*

cautious about	serious about
concerned about	unsure about
nervous about	worried about

5 **TALK** to a partner about the situations in Activity 1 on page 120. Use *There is* or *There are* with *in effect* and *because of*.

Example: *There is a blizzard advisory in effect because of heavy snow and low visibility.*

The adjective phrase *in effect* means "happening now" and is often heard in weather reports.

> There is a hurricane warning in effect.
> There are mudslide alerts in effect.

6 **WRITE** a sentence about what is happening in each photo. Use the verb *be* with one item from each box.

Adjective + Preposition	Gerund	Noun
concerned about	getting caught in	a blackout
responsible for	preventing	a hurricane
upset about	having	a wildfire
worried about	preparing for	a severe thunderstorm

These women are upset about …

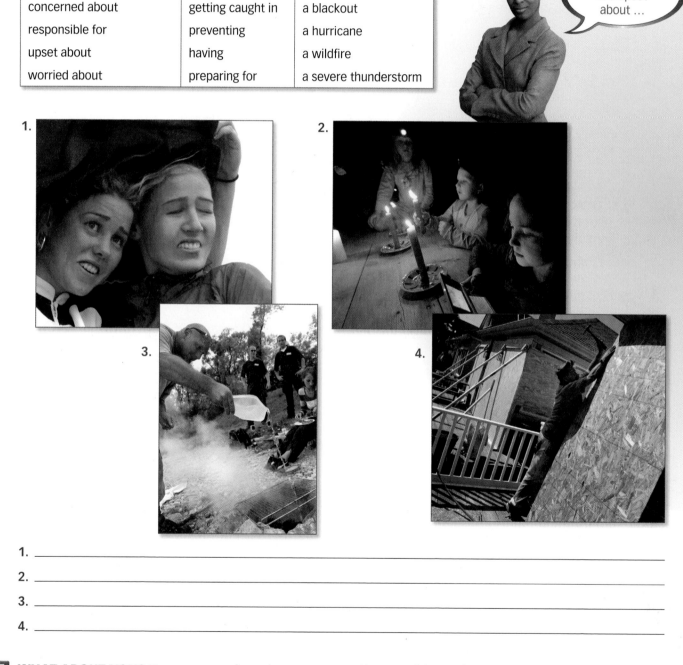

1.

2.

3.

4.

1. _____

2. _____

3. _____

4. _____

7 **WHAT ABOUT YOU?** Have you ever been in a severe weather condition? Where were you? What precautions did you take? Talk with a partner.

LESSON 3: Listening and Conversation

1 LISTEN LIsten to the conversation. Then listen to the question. Fill in the correct answer. Replay each item if necessary.

TCD3, 19–24

1. (A) (B) (C)   4. (A) (B) (C)

2. (A) (B) (C)   5. (A) (B) (C)

3. (A) (B) (C)   6. (A) (B) (C)

2 LISTEN to an announcer give a national weather report. What does she say about weather in an area near you, or an area you are familiar with?

TCD3, 25

3 LISTEN again. Write the letters of the precautions on the lines. Then check your answers with a partner.

TCD3, 26

_____ 1. flash flood   **a.** leave the area quickly

_____ 2. hurricane   **b.** evacuate the area immediately

_____ 3. tornado   **c.** get to higher ground right away

_____ 4. mudslides   **d.** find shelter as soon as possible

_____ 5. wildfires   **e.** find a safe place on the first floor

4 TALK with a partner. Take turns giving weather reports using the map and the information in the chart below.

Example: *Here's today's forecast for the South-east. There are severe thunderstorms in the area and a hurricane alert in effect for today. We recommend taking precautions. We advise against traveling on the highways.*

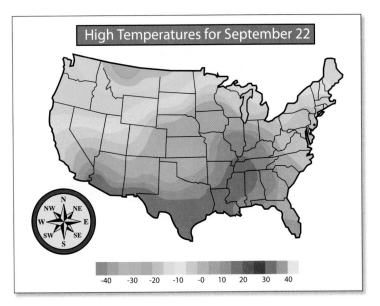

High Temperatures for September 22

There is/are . . . in effect	We recommend / We advise against
a power outage warning	conserving water
blizzard conditions	exercising outdoors
drought conditions	finding shelter immediately
a smog advisory	cutting down on your use of energy
a tornado alert	driving with your hazard lights on

5 ROLE-PLAY. Imagine you and your partner are listening to one of the weather reports from Activity 4. Discuss what you are concerned about, and decide what you should do.

6 **LISTEN** to the conversation.

Chris: Today we're going to review <u>earthquake</u> preparedness procedures.

Pat: We recommend practicing these procedures: <u>Drop under a sturdy desk or table, hold on, and protect your eyes by pressing your face against your arm.</u>

Chris: Practicing will make these actions more automatic.

Pat: Responding quickly can help protect you from injury. Talk to your family about <u>earthquake</u> preparedness.

7 **PRACTICE** the conversation from Activity 6 with a partner. Then make new conversations with the information below.

Preparedness for a	Recommendation
hurricane	Stay away from windows. If you cannot evacuate, go to a low floor in your home. Protect yourself by lying under a strong table.
mudslide	Stay alert. Listen for strange sounds in your home or building. If it is safe, evacuate the area immediately.

Math Skills: Converting Fahrenheit and Celsius Temperatures

To convert degrees (°) Fahrenheit to Celsius, follow these steps.

Step 1 Take the temperature in °F and subtract 32.   (90°F – 32 = 58)

Step 2 Take that number and divide by 9.   (58 ÷ 9 = 6.44)

Step 3 Take that number and multiply it by 5 to get °C.   (6.44 × 5 = 32.22)

1. Convert 98°F to Celsius. _____°C
2. Convert 70°F to Celsius. _____°C
3. Convert 55°F to Celsius. _____°C
4. Convert 20°F to Celsius. _____°C

8 **TALK** with a partner. In the U.S., we often use weather to make "small talk." Use the conversation strategies to talk with your partner about the weather today. Then discuss weather in your native country. How hot does it get in the summer? How cold does the temperature usually get in the winter?

It's freezing today, isn't it?

It sure is.

Conversation Strategy

Making Small Talk about Weather

It's freezing today, isn't it?

It's a scorcher today!

Can you believe this weather?

It's raining cats and dogs today.

What a beautiful day.

It looks like rain, doesn't it?

TCD3, 28

1 **GRAMMAR PICTURE DICTIONARY.** Who helps when there is a disaster? Listen and read.

1. The Federal Emergency Management Agency (FEMA) is a government organization that helps with evacuating victims of **natural disasters**. FEMA also helps victims after a **crisis**.

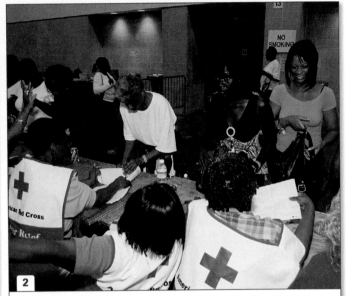

2. The American Red Cross is a volunteer organization that helps people during emergencies. They focus on providing **disaster relief** to victims all over the world.

3. The Environmental Protection Agency (EPA) works on removing **toxic waste** from the rivers and streams. This government group **believes in** keeping water clean and the environment safe.

4. The Natural Resources Defense Council (NRDC) **focuses on** protecting the Earth and its **resources**. It works on finding solutions to **global warming**.

2 **READ** the sentences from Activity 1 with a partner.

3 **NOTICE THE GRAMMAR.** Underline the verb + preposition combinations. Circle the gerunds.

Gerunds as Objects of a Verb + Preposition

A gerund can follow a verb + preposition.

Subject	Verb + Preposition	Gerund + Phrase
They	focus on	**saving** the environment.
I	plan on	**helping** the victims.
He	works on	**solving** the global warming problem.
She	cares about	**protecting** our water.
I	believe in	**helping** other people.
They	help with	**cleaning** up after a tornado.

4 **READ** the information about American Red Cross volunteers. Fill in the correct form of the verb + preposition + gerund.

> ### The American Red Cross: What We Do! ✚
>
> The American Red Cross is a disaster relief organization. During a crisis, we ___*help with setting up*___
> (help with / set up) shelters and with _____ (supply) important emergency
> items. Our team also _____ (work on / send) warm blankets, water, and
> meals to the disaster area. We _____ (care about / make) victims feel
> comfortable. Our hundreds of volunteers _____ (help with / feed)
> people and with _____ (hand out) the supplies. During a crisis,
> we _____ (focus on / provide) first-aid and medical care to the victims.

5 **WRITE** sentences to answer the questions about the organizations described in Activity 1. Use a verb + preposition + gerund.

1. What does the NRDC focus on?

    ___*The NRDC focuses on saving the environment.*___

2. What does FEMA work on?

    _____

3. What does the American Red Cross help with?

    _____

4. What does the EPA focus on?

    _____

5. What does the NRDC believe in?

    _____

LESSON 5: Grammar Practice Plus

TCD3, 29
SCD33

1 **LISTEN** to the statements. As you listen, match the statement with the photo below. Then take turns reading the sentences with a partner.

_B_ 1. We **believe in** providing disaster relief all over the world. By giving emergency assistance during a crisis, we make a difference!

_____ 2. I **focus on** preventing serious wildfires. Protecting our forests is very important to me.

_____ 3. We **focus on** rescuing victims in any situation. Finding and helping victims are our priorities.

_____ 4. We **count on** receiving donations to support our organization. Volunteering time to build homes is one way we help people.

_____ 5. We **focus on** transporting hazardous materials in the U.S. Checking for toxic waste and dangerous materials is our job.

_____ 6. I **care about** protecting wildlife. I help wildlife when they are injured or in danger.

A.
U.S. Department of Agriculture (USDA) Forest Ranger

B.
American Red Cross

C.
Hazardous Materials Safety (HazMat) worker

D.
Search and Rescue Teams

E.
U.S. Fish & Wildlife Service worker

F.
Habitat for Humanity builders

2 **TALK** with a partner about the organizations in Activity 1. Who do you think are government workers? How do you know? Who are volunteer workers? Which organizations are you already familiar with?

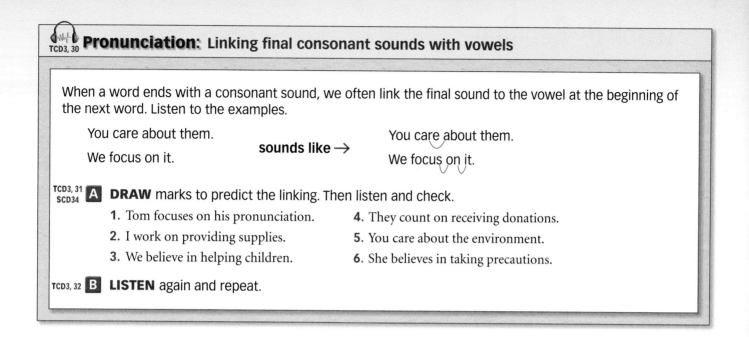

TCD3, 30 Pronunciation: Linking final consonant sounds with vowels

When a word ends with a consonant sound, we often link the final sound to the vowel at the beginning of the next word. Listen to the examples.

You care about them.   sounds like →   You care about them.

We focus on it.   We focus on it.

TCD3, 31 SCD34 **A** **DRAW** marks to predict the linking. Then listen and check.

1. Tom focuses on his pronunciation.   4. They count on receiving donations.
2. I work on providing supplies.   5. You care about the environment.
3. We believe in helping children.   6. She believes in taking precautions.

TCD3, 32 **B** **LISTEN** again and repeat.

TCD3, 33 **3** **LISTEN** to an interview on a TV talk show. Listen for the four problems the guest talks about and write them in the correct column in the chart.

Where was the problem?	What was the problem?	Who helped solve the problem?	How did they help?
Louisiana	Hurricane Katrina	The National Resources Defense Council	
Northern California			
Wisconsin			
New York			

4 **LISTEN** again and fill in the rest of the chart. Then talk with a partner or in a group about the situations from the interview. Can you remember how each organization helped?

5 **WRITE.** Check your answers in Activity 4 with a partner. Write sentences about what each organization is and what they do after a natural disaster.

Example: *The NRDC is involved in cleaning up the area after a natural disaster.*

6 **WHAT ABOUT YOU?** Volunteers give their time without payment. Why do you think people volunteer? What organization are you interested in volunteering for? Talk with a partner.

LESSON 6: Reading

1 **THINK ABOUT IT.** What things do people do to hurt the environment? What things do companies do to hurt the environment?

2 **BEFORE YOU READ.**

A. PREVIEW. Read the title and look at the pictures.

> **READING FOCUS: Scan for specific information**
>
> We scan articles and other types of texts when we must answer questions about what they say. *Scanning* means reading quickly to find the answers. After scanning, we read the text again more carefully.

B. SKIM the article. Read the first sentence of each paragraph. Then read the questions below. Which paragraph is each answer in?

1. Who was the first "spokesperson" for the forests?
2. When did Earth Day begin?
3. What did former Vice President Al Gore do to make people aware of global warming?

Reading Strategies Summary

Use prior knowledge.
Preview.
Skim for main ideas.
▶ **Scan for specific information.** ◀

C. SCAN the article and write the answers to the questions in Activity 2B.

3 **READ** the article. Check the answers you wrote in Activity 2C with a partner.

4 **AFTER YOU READ.**

A. VOCABULARY. Find these words in the text. Match them with their meanings.

___e___ 1. public service campaign

_____ 2. activism

_____ 3. activist

_____ 4. participants

_____ 5. raise awareness

a. increase people's knowledge about an issue

b. a person who works hard to change a situation

c. people who join or are part of an activity

d. the act of working hard to change a situation

e. information that makes people pay attention to an issue

B. WRITE answers to the questions below.

1. Why did Senator Nelson create Earth Day?
2. What happened because of Senator Nelson's efforts?
3. Why did the USDA create "Woodsy Owl"?
4. What two things happened due to Al Gore's environmental activism?

Raising Public Awareness about Environmental Issues

STARTING IN THE MID-1940s, a fictional* character named Smokey Bear was created. He was part of a public service campaign to stop forest
5 fires. His posters and radio announcements focused on educating both children and their parents. Smokey's
10 slogan* was "Only You Can Prevent Forest Fires."

During the '60s and
15 '70s, many Americans began thinking about environmental activism. Wisconsin state Senator and environmental activist Gaylord Nelson established Earth Day on April 22,
20 1970. On Earth Day, people plant trees, clean up and improve parks, and take part in demonstrations to show support for the environment. Almost 20 million people around the U.S. participated in the first celebration. Today, Earth Day is the
25 largest non-religious holiday in the world with over 175 countries and nearly 500 million participants. Because of Senator Nelson's efforts, the U.S. Congress passed laws that were concerned with improving our drinking water, preserving wildlife,
30 and keeping our air clean. The Environmental Protection Agency (EPA) was started in July of 1970 to protect the environment and support these laws.

In the 1970s, some organizations started
35 broadcasting public service announcements to raise awareness of problems like wildfires, toxic waste, and oil spills. The United States Department of Agriculture Forest Service (USDA-Forest Service) created a mascot* named Woodsy Owl. Woodsy's
40 slogan was "Give a hoot, don't pollute!"

In addition to the EPA and the USDA, many other groups like Greenpeace and the Natural Resources Defense Council are working to find solutions to environmental problems. Politicians such as former
45 Vice President Al Gore have also begun tackling* environmental issues.

In 2005, Gore made a film called *An Inconvenient Truth*. It is about the issue of global warming, which is a result of air pollution. In 2007, he received the
50 Nobel Peace Prize for his efforts in raising public awareness about the dangers of global warming.

---

fictional (adj.): imaginary or not based on fact

slogan (n.): a saying or short phrase

mascot (n.): a group or team's good luck symbol (usually an animal or character)

tackle (v.): try to solve a difficult problem

LESSON 7: Writing

1 **THINK ABOUT IT.** Talk about these questions with your class.

1. What are three things we can do to help protect the environment?

2. What do environmental activists do?

3. What do you think it means to be "green"?

2 **BEFORE YOU WRITE.**

A. DISCUSS. Look at the pictures with a partner.
What do you think each group does?
Why do you think they are called "green groups"?

The Nature Conservancy (protecting nature and land)

The National Wildlife Federation— (educating people about nature; reversing global warming; protecting wildlife habitats)

Greenpeace (protecting our environment; standing up for our health)

B. LISTEN to a talk about green groups. Read the statements and check ☑ *True* or *False*.

	True	False
1. Greenpeace is focused on protecting nature and our environment.	☐	☐
2. Greenpeace activists never demonstrate against the government.	☐	☐
3. The Nature Conservancy and Greenpeace work on finding solutions to global warming.	☐	☐
4. The Nature Conservancy is against renewing forests by planting trees after wildfires have damaged them.	☐	☐
5. The National Wildlife Federation is focused on protecting endangered wildlife such as eagles, polar bears, and wolves.	☐	☐
6. The National Wildlife Federation is not interested in solving the problems of global warming.	☐	☐

TCD3, 34

C. TALK in a group. Which environmental issues are you worried about? Why?

> **WRITING FOCUS: State your purpose**
> When you write a formal letter of request, start your letter with a clear statement of your purpose.
> **Example:** I am writing to request your support of the Clean Air Act.

D. READ the letter to a senator from a green group's website. <u>Underline</u> the places in the letter where the writer did the following:

1. stated his purpose

2. said what the problem is

3. explained why it is important

4. gave reasons to support his opinion

The Honorable Senator Smith
Rm.#100 Senate Office Building
United States Senate
Washington, DC 20510

Dear Senator Smith,

I am writing to request your support of the Beach Protection Act. Because of toxic waste, many of our nation's beach waters have become contaminated. We are concerned about toxic waste harming swimmers, destroying the environment, and damaging the coasts. People need information about unsafe water due to pollution and bacteria.

The Beach Protection Act is for using better methods and for testing the water. This Act would give money to programs in states and local communities. It would help identify and clean up the sources of pollution.

Please support this important legislation right away, and do all you can to encourage leaders to support and vote for this bill. Thank you for your attention to this matter.

Sincerely,

Homer Peterson

---

 3 **WRITE** a letter to your local government official or your state senator explaining what you would like to change in your community or state.

1. Say what the issue or problem is, and explain why it is important (your purpose).

2. State your opinion.

3. Give two reasons to support your opinion using *because of* or *due to*.

4. Thank the reader for his or her attention.

4 **AFTER YOU WRITE.**

A. **EDIT** your letter. Ask yourself these questions.

1. Did I use a greeting and closing?

2. Did I explain the reason for my letter?

3. Is the spelling correct? Check the words in a dictionary if you are not sure.

4. Is the punctuation correct? Check commas, apostrophes, and periods.

B. **REWRITE** your letter with corrections.

Tip

When you write to a government official, you should use a title in your greeting:
 	
    Dear Assemblyman Smith,
 	
    Dear Congressman Jones,
 	
    Dear Senator Brown,
 	
You should refer to a government official in the address as:
 	
    The Honorable (full name)
 	
Then write the address, city, state, and zip code below the official's name.
 	
See Unit 1 page 19 for more about letters.

Career Connection

1 **THINK ABOUT IT.** How can companies be sure that their employees stay safe during a natural disaster? What do you know about how to stay safe in an earthquake?

2 **READ** the following company memo on updated emergency evacuation procedures for earthquakes. What precautions have they taken? What can employees do to stay safe during and after an earthquake?

Medix **Pharmaceuticals**

To: Medix Pharmaceuticals Employees
From: Human Resources Department
Re: Earthquake Safety Information

Medix is serious about being prepared for an earthquake. We have recently updated our facilities because we care about protecting our employees and their well-being.

- Wherever possible, we have secured* cabinets, bookcases, and heavy objects.
- There are first-aid kits with items such as bandages, antibiotic ointment*, burn cream, and eye drops located by the elevators, and in the kitchens on each floor.
- We have a supply of 5-gallon water tanks and canned foods in all of the kitchens.

As a reminder, here are a few safety guidelines to follow in the event of an earthquake:

During an earthquake
If you feel an earthquake, get under a desk or strong table. Stay under the desk, even if it moves. Don't go near windows, bookcases, filing cabinets, hanging plants, or other heavy objects that could fall. If you are not near a desk or table, put your body against an inside wall and cover your head with your arms. Do not use the elevators. If you are outside, move to a clear area as far from the building and trees as possible.

After an earthquake
Stay calm. Be prepared for aftershocks*, and have a plan for where you will go when they happen. Check for injuries*. If you are injured, take care of yourself before helping another person. Help put out any small fires you see. Only use the telephone for emergency calls. Make sure you remember to eat, and drink water.

---

secure (v.): fix something so that it cannot easily move

antibiotic ointment (comp. noun): medicine you put on cuts or burns so that they can heal faster

aftershock (n.): when the ground shakes a little after an earthquake

injury (n.): sign that you have hurt yourself, like a cut or a burn

3 **COMPLETE.** Circle the correct answer to complete each sentence. Then compare your answers with a partner's.

1. There are first aid kits _____.
   a. in all of the bathrooms in the building
   b. at the nurse's station
   c. in the kitchen and by the elevators

2. During an earthquake, you should _____.
   a. run outside
   b. get under a sturdy table or desk
   c. go to the doorway

3. If you are outside during an earthquake, _____.
   a. go to an open area away from trees or buildings
   b. get under a tree
   c. run inside

4. If you see a small fire after an earthquake, _____.
   a. call the fire department
   b. run
   c. put out the fire yourself

4 **WHAT ABOUT YOU?** What precautions have you taken for earthquakes? Are there other natural disasters in your area, such as tornados, hurricanes, or blizzards? What precautions can you take for them?

Check Your Progress!

Skill	Circle the answers.	Is it correct?
A. Use gerunds as objects of adjective + preposition.	1. Sara was nervous about **flying / to fly** during a thunderstorm. 2. The mayor is serious about **to provide / providing** shelter for people during the hurricane. 3. Farmers are excited about **to get / getting** rain after a long drought. 4. The man was concerned about **driving / to drive** in the blizzard.	☐ ☐ ☐ ☐
	Number Correct	0 1 2 3 4
B. Use gerunds as objects of verb + preposition.	5. Habitat for Humanity helps **with building / on building** new homes 6. During a tornado warning, we focus **on getting / about getting** to a safe place. 7. We must all **work on / work to** saving water. 8. City officials are beginning to **care about / care for** reducing smog.	☐ ☐ ☐ ☐
	Number Correct	0 1 2 3 4
C. Understand terms used to discuss weather and natural disasters.	9. The **blizzard / earthquake** last week shook the ground. 10. The **droughts / tornados** in our town caused power outages. 11. The **forest / advisory** said it was going to be a beautiful day. 12. We evacuate the area when there is a **thunderstorm / mudslide**.	☐ ☐ ☐ ☐
	Number Correct	0 1 2 3 4
D. Talk about relief organizations.	13. The American Red Cross focuses on **building homes / offering emergency assistance** after a disaster. 14. A USDA Forest Ranger concentrates on **preventing wildfires / caring for injured animals**. 15. The NRDC focuses on **protecting the environment / rescuing victims**. 16. A **Hazardous Materials worker / U.S. Fish and Wildlife worker** is concerned with inspecting radioactive materials.	☐ ☐ ☐ ☐
	Number Correct	0 1 2 3 4

COUNT the number of correct answers above. Fill in the bubbles.

Chart Your Success					
Skill	Need Practice	Okay	Good	Very Good	Excellent!
A. Use gerunds as objects of adjective + preposition.	⓪	①	②	③	④
B. Use gerunds as objects of verb + preposition.	⓪	①	②	③	④
C. Understand terms used to discuss weather and natural disasters.	⓪	①	②	③	④
D. Talk about relief organizations.	⓪	①	②	③	④

UNIT 9 Community Crossroads

LESSON 1: Grammar and Vocabulary

1 GRAMMAR PICTURE DICTIONARY. What's happening around town? Listen and read.

TCD3, 35
SCD35

1
The **crossing guard** allows **pedestrians** to cross the street safely.

2
The traffic rule doesn't permit drivers to turn left during **rush hour**.

3
Traffic laws require all drivers to drive slowly in a **school zone**.

4
A **guide dog** helps a **visually impaired person** cross the street more confidently.

5
A **wheelchair lift** allows **handicapped passengers** to get on a bus easily.

6
The **driver education** teacher helped his students study for the learner's permit exam.

2 READ the sentences from Activity 1 with a partner.

3 NOTICE THE GRAMMAR. Circle the verbs. Underline the infinitives or base forms that follow objects.

134 | Getting around town. • Causative verbs.

Causative Verbs

Use a causative verb to show that someone caused, helped, or allowed something to happen.

Most common causative verbs are followed by object + infinitive. Some examples are *allow, enable, permit,* and *require.*

Subject	Verb	Object	Infinitive	
The teacher	requires	his students	to study	for an hour every day.
The parents	allow	their sons	to ride	bikes to school.

The causatives *let, make,* and *have* are always followed by object + base form.

Subject	Verb	Object	Base Form	
Janet	let	her daughter	take	the bus yesterday.
She	made	her son	study	for the exam.
Tom	had	the mechanic	change	the tires.

> *Help* can be followed by object + infinitive or by object + base form.
>
> The crossing guard *helps* pedestrians **to cross / cross** the street.

---

4 COMPLETE. Circle the infinitive or the base verb to complete the sentences.

1. The law requires all drivers **(to drive)** / **drive** slowly in a school zone.
2. The crossing guard lets pedestrians **to cross** / **cross** the street safely.
3. He will have the mechanic **to check** / **check** his car tomorrow.
4. The law allows visually impaired passengers **to bring** / **bring** guide dogs on the bus.
5. She always makes the children **to hold** / **hold** hands while crossing at an intersection.
6. A wheelchair lift allows handicapped passengers **to get on** / **get on** the bus.

5 COMPLETE the sentences with the correct form of the verb.

1. The traffic rule ___*allows*___ (allow) drivers ___*to turn*___ (turn) left at the intersection after rush hour.
2. The driver education teacher _____ (help) his students _____ (practice) parking last week.
3. Guide dogs _____ (help) visually impaired pedestrians _____ (cross) the street.
4. The handicapped passenger _____ (have) the bus driver _____ (lower) the wheelchair lift before he got on the bus.
5. The crossing guard usually _____ (make) the children _____ (hold) hands while crossing the street.

6 WHAT ABOUT YOU? Talk with a partner. What did your parents make you do when you were a child? What did they let you do?

> My parents let me ride the bus by myself when I was ten years old.

LESSON 2: Grammar Practice Plus

1 **TALK** with a partner. What are people doing? Use the words in the box to talk about the picture.

fire hydrant
parking meter
road construction
tow-away zone
wheelchair access ramp

2 **LISTEN** to statements about the people in the picture. Write the number next to the correct name.

TCD3, 36

_____ Howie   _____ Luz   _____ Martina and Ben   __1__ Rita

_____ Lina and Ralph   _____ Tom   _____ Carla and Sue   _____ Tony

3 **WRITE** sentences about the people in Activity 2. Use the causative verbs with the verbs on the right to make new sentences.

1. The mother / her son / the bus by himself.

   The mother let her son take the bus by himself.

2. The traffic officer / pedestrians / the road construction.

3. The driver education teacher / her student / parking at the parking meter.

4. The wheelchair access ramp / the handicapped student / the school.

5. The guide dog / the visually impaired woman / the street.

6. The traffic officer / Sue / a fine for parking / in a tow-away zone.

7. The traffic law / Tony / at the intersection during rush hour.

8. The traffic officer / Howie / a fine / for parking near the fire hydrant.

allow	cross
enable	enter
help	go around
let	park
make	pay
permit	practice take
	turn left

Passive Causatives *Get* and *Have*

Use *get* and *have* to show that someone made another person do something.

Subject	Verb	Object	Past Participle
I	had	my hair	done.
He	got	his car	repaired.
We	are having	our house	painted.

4 **COMPLETE** the sentences with the past participle of the verbs in parentheses.

1. She is having her bicycle _____ *fixed* _____ (fix) before she rides it home.

2. I usually have my hair _____ (do) by the hairdresser.

3. He had the wheelchair lift _____ (lower) before he got on the bus.

4. They got their car _____ (repair) at the gas station.

5. He always gets his hair _____ (cut) before an important date.

6. We got our car engine _____ (check) last week.

5 **WRITE** sentences with the words below.

1. I / have / computer / fix / last week   *I had my computer fixed last week.*

2. He / get / hair / cut / yesterday   _____

3. He / have / kitchen sink / repair / last month   _____

4. We / get / car / repair / yesterday   _____

5. She / have / hair / do / last night   _____

6 **COMPLETE** the sentences with the correct form of *be + allowed*.

> The verb *allow* is often used in the passive voice. *Allow* has the same meaning as *permit*.
>
> You're not *allowed to park* there.
> We *are allowed to turn* left here.

1. Drivers _____ *are not allowed to park* _____
   (not / allow / park) near a fire hydrant.

2. You _____
   (not / allow / turn) left during rush hour.

3. Julie _____
   (allow / drive) her father's car.

4. Children _____ (not / allow / cross) the street by themselves.

5. She _____ (allow / ride) the bus alone.

6. We _____ (not / allow / smoke) in the restaurant.

7 **WHAT ABOUT YOU?** Write sentences with *allow* about your community, work, or family.

Example: *We're not allowed to use cell phones in the library.*

LESSON 3: Listening and Conversation

TCD3, 37–42

1 **LISTEN** to the question. Then listen to the conversation. Listen to the question again. Fill in the correct answer. Replay each item if necessary.

1. Ⓐ   Ⓑ   Ⓒ   4. Ⓐ   Ⓑ   Ⓒ

2. Ⓐ   Ⓑ   Ⓒ   5. Ⓐ   Ⓑ   Ⓒ

3. Ⓐ   Ⓑ   Ⓒ   6. Ⓐ   Ⓑ   Ⓒ

TCD3, 43

2 **LISTEN** to the conversation. Read the statement and check ☑ *True* or *False*.

	True	False
1. The woman was surprised because the man was late.	☐	☐
2. The man turned left at the intersection during rush hour.	☐	☐
3. The man was late because a school bus broke down.	☐	☐
4. The man is a mechanic.	☐	☐
5. The woman cancelled her appointment.	☐	☐

3 **LISTEN** again and write answers to the questions. Then tell a partner.

1. Why was the man late?

2. Why did the man go to the gas station?

3. Why was the woman going to get her hair done?

4 **ROLE-PLAY.** Imagine that you are a traffic officer. Your partner is a new resident in town. Make a dialogue about each sign.

5 **LISTEN** to the conversation.

TCD3, 44
SCD36

A: You were late this morning, weren't you?

B: Yes. I had to take care of a problem.

A: Oh. What's going on?

B: My car didn't start yesterday.

A: So how did you get here today?

B: I had my friend pick me up.

A: I see. What did you do about your car?

B: I had a mechanic help me and I got it repaired.

6 **PRACTICE** the conversation from Activity 5 with a partner. Use the information in the chart to make new conversations.

Problem	What you did	Solution
1. My bicycle had a flat tire	had a bicycle repairman look at it	got the tire changed
2. My license expired	had my friend drive me to the Department of Motor Vehicles	got it renewed
3. My truck broke down	had my truck taken to the gas station	got it fixed

Pronunciation: Reduction of *To*

TCD3, 45

The words *to*, *two*, and *too* are all pronounced the same way. However, when *to* is used in a sentence, it is reduced. Listen to the examples. Pay attention to the underlined words.

They have to take two exams.   He wants to take the driving class, too.

TCD3, 46
SCD37
A. **CIRCLE** the word *to* in each sentence below. Then listen to the sentences.

1. You're not allowed to turn left here.

2. Only students 16 and older are permitted to take the driving class.

3. The laws require drivers to drive slowly.

4. The wheelchair lift allows passengers in wheelchairs to get on the bus.

TCD3, 47 **B.** **LISTEN** again and repeat.

7 **WHAT ABOUT YOU?** Think about problems in your community or neighborhood. Use the conversation strategies to propose solutions to your partner.

We're not allowed to park on my street.

Why don't you rent a space in a parking garage?

Conversation Strategy

Proposing Solutions

Why don't you . . . ?

You might as well . . .

Would you mind if . . . ?

Let's try . . .

LESSON 4: Grammar and Vocabulary

1 **GRAMMAR PICTURE DICTIONARY.** What are these people talking about? Read and listen. Listen and read.

TCD3, 48
SCD38

1

A: I need <u>to renew</u> my car registration.

B: Did you remember <u>to bring</u> **proof of insurance**?

A: Yes, but I forgot <u>to bring</u> my registration card.

2

A: Hi. I just moved and I haven't gotten any mail lately.

B: Do you remember filling out a **change of address** form?

A: No. I don't remember doing that.

3

A: I still remember taking my **road test**. I was so nervous.

B: Well, I'll never forget riding with you for the first time. I was terrified!

4

A: Uh-oh. We've got **engine trouble**.

B: We'd better stop to call a **tow truck**. That gas station is closed.

5

A: Excuse me. We need to find the **Visitor Information Center**. Do you know where it is?

B: It's on that corner. You can stop to pick up a map while you're there.

6

A: Excuse me. Could you tell us where **Town Hall** is?

B: Sorry, I can't stop running! Ask someone at that **convenience store**.

2 **PRACTICE** the conversations in Activity 1 with a partner.

3 **NOTICE THE GRAMMAR.** Find the verbs that are followed by gerunds or infinitives. Circle the gerunds. <u>Underline</u> the infinitives.

Verbs That Take Gerunds or Infinitives

Many verbs can take a gerund or an infinitive with no change in meaning. With some verbs, the meaning changes. The verbs *forget*, *remember*, and *stop* change in meaning with a gerund or infinitive.

Verb + Infinitive	Verb + Gerund
I always **stop to look** for traffic. (I stop doing one thing in order to do another.)	I **stopped driving** my son to school. (I used to drive him, but I don't anymore.)
I **remembered to bring** the letters. (I didn't forget to bring them.)	I **remember mailing** the letters. (I remember the act of mailing the letters.)
I **forgot to go** to the Visitor Center. (I intended to go, but I forgot.)	I'll never **forget seeing** it for the first time. (I will always remember this.)

4 COMPLETE the conversations with a gerund or an infinitive. Then practice reading the conversations with a partner.

1. *A:* I have to get my vehicle registration renewed. What do I need to have with me?

    B: Remember _____*to bring*_____ (bring) your proof of insurance and registration card.

2. *A:* I'll see you later. I have to pick up my son from high school.

    B: Oh. I thought you stopped _____ (drive) him to and from school after he passed his road test.

3. *A:* Why did you stop at the Visitor Information Center?

    B: I was lost and I forgot _____ (take) a map with me.

4. *A:* We've got engine trouble. Do you see a gas station near here?

    B: No. I think we'd better stop _____ (call) a tow truck right now.

5. *A:* Where are the car keys? I have to take the car to the gas station.

    B: I remember _____ (put) them on the kitchen table.

6. *A:* Do you remember that restaurant we went to in New York? It was great, wasn't it?

    B: It sure was. I'll never forget _____ (eat) such delicious food.

5 WRITE three sentences with the verb *remember* + gerund. Then write three sentences with *never forget* + gerund.

Example: *I remember taking my road test when I was 16.*

I'll never forget seeing snow for the first time.

6 WHAT ABOUT YOU? Think of things in your home that you sometimes forget to do, usually remember to do, and always remember to do. Talk with a partner.

I always remember to turn off the lights before I leave home.

LESSON 5: Grammar Practice Plus See P222

TCD3, 49

1 **LISTEN** to the conversations. Sam is moving to a new apartment and has to get things done today! Match the letter in the map with the name of each place Sam went.

- _c_ **1.** hardware store
- _____ **2.** post office
- _____ **3.** Department of Motor Vehicles
- _____ **4.** parking lot
- _____ **5.** moving van rental service
- _____ **6.** Chamber of Commerce
- _____ **7.** convenience store

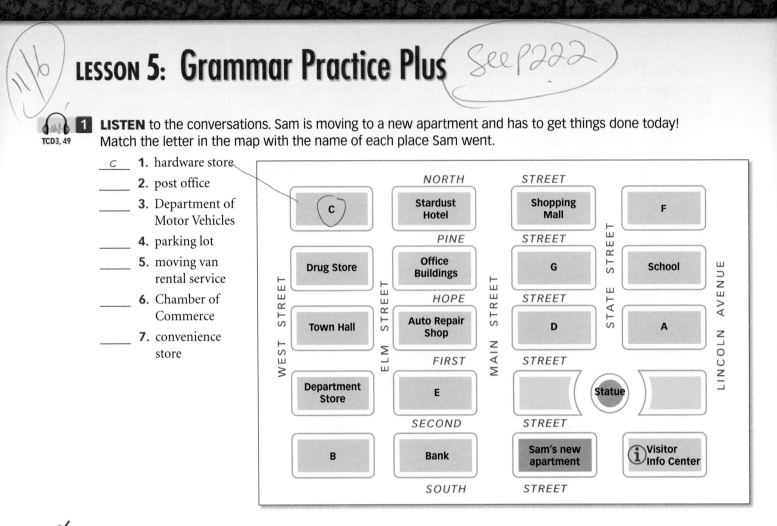

2 **WRITE.** Read Sam's "to-do" list. Write sentences to say where Sam needs to go to do each of the things on his list.

Example: *Sam needs to go to the hardware store to buy paint and light fixtures.*

To Do:
- ☑ Buy paint and light fixtures
- ☐ Pick up milk, bread, and coffee
- ☐ Fill out change-of-address form
- ☐ Reserve a moving van
- ☐ Drop off car for tune-up and new tires
- ☐ Get information about a business license
- ☐ Renew vehicle registration

3 **ROLE-PLAY.** Take turns asking and answering the questions. Use the map in Activity 1.

1. *A:* Where can I get my tires changed?

2. *A:* I need to have my new apartment painted. Can you tell me where the hardware store is?

3. *A:* I need to get my license renewed. Where is the DMV?

4. *A:* I forgot to buy milk. Do you know where a convenience store is?

Example: *A:* Where can I get my tires changed?
   B: There is an auto repair shop on the corner of Hope and Main streets.
   A: Thanks.
   B: My pleasure!

Conversation Strategy

Responding Politely to Thanks
You're welcome!
My pleasure.
It's nothing.
Don't mention it.
No problem.

4 **LISTEN** to the conversation. As you listen, put a check ☑ under Sam or Mrs. Peterson.

TCD3, 50

	Sam	Mrs. Peterson
1. forgot to take the keys	☐	☑
2. forgot to bring proof of insurance	☐	☐
3. forgot to get a winter coat	☐	☐
4. remembered seeing sales at the shopping mall	☐	☐
5. Needs to get information about a business license	☐	☐
6. remembered getting a marriage license at Town Hall	☐	☐
7. stopped driving and started taking the bus	☐	☐
8. has to call the mechanic	☐	☐

5 **WRITE** five sentences from the information in Activity 5 about what Sam and Mrs. Peterson forgot or remembered, and where they stopped.

Example: *Mrs. Peterson remembered getting a marriage license at Town Hall.*
Sam forgot to get a winter coat.

6 **TALK** to a partner. Ask and answer questions about the conversation.

1. What happened to Sam this morning?
2. What did Mrs. Peterson stop doing last year?
3. Why did Mrs. Peterson remember going to Town Hall?
4. What does Sam need to do when he gets home?

Math: Interpret Statistical Information

A. READ the statistics about transportation in Sam's new town. Note: a *household* is usually a family.

Total Number of Residents	Number of Households	Percentage of Residents Who Have Cars	Percentage of Residents Who Take Public Transportation
211,680	70,560	85%	33%

B. CALCULATE the answers.

1. What is the average number of people per household? Calculate the average by dividing the number of residents by the number of households. _____

2. Calculate the number of residents who have cars. Multiply the number of residents by .85. _____

3. Calculate the number of residents who ride public transportation. Multiply the number of residents by .33.

_____

---

7 **WHAT ABOUT YOU?** Talk to a partner about your community. Where do you go in your community when you need to get things done? Where do you go shopping? Where do you get your hair cut? Do you take public transportation or do you drive?

LESSON 6: Reading

1 **THINK ABOUT IT.** Have you ever been in a car accident? What happened? Did the police come?

2 **BEFORE YOU READ.** Preview the article on the next page. Look at the title and the pictures. What is the article about?

3 **READ** the article. What happened? What was the cause of the accident?

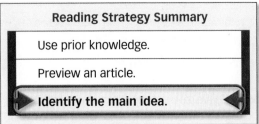

Reading Strategy Summary

Use prior knowledge.

Preview an article.

▶ **Identify the main idea.** ◀

4 **AFTER YOU READ.**

A. VOCABULARY. <u>Underline</u> each word of phrase in the article. Read the paragraph again. Then match the word or phrase with its meaning.

_____ **1.** vehicles

_____ **2.** responders

_____ **3.** fatalities

_____ **4.** authorities

_____ **5.** jackknifed

a. people with official power—police or government officials

b. folded into a deep v-shape

c. cars and trucks

d. deaths

e. people who came to help

B. READ the article again. What is the main idea of each paragraph? Discuss with a partner.

C. SCAN the article to answer the following questions.

1. When did the accident happen?

2. What was the weather like that day?

3. How many vehicles were involved in the accident?

4. What do police believe caused the accident?

5. How many people were hurt? What happened to them? Did anyone die?

> **READING FOCUS: Identify the main idea**
>
> As you read each paragraph or section of an article, ask yourself, "what is the main idea?" Identifying the main idea will help you remember and understand the most important points in the article.

Accident Requires Interstate 70 to Close for Eight Hours

January 22, 2010

Denver, Colorado -- Early this morning, police permitted cars to reenter Interstate 70 near Vail, Colorado, after they were able to clean up a car accident involving 60 vehicles during the Friday afternoon rush hour. Interstate 70 is Colorado's main east-west highway and was required to close for almost eight hours following the crash. The accident forced many travelers to find hotel rooms in the Vail area to stay in until the highway was reopened.

Police and emergency responders arrived immediately at the scene of the crash. They were surprised to find very few injuries and no fatalities from such a large crash. Throughout the night, police authorities had drivers bused to nearby towns. Other emergency responders spent the night clearing the numerous vehicles that were in the crash.

Although the accident happened during snowy weather, authorities are still not sure of the exact cause of the accident. Colorado State Trooper Jack Meyer said that authorities believe a semi truck jackknifed in the road, folding into a deep v-shape, and that this is what caused the original crash. After that, the snowy road conditions made it impossible for other cars and trucks to stop quickly enough to avoid the crash.

Joey Johnson was in one of the first cars that stopped in time to avoid the crash. "It was a terrible wreck – cars and trucks everywhere," Johnson said. Johnson said he saw three semi trucks jackknifed at the front of the crash, with at least 20 cars crashed in between. It looked like there were two or three more sets of crashes further down the road, with cars on top of each other.

Twelve people with broken bones, bruises and scrapes were required to go to Vail Community Hospital, about 15 miles from the scene of the accident, said hospital spokesperson Dave Gioto. All were in fair condition when they arrived at the hospital. They were all treated and able to leave the hospital by the following morning. "We are amazed and pleased by how few and minor the injuries were after such a large car accident," said Gioto.

Police encourage drivers to avoid driving whenever possible during snowstorms. "If you have to drive in snowy conditions, use a slow speed and be sure to keep a large distance between you and the vehicle in front of you," advises Officer Meyer.

LESSON 7: Writing

1 **THINK ABOUT IT.** How do car insurance companies help people who have been in an accident? What do people have to do after they have an accident to get help from their insurance companies?

2 **BEFORE YOU WRITE.**

A. DISCUSS. Look at the picture on page 145 with a partner. Describe what happened.

B. LISTEN to a conversation about another car accident. Read the statements and check ☑ *True* or *False*.

TCD3, 51

	True	False
1. Two of the people in the accident were hurt.	☐	☐
2. Tom's car hit the other car from behind.	☐	☐
2. They called the police, but they never came.	☐	☐
4. Tom's car is fine, so he's just going to drive it home.	☐	☐

> **WRITING FOCUS: Make a numbered list to sequence an event**
>
> Make a numbered list to write about the details of an event. This is especially important on forms, when it is important to stress the order in which the events happened.

C. COMPLETE. Read the insurance form that Tom filled out and fill in any missing details. Then listen again to check your answers.

http://www.onlineclaimsreporting.net

Assure Online Claim Report

State where the accident occurred: Florida
Date and time of the accident: March 30, 2010 / _____ p.m.
General description of what happened:
1. I was in my car, waiting at a _____ behind another car.
2. The light turned _____ and the car in front of me started to go, but then stopped quickly for a _____ in the crosswalk.
3. I put on my brakes, but couldn't _____ in time.
4. I hit the car from _____.
Location where your vehicle was towed: Pete's Body Shop on _____
Police Department involved (if any) and accident report number: _accident report # 80560_
Contact information for the other people involved (name, address, phone number, email address): _____ / 555-320-9012 / mchang@yippee.com
License plate numbers for the other vehicles involved: AO8 9H7
Insurance information for the other vehicles involved: Genco Auto Insurance

3 **WRITE.** Imagine you were one of the cars in the accident described in the reading on page 145. Fill out the insurance form. Be sure to make a numbered list to describe what happened.

Assure Online Claim Report

State where the accident occurred:
Date and time of the accident:
General description of what happened:
1. 2. 3. 4.
Location where your vehicle was towed:
Police Department involved (if any) and accident report number:
Contact information for the other people involved (name, address, phone number, email address)
License plate numbers for the other vehicles involved:
Insurance information for the other vehicles involved:

4 **AFTER YOU WRITE.**

A. **DISCUSS.** Share your insurance claim with a partner. What questions does your partner have about the accident? How can you improve your insurance claim form?

B. **EDIT** your insurance claim form. Ask yourself these questions:

1. Did I sequence the events of the accident correctly?

2. Do I need to add any information?

3. Is the spelling correct? Check the words in a dictionary if you are not sure.

4. Is the punctuation correct? Check commas, apostrophes and periods.

5. Did you use verbs + gerunds or infinitives correctly?

C. **REWRITE** your insurance claim form, making corrections.

Career Connection

1 THINK ABOUT IT. Look at the picture. What are the workers doing to solve their problem? What does *collaborate* mean?

🎧 **2 LISTEN** to a discussion among engineers and line workers at an auto plant. What problem are they discussing? Choose the correct answer.

TCD3, 52

a. a late shipment

b. a broken machine

c. a training program

3 LISTEN again. Pay attention to the names of the speakers. Then complete the sentences with the correct name.

Nancy	Ray	Carl

1. _____ is worried about a late shipment.

2. _____ wants to wait for an engineer.

3. _____ doesn't really want to try to fix the machine.

4. _____ wants to call Gary.

5. _____ doesn't want to bother Gary on his vacation.

6. _____ decides to call Gary.

4 DISCUSS. How did Carl, Ray, and Nancy decide to solve their problem? How were they different in how they tried to do it? Discuss with a partner.

5 TALK with a partner about the ways that people try to solve problems. When there's a problem at work, do you think it's best to collaborate in a group, work as individuals, or wait for a supervisor's decision?

6 WHAT ABOUT YOU? Think about a situation where you had a problem in your job. How did you solve the problem? Can you think of any other ways you could have solved the problem?

Check Your Progress!

Skill	Circle the answers.	Is it correct?
A. Use causative verbs.	1. The law requires each bus **have** / **to have** a wheelchair lift. 2. His mother doesn't let him **cross** / **to cross** the street alone. 3. She makes the children **hold** / **to hold** hands crossing the street. 4. I had my friends **fix** / **fixed** my bicycle.	☐ ☐ ☐ ☐
	Number Correct	0 1 2 3 4
B. Use the verbs *forget, remember,* **and** *stop.*	5. I forgot **to go** / **going** to the convenience store. We still need milk. 6. I stopped **to eat** / **eating** ice cream, so I lost weight. 7. I remember **to go** / **going** to my aunt's house when I was a child. 8. Did you stop **to see** / **seeing** Town Hall? It's a beautiful building.	☐ ☐ ☐ ☐
	Number Correct	0 1 2 3 4
C. Talk about getting around town.	9. The wheelchair lift is for **disabled** / **visually impaired** passengers. 10. You can't park at a **parking meter** / **fire hydrant**. 11. The **crossing guard** / **road construction** caused a traffic jam. 12. You should drive slowly in the **tow-away zone** / **school zone**.	☐ ☐ ☐ ☐
	Number Correct	0 1 2 3 4
D. Talk about things in the community.	13. I moved. I need to fill out a **change-of-address** / **registration** form. 14. You can take a **road test** / **proof of insurance** to receive a license. 15. What's that noise? I think my car has engine **rush hour** / **trouble**. 16. I think they give away free maps at the **visitor information center** / **convenience store**	☐ ☐ ☐ ☐
	Number Correct	0 1 2 3 4

COUNT the number of correct answers above. Fill in the bubbles.

Chart Your Success					
Skill	Need Practice	Okay	Good	Very Good	Excellent!
A. Use causative verbs.	⓪	①	②	③	④
B. Use the verbs *forget, remember,* **and** *stop.*	⓪	①	②	③	④
C. Talk about getting around town.	⓪	①	②	③	④
D. Talk about things in the community.	⓪	①	②	③	④

LESSON 1: Grammar and Vocabulary

1 **GRAMMAR PICTURE DICTIONARY.** What did the instructor say about home safety? Listen and read.

TCD4, 2
SCD39

1

You need handrails on your stairways.

A: How was the home safety class? What did the instructor say?
B: She taught us a lot. She said we needed handrails on all of our stairways.

2

You need to have an emergency escape plan, and the whole family needs to practice once a year.

Window   Window
Room 1   Room 2
Room 3
Kitchen
Meeting Place

A: What else did she say?
B: She said we needed to have an emergency escape plan, and the whole family needed to practice once a year. Let's have a **fire drill** next week so we know what to do if there's a fire.

3

Carbon monoxide is a deadly gas that collects when fuels like wood and kerosene are burned.

A: Did she say anything about **safety devices**?
B: Yes. She talked about **smoke detectors** and **carbon monoxide detectors**. She said carbon monoxide was a deadly gas that collects when fuels like kerosene are burned.

4

You can keep your children safe by using outlet covers and child-safety locks.

A: Did you learn anything about making the house safe for the new baby?
B: Yes, she said we could keep our children safe by using **outlet covers** and **child-safety locks**.

2 **PRACTICE** the conversations in Activity 1 with a partner.

3 **NOTICE THE GRAMMAR.** Look at the blue parts of the sentences above. Then look at what the teacher says. How are the sentences different? Then circle the differences in speaker B's sentences.

Reported Speech

When you want to report what someone said, you can use reported speech. Use *said* to introduce the person's words and ideas. The verb usually changes when you use reported speech. *That* can be omitted in reported speech without changing the meaning.

Direct Quotation	Reported Speech
Simple Present ➝	**Simple Past**
Jan said, "I *have* some cabinet locks."	Jan said (that) she *had* some cabinet locks.
She said, "You *can borrow* my cabinet locks."	She said (that) I *could borrow* her cabinet locks.
Present Continuous ➝	**Past Continuous**
Ed said, "I'*m talking* to the doctor."	Ed said (that) he *was talking* to the doctor.
Stan said, "We'*re having* a fire drill."	Stan said (that) they *were having* a fire drill.
Future with *Be Going to* and *Will* ➝	***Was/Were Going to* and *Would***
Joe said, "I'*m going to do* it later."	Joe said (that) he *was going to do* it later.
May said, "I'*ll help* you."	May said (that) she *would help* me.
Simple Past ➝	**Past Perfect**
Ann said, "He *took* a safety class."	Ann said (that) he *had taken* a safety class.
David said, "You *weren't* too noisy."	David said (that) we *hadn't been* too noisy.
Present Perfect ➝	**Past Perfect**
Lee said, "I'*ve been* here before."	Lee said (that) he *had been* there before.
Bo said, "He *hasn't asked* for my advice."	Bo said (that) he *hadn't asked* for her advice.

You may have to change words like pronouns, possessives, and *here* to report the speaker's original meaning. For example: Jack said, "**My** brother and I have eaten **here** several times." Jack said (that) **he** and **his** brother had eaten **there** several times.

---

4 **WRITE** reported speech for each direct quotation.

1. Susan said, "I'm installing child-safety locks on our kitchen cabinets."

   Susan said that she was installing child-safety locks on their kitchen cabinets.

2. Terry said, "We have a fire drill twice a year at our house."

3. He said, "I didn't buy a carbon monoxide detector."

4. Chuck said, "I'm building a handrail for our stairs."

5. Sarah said, "I've never used outlet covers before."

6. Aaron said, "My medicine cabinet has a child-safety lock on it."

5 **WHAT ABOUT YOU?** Interview a classmate and ask the questions below. Write down your classmate's answers as direct quotations. Then share the information with the class using reported speech.

Example: *"I have a carbon monoxide detector and a smoke detector."*

> John said that he had a carbon monoxide detector and a smoke detector.

1. What kinds of safety devices do you have in your house?

2. Does your family have fire drills? Why or why not?

LESSON 2: Grammar Practice Plus

1 **TALK** about the safety problems in the picture.

2 **LISTEN** to the conversation. Then write the correct number next to each word below.

_____ burn hazard

_____ electrical cord

_____ electrical outlet

_____ child-safety gate

_____ toxic cleansers

_____ choking hazard

3 **COMPLETE** each sentence with a vocabulary word from Activity 2.

1. Hard candy can be a _____ *choking hazard* _____ for small children.

2. The _____ are not being used. Stairs can be dangerous for small children.

3. The children can reach those pans on the stove. They're a _____ .

4. The children can easily reach the _____ under the sink.

5. There are too many _____ plugged into one _____ .

Reported Speech with *say* and *tell*

Use *said* or *told* to introduce a person's words and ideas. Follow *told* with a noun, a name, or an object pronoun (me, you, him, her, us, them).

Doris **said**, "The candy is a choking hazard.."

Doris **said** (that) the candy was a choking hazard.

Doris **told** her daughter (that) the candy was a choking hazard.

Doris **told Mia** (that) the candy was a choking hazard.

Doris **told her** (that) the candy was a choking hazard.

4 WRITE. Use the information from Activity 3 to write six things that Doris told Mia. Use reported speech. Write 3 sentences with *said*, and 3 sentences with *told*.

Example: *Doris said the candy was a choking hazard.*

5 TALK with a partner. Look at the sentences in Activity 3. What should Mia do to fix each problem? Write your partner's answers. Then tell another classmate what your partner said.

What do you think Mia should do about the candy?

My partner said that Mia should put the candy somewhere else, so the children can't reach it.

Math: Subtracting Decimals

A READ the chart below. It shows that in Westfield accidents decreased from 1988 to 2008 because of new technologies and safety measures. Calculate the decrease from 1988. Subtract the 2008 number for each category.

Example:
```
falls  0.95
      -0.35
       0.60
```

1. Falls _____
2. Car Accidents _____
3. Bike Accidents _____
4. Burns from Fire _____
5. Poisonings _____

B CALCULATE. Which category had the largest decrease?

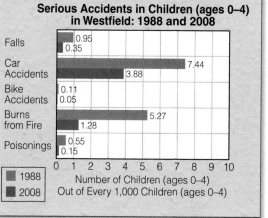

Serious Accidents in Children (ages 0–4) in Westfield: 1988 and 2008

Falls: 0.95 / 0.35
Car Accidents: 7.44 / 3.88
Bike Accidents: 0.11 / 0.05
Burns from Fire: 5.27 / 1.28
Poisonings: 0.55 / 0.15

0 1 2 3 4 5 6 7 8 9 10

■ 1988
■ 2008

Number of Children (ages 0–4) Out of Every 1,000 Children (ages 0–4)

LESSON 3: Listening and Conversation

TCD4, 4–9

1 **LISTEN** to the conversation. Then listen to the question. Fill in the correct answer. Replay each item if necessary.

1. (A) (B) (C)   4. (A) (B) (C)
2. (A) (B) (C)   5. (A) (B) (C)
3. (A) (B) (C)   6. (A) (B) (C)

TCD4, 10

2 **LISTEN** to the conversation. Then (circle) the correct words to complete the message slip.

> This message is for: (1)___*Jack / Stan*_____
>
> Date: _*4/14/08*_____   Time: ____*10:10*_____ ☑A.M. ☐P.M.
>
> (2)_*Jack / Stan called.*_____
>
> (3)
> *He isn't coming to work / is going to be late.* He fell and
> (4)   (5)
> *broke / sprained* his ankle. He's at *home / the hospital*
> (6)
> right now. *I'll visit / call* him later to see how he is.
>
> _____
>
> _____
>
> Message taken by: (7)___*Mia / Laura*_____

3 **LISTEN** again to the conversation between Laura and Jack. Then complete the following conversation between Laura and her boss, Stan.

Laura: Good morning, Stan. Jack called. He said he (1) _____*wasn't coming*_____(not come) to work today.

Stan: Did he say why?

Laura: Yes. He said he (2) _____ (fall and break) his ankle.

Stan: That's terrible. How did it happen?

Laura: He told me he (3) _____ (trip) on some toys on the stairs.

Stan: Is he at home?

Laura: No. He said he (4) _____ (be) at the hospital. He told me Mia

(5) _____ (drive) him there.

Stan: Did he say anything else?

Laura: No. I told him I (6) _____ (call) him later.

Stan: Okay. Let me know when you call him. I'd like to speak with him.

Take a phone message. • Role-play a conversation.

4 **LISTEN** to the conversation.

TCD4, 11
SCD40

A: So, what did your mother say?

B: She said that I had to check the smoke detector once a year to make sure it's working.

A: Oh, what else did she say?

B: She said that there were too many electrical cords plugged into one outlet. She told me that fire was the third leading cause of injury in the home last year.

A: Oh, wow, really? Did she say anything else?

B: Yes. She told me that she was coming back next month to check up on me!

5 **ROLE-PLAY.** Imagine that you had these conversations with Linda and Jack. Then work with two classmates. Take turns telling each other what Linda and Jack said to you. Use the conversation in Activity 4 as a model.

Conversation 1	Conversation 2
Linda: "I had an accident in my house two years ago."	**Jack:** "We're going to take a home-safety class next month."
You: "What happened?"	**You:** "Really? Why?"
Linda: "There were electrical cords underneath a rug in the living room. They caught on fire."	**Jack:** "We want to learn how to make our home safe for kids. We're going to have a baby!"
You: "How scary!"	**You:** "Congratulations! When is the baby due?"
Linda: "I learned my lesson that day!"	**Jack:** "The baby is due in April."

6 **WHAT ABOUT YOU?** Talk with a partner. Tell each other three things you want to do to improve your home safety. Take notes about your partner's ideas.

> Michael – going to get a carbon monoxide detector
>   – needs to . . .

7 **TALK** with a different partner and tell him or her what your partner in Activity 6 said. Use reported speech.

> Michael told me that he was going to get a carbon monoxide detector.

LESSON 4: Grammar and Vocabulary

1 GRAMMAR PICTURE DICTIONARY. What did this man do for his health? Listen and read.

TCD4, 12
SCD41

1 Last year, I **found out about** an exercise group in my neighborhood. The group met three times a week for an hour.

2 My doctor told me I needed to lose some weight, so I **signed up** on Monday. The group's instructor created an exercise plan for me.

3 The exercises were really difficult. I wanted to **give up** several times.

4 Then I **thought** it **over**. I decided that I really wanted to lose weight and be healthy, so I didn't quit.

5 I **followed through with** my plan, even though it was extremely difficult.

6 In the end, the plan really **paid off**. I lost 50 pounds, and I feel great!

2 READ the sentences in Activity 1 with a partner.

3 NOTICE THE GRAMMAR. Match the phrasal verbs with the words that have the same meaning.

_d_ **1.** follow through with   **a.** have a successful end
_f_ **2.** give up   **b.** join
_b_ **3.** sign up   **c.** hear or read about
_c_ **4.** find out about   **d.** complete
_a_ **5.** pay off   **e.** consider carefully
_e_ **6.** think over   **f.** quit

Phrasal Verbs

A phrasal verb is a two- or three-word verb that includes a main verb and a particle.
A particle looks like a preposition, but it isn't a preposition when it's part of a phrasal verb.

Some phrasal verbs cannot be separated in a sentence. If an inseparable phrasal verb takes an object, the object comes after the the phrasal verb.

Inseparable Phrasal Verbs

count on (trust)	I can **count on** her to buy healthy food.
fall for (believe)	Sue didn't **fall for** his excuses.
come back (return)	I **came back** from the gym at 5:30.
show up (arrive)	Ed **showed up** early for the yoga class.

Some phrasal verbs can be separable or inseparable. Notice the placement of the object.

Separable Phrasal Verbs

With most separable phrasal verbs, an object noun can come either after the particle, or between the verb and the particle. If the object is a pronoun, it must come between the verb and the particle.

use up (use completely)	I **used up** all my cell phone minutes this month. I **used** all my cell phone minutes **up** this month. I **used** them **up** this month.
look up (look for information)	We **looked up** the information online. We **looked** the information **up** online. We **looked** it **up** online.

With some phrasal verbs, the object must come between the verb and the particle.

talk into (convince)	Dan **talked** me **into** going for a run.
start over (begin again)	Let's **start** the exercise **over**.

4 COMPLETE. Read the sentences. Then complete each sentence with the words in parentheses and the correct particle. Pay attention to word order. When you are finished, ask and answer the questions with a partner.

1. Has anyone ever ___talked you into___ buying something you didn't want?
   (talk / you)

2. Where do you usually ___look up phone numbers?___ ?
   (look / phone numbers)

3. When have you needed to ___count on your friends.___ ?
   (count / your friends)

4. How do you ___find out about events___ that are happening in your city?
   (find / about / events)

5. Have you ever ___fallen for a story___ that wasn't true?
   (fallen / a story)

5 WHAT ABOUT YOU? Ask and answer the questions in Activity 4 with a partner.

LESSON 5: Grammar Practice Plus

10/24

Used to, Be Used to

Used to and *Be Used to* have completely different meanings.

> Remember, *used to* is followed by the base form of a verb, and *be used to* is followed by the *-ing* form of a verb, or by a noun or pronoun.

Use *used to* (*didn't + use to*) + verb to talk about past habits.

> I **used to** eat a lot of junk food, but now I eat well.
> Sara **didn't use to** like running, but now she runs every day.

Use *be + used to* (*be + not used to*) + noun or pronoun to talk about things you already know about, or do.

> Jill's exercise plan was really hard at first, but she**'s used to** it now.
> I**'m not used to** waking up early. I usually wake up after 10:00.

1 **READ** the paragraphs below. Fill in each blank with *used to*, *didn't use to*, *be + used to*, or *be + not used to*.

Five years ago, I had a lot of unhealthy habits. I ___used to___ drink five to ten sodas a day. I ___didn't use___ eat fruits or vegetables. I also ___used to___ smoke a lot of cigarettes. My wife always ___used to___ ask me to quit, but I didn't listen. Because of my smoking, I had trouble breathing, and I couldn't run around and play with my kids. I missed out on a lot. My wife was worried about my health and after a while, she talked me into joining a gym. I signed up for exercise classes, but after a month, I dropped out. I ___wasn't used to___ all that exercise!

But then I found out that I had diabetes. My doctor told me that if I didn't change my habits, I wasn't going to live to see my children grow up. Now I eat fruit and vegetables instead of junk food. I ___used to___ get tired after running for five minutes, but now I ___am used to___ running five miles a day. When someone offers me a cigarette, I turn it down. I look forward to living a healthy life for my kids *and* my grandkids.

2 **VOCABULARY.** Find and <u>underline</u> the phrasal verbs below in the paragraph in Activity 1. Then match each phrasal verb with the correct definition.

_d_	**1.** miss out on	**a.** to be excited about something that is going to happen
_e_	**2.** drop out	**b.** grow from child to adult
_b_	**3.** grow up	**c.** refuse or reject something
_c_	**4.** turn down	**d.** not be able to do something that you want to do
_a_	**5.** look forward to	**e.** quit doing a group activity or belonging to a group

3 **WRITE** each phrasal verb from Activity 1 in the correct place in the chart below.

Separable	Inseparable

TCD4, 13 **Pronunciation:** *Used to* and *Be Used to*

It can be difficult to hear the difference between *used to* and *be used to*. To hear the difference, pay attention to the context of the speaker's sentence. Is the speaker talking about something he or she did (or didn't do) in the past, or is he or she talking about being accustomed to doing something?

TCD4, 14
SCD42 **A** It also helps to pay attention to the word that comes after *used to* or *be used to*. Listen and repeat these examples.

I **used to** exercise every day. I**'m used to** exercising every day.

TCD4, 15 **B** **LISTEN** to the sentences. Circle the phrase that you hear.

1. I didn't use to	I'm not used to		**4.** I used to	I'm used to
2. I used to	I'm used to		**5.** I used to	I'm used to
3. I didn't use to	I'm not used to		**6.** I didn't use to	I'm not used to

4 **LISTEN** and complete the chart below. Check ☑ the correct column for each item.
TCD4, 16

	Past	Present
1. exercise every day	✓	
2. play basketball or soccer in the afternoons		
3. in great shape		
4. eat fast food for dinner		
5. not used to exercising		
6. able to run five miles without getting tired		
7. sign up with a gym in her neighborhood		

5 **WHAT ABOUT YOU?** Complete the sentences below with *used to, didn't use to, am used to,* or *am not used to* to make them true about yourself.

1. I _____ eat a lot of junk food when I was young.

2. I _____ exercise a lot when I was young.

3. I _____ exercising every day.

4. I _____ cooking my own meals.

5. I _____ eating well.

LESSON 6: Reading

1 THINK ABOUT IT. When your doctor gives you a new medication, what questions do you ask him or her? Write your ideas here.

1. _____

_____

2. _____

_____

3. _____

_____

Reading Strategy Summary

Preview the text.

Make Inferences.

Use context to guess the meaning of new words.

2 BEFORE YOU READ. Preview the advertisement. Look at the picture and the different parts of the advertisement. What product is advertised?

3 READ the advertisement on the next page. Did you correctly guess what the advertisement is about?

4 AFTER YOU READ.

A. **ANSWER** the questions with a partner.

1. What is the name of the medication in the advertisement?
2. What is the medication for?
3. Why did the man go to see his physician?
4. What advice did the physician give to the man?
5. How often should a person take this medication?
6. What are some possible side effects of this medication?
7. What might happen if someone has an allergic reaction to Fumenol?

B. **REREAD** the advertisement and underline any words you do not know. With a partner, choose five words from the advertisement. Write them below, and use the context to guess the meaning of each word. Write your guesses below. Then use a dictionary to look up the word and find out if you were correct.

READING FOCUS: Use context to guess the meaning of new words

When you don't know the meaning of a word, read the complete sentence with the word in it, and one or two sentences before and after it. Then try to guess the meaning.

1. _____
2. _____
3. _____
4. _____
5. _____

" I was only 43—I didn't want to die! I decided to make a change . . . with *Fumenol*. "

When I was in my 20s, I used to eat whatever I wanted. I used to smoke a lot, too. I didn't worry about my health at all.

But then when I was 43, I had a heart attack. My physician said that I had to change my lifestyle*. He wanted me to give up fatty foods, alcohol, and cigarettes. I took some time to think over what he had said. I was only 43—I didn't want to die! I decided to make a change.

The first thing I wanted to do was to find out about ways to quit smoking. I was used to smoking about two packs a day. I had tried a dozen* different programs to quit smoking, but I could never follow through with them.

I asked my physician what to do. He said that I should try this new drug, Fumenol. My doctor's advice* has really paid off for me. Fumenol helped me stop smoking in just three weeks. Maybe it can help you, too.

Don't let your life slip away from you. Find out about *Fumenol*, and stop smoking today.

WARNING: If you experience chest pain when taking Fumenol, call your physician immediately.

HOW TO USE: Take Fumenol three times each day. Take with meals and a full glass of water to prevent nausea.

SIDE EFFECTS: Some patients experience nausea*, dizziness*, or tiredness when they begin taking Fumenol. If these symptoms last longer than three days, contact your physician.

PRECAUTIONS: Fumenol should not be taken by people who have chronic* liver or kidney problems. Some users experience an allergic reaction to this drug. Symptoms include: rash*, itching, swelling*, and shortness of breath*. If you experience an allergic reaction to this drug, seek medical help immediately.

---

lifestyle (n.): the way that a person lives

dozen (n.): twelve

advice (n.): an idea or ideas to help make something better

nausea (n.): a feeling of sickness in the stomach

dizziness (n.): a spinning feeling in the head

chronic (adj.): lasting a long time

rash (n.): a red or bumpy area on the body

swelling (n.): area of the body that becomes bigger

shortness of breath (n.): difficulty breathing

LESSON 7: Writing

1 **WARM UP.** Every January, people make New Year's resolutions, or promises to themselves. These promises are often about a healthier lifestyle. Have you ever made a New Year's resolution about your health? What was it?

2 **BEFORE YOU WRITE**

    A. THINK about health habits that people often want to change. Make notes about ways that people can improve their health.

THINGS TO CHANGE OR STOP	THINGS TO DO MORE
stop smoking	*eat more fruit*

    B. WRITE. Imagine that a friend (or family member) wants to live a healthier lifestyle. He or she asks for your advice. Write your ideas in the chart. Give several suggestions.

What change should your friend make?	Why should he or she make this change?	How can he or she make this change?
You should eat more fruit.	*Fruit has vitamins that the body needs.*	*You should eat an apple instead of potato chips.*

    C. READ the New Year's resolution that Victor wrote. <u>Underline</u> the sentences that answer these questions:

      • What?   • Why?   • How?

This year, I must exercise more. I can't do all the things I used to do. I used to lift weights, but now I can hardly pick up my son. I used to have lots of energy, but now I'm tired all the time. I have to make a fitness plan and follow through with it. My doctor said that I should sign up for the gym. I'll have to find out how much a gym membership costs and pick up an application. Then I'll talk it over with my friend Ray. If he signs up, too, I won't give up so easily. It's easier to work out when you do it with a friend.

3 **WRITE** three New Year's resolutions about your own health. Follow the steps below.

1. In the first column, write about health habits that you want to improve or change. Begin your sentence with *I must / I should / I have to*.

2. In the second column, give reasons about why you should change each health habit.

3. In the final column, tell what you can do to make each change happen.

4. When you have finished the chart, write a paragraph for each resolution.

> **WRITING FOCUS: Identify problems and solutions**
>
> One way to organize writing is by presenting problems and solutions. First, tell *what* the problem is and explain *why* it is a problem. Then tell *how* to fix the problem. That is the solution.

What to change / improve	Why change / improve	How to change / improve
Resolution 1		
Resolution 2		
Resolution 3		

4 **AFTER YOU WRITE**

A. **EDIT** your paragraphs. Ask yourself these questions.

1. Are the problem and solution stated clearly?
2. Is there any information that is not about the topic?
3. Is the information in the right order?
4. Do I need to add any information?
5. Is the punctuation correct? Check commas, apostrophes, and periods.
6. Did you use phrasal verbs? If so, are they correct?
7. Did you use reported speech? If so, is it correct?

 B. **REWRITE** your paragraphs with corrections.

C. **DISCUSS** your work with a partner. Read each other's resolutions. Then ask and answer questions about each other's ideas.

Career Connection

1 **THINK ABOUT IT.** What kinds of things do nurses do at a hospital? What kinds of skills do you think a nurse has that can transfer to other departments in a hospital or private doctor's office?

2 **READ** this online job advertisement and application form. Nina is applying for a case manager's position at Children's Hospital. As you read, match the numbered words to the correct definition.

CASE MANAGER, Children's Hospital.
Description: Coordinates patient care from admission to (1)**discharge**. Acts as a (2)**liaison** between patient's family and medical team.

Requirements: Registered Nurse (RN) with 3+ years of case management experience. Administrative experience required. Experience preferred in the following clinical areas: (3)**Intensive** Care/Critical Care Unit; Emergency/(4)**Trauma**; Pediatric Care.

APPLICATION FORM
NAME: Nina Escobar

Describe your nursing experience.

I was an RN for 4 years at University Hospital, where I worked in the following departments: Cardiology, Pediatrics, Pediatrics Intensive Care Unit, Respiratory Acute Care Unit.

Describe your previous case management experience.

I worked as a case manager for 3 years at City Hospital, where I served as a patient liaison in the Pediatrics Department. In that position, I helped families fill out insurance paperwork, and I followed up on patient complaints. Often, the families wanted to talk over their options with me. This was the most (5)**rewarding** part of the job—I like helping people during difficult times.

What skills and qualities make you a good candidate for this position?

My manager at City Hospital said that I was the person she counted on most in times of crisis. She trusted me to make important decisions on my own, when needed. I am used to working independently and I am able to make decisions quickly. These are the strengths that I can offer Children's Hospital.

_____ **A.** a wound or shock to the body caused suddenly
_____ **B.** release from the hospital
_____ **C.** someone who helps with communication between two people or groups
_____ **D.** serious, extreme
_____ **E.** satisfying, bringing happiness for something a person has done

3 **WRITE.** Compare three things from Nina's experience and qualifications to the job description in the advertisement. Do you think Nina's qualifications match those asked for in the job description?

Nina's Experience	Job Description
Nina wrote that she had 3 years of case management experience.	The ad stated that it required 3 or more years of case management experience.

4 **ROLE-PLAY** a scene between Nina and the hiring supervisor at Children's Hospital. Interview Nina. Ask her how her qualifications will transfer to this job.

Supervisor: Nina, tell me about your work as a case manager.

Nina: I worked for 3 years as a patient liaison in the Pediatrics Department at City Hospital. I helped explain medical options to the children's parents.

5 **WHAT ABOUT YOU?** What skills do you have from your previous experience or from your educational background that could transfer easily to a job you would like to have? Talk with a partner.

Check Your Progress!

Skill	Circle the answers.	Is it correct?
A. Use reported speech.	**1.** Ann: "I have some." Ann said she **had** / **have** some. **2.** Joe: "I didn't see you." Joe said he **hadn't seen** / **didn't see** me. **3.** Ed: "I'm waiting for Sue." Ed said **he** / **I** was waiting for Sue. **4.** Kim: "We're going to your house." Kim said they were going to **her** / **my** house.	☐ ☐ ☐ ☐
	Number Correct	0 1 2 3 4
B. Use phrasal verbs.	**5.** Did they talk **into you** / **you into** buying expensive equipment? **6.** The number was easy to find. We looked **it up** / **up it** online. **7.** Let's start **over the exercises** / **the exercises over**. I'm not tired yet. **8.** I can count **her on** / **on her** to be on time.	☐ ☐ ☐ ☐
	Number Correct	0 1 2 3 4
C. Talk about safety.	**9.** Hold onto the **locks** / **handrails** when you walk down the stairs. **10.** **Outlet covers** / **cabinet locks** protect kids from getting shocked. **11.** Carbon monoxide is a deadly **gas** / **smoke**. **12.** We have a baby, so we need new safety **devices** / **detectors**.	☐ ☐ ☐ ☐
	Number Correct	0 1 2 3 4
D. Talk about health.	**13.** I found out **about** / **on** a yoga class that I want to take. **14.** Ken signed **in** / **up** for an exercise class that starts next week. **15.** That class really paid **out** / **off**. I've lost 10 pounds already. **16.** You should **follow through with** / **look forward to** your exercise plan if you want to lose weight.	☐ ☐ ☐ ☐
	Number Correct	0 1 2 3 4

COUNT the number of correct answers above. Fill in the bubbles.

Chart Your Success					
Skill	Need Practice	Okay	Good	Very Good	Excellent!
A. Use reported speech.	⓪	①	②	③	④
B. Use phrasal verbs.	⓪	①	②	③	④
C. Talk about safety.	⓪	①	②	③	④
D. Talk about health.	⓪	①	②	③	④

LESSON 1: Grammar and Vocabulary

TCD4, 17 SCD43

1 GRAMMAR PICTURE DICTIONARY. What are people doing for their careers? Listen and read.

1

A: Is it hard to **conduct a job search** online?

B: Not really. If you look on some job websites, you can find lots of **opportunities** to **pursue**.

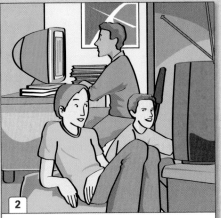

2

A: What is Carlos working on?

B: He's **updating** his **résumé**. He'll be able to apply for the job tomorrow if he gets the résumé done tonight.

3

A: I need to **build a stronger résumé**.

B: If you bring your résumé to the career advisor, she will **evaluate your credentials** and give you **feedback**.

4

A: Do you think it's okay if I tell my boss about my idea for increasing sales?

B: Sure. If you tell her, she will see that you **take the initiative**.

5

A: If I **identify my strengths and weaknesses**, I can choose the right career for myself.

B: That's right. You'll be able to **take steps** to improve your skills, too.

6

A: That **professional development** course is expensive! How can you afford it?

B: I can **cover the costs** if I save money carefully.

2 PRACTICE the conversations in Activity 1 with a partner.

3 NOTICE THE GRAMMAR. Circle *if* and underline the clause that follows. What form is the verb: past, present, or future?

Real Conditionals: Present and Future

Real conditionals describe a situation and the result of the situation. Real conditionals include an *if*-clause and a main clause. The *if*-clause can come before or after the main clause. When the *if*-clause is first, use a comma after it.

Statements and Questions about the Present

Use the present tense in the *if*-clause and in the main clause to describe something that usually happens in a specific situation.

If-Clause	Main Clause
If I **am** late,	my boss **gets** mad.
If Melissa **works** hard,	she **finishes** her tasks quickly.
If you **leave** early,	do your coworkers **get** angry?

Statements and Questions about the Future

Use the present tense in the *if*-clause and the future tense or a modal in the main clause to describe something that will happen in the future if something else happens first.

If-Clause	Main Clause
If Carlos **works** on his typing skills,	he's **going to get** a promotion.
If Melissa **doesn't check** her email,	she **won't get** the news from our meeting.
If he **gets** a raise,	he **can buy** a new car.
If we **don't turn in** the assignment,	what **will** the boss **say**?

---

4 **MATCH** the clauses to make sentences.

1. If Melissa gives helpful feedback, __d__

2. If Harris and Michael build stronger résumés, _____

3. If Sara takes the initiative, _____

4. If Antonio takes steps to improve his computer skills, _____

5. If Elena and Susan can cover the costs, _____

6. If her sister gets a job in New York, _____

a. he may receive a promotion.

b. Luz will conduct a job search in New York, too.

c. they will take a professional development course together.

d. her employees will be happier.

e. she will receive a promotion.

f. they will be able to pursue new opportunities.

5 **WHAT ABOUT YOU?** Complete the sentences about you. Then talk with a partner.

1. If I update my résumé, I can _____.

2. If I identify my strengths and weaknesses, I can _____.

3. I will improve my credentials if I _____.

4. I can find a great job if I _____.

5. If I take steps to improve my English, I will _____.

LESSON 2: Grammar Practice Plus

1 TALK about the people at the job fair. What are they doing?

2 LISTEN and look at the picture. Write the number of the person next to each word.

TCD4, 18

_____ assertive   _____ demanding   _____ impressed

_____ prepared   _____ professional   _____ sloppy

3 WRITE the words from Activity 2 next to their meanings.

1. _prepared_: having everything that is needed; being ready and organized

2. _____: being confident; not being afraid to state your opinion or take a leadership role

3. _____: expecting a lot of someone or something, expecting too much

4. _____: not careful; messy, disorganized

5. _____: feeling admiration or respect for someone or something

6. _____: showing excellence at your work; showing good training

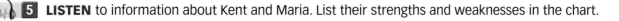

4 **COMPLETE** the sentences with the vocabulary from Activity 2.

1. If Luis is too _____*demanding*_____ about the display, his employees won't like working for him.

2. Maria was _____ with her business card and résumé, so she is showing one of her strengths.

3. Chris will be _____ with Maria if she has a strong résumé.

4. If Kent is _____ about his strengths, Allison will probably give him good feedback.

5. If Kirk identifies his own weaknesses, he will take steps to not be so _____ .

6. Jana will only accept a job if her supervisor is as _____ as she is.

5 **LISTEN** to information about Kent and Maria. List their strengths and weaknesses in the chart.

TCD4, 19

Kent		Maria	
Strengths	**Weaknesses**	**Strengths**	**Weaknesses**
assertive	needs more work experience		

6 **WRITE** three sentences about Kent and three sentences about Maria. Use the real conditional.

Example: *If Kent is assertive, he will get good feedback from the company.*

1. _____.
2. _____.
3. _____.
4. _____.
5. _____.
6. _____.

7 **WHAT ABOUT YOU?** Think about your strengths and weaknesses. Then complete the sentences and talk with a partner.

1. If I want to build a stronger résumé, I need to _____.

2. I can conduct a job search, if _____.

3. If I'm not assertive, I _____.

4. If I'm sloppy with my work, _____.

5. If I'm not prepared for class, _____.

LESSON 3: Listening and Conversation

TCD4, 20–25

1 **LISTEN** to the conversation. Then listen to a question. Fill in the circle for the correct answer. Replay each item if necessary.

1. Ⓐ   Ⓑ   Ⓒ   4. Ⓐ   Ⓑ   Ⓒ

2. Ⓐ   Ⓑ   Ⓒ   5. Ⓐ   Ⓑ   Ⓒ

3. Ⓐ   Ⓑ   Ⓒ   6. Ⓐ   Ⓑ   Ⓒ

TCD4, 26

2 **LISTEN** again. Check ☑ the strengths for each person.

	Jim	Jan	Sam	Ann	Ed	Mary
confident						
friendly						
helpful						
prepared	✓					
professional						

TCD4, 27

3 **LISTEN** to the two managers continue their discussion about Mary. Then check ☑ *True* or *False* for each statement.

	True	**False**
1. The managers want to give Mary a promotion.	☐	☐
2. The managers are confident in Mary's leadership skills.	☐	☐
3. The managers think Mary needs more experience.	☐	☐

TCD4, 28 **Pronunciation:** Rhythm of Thought Groups

Thought groups are phrases that are grouped by meaning and by grammatical structure. There is often a small pause between thought groups. Listen for the thought groups in the following examples.

If I ride my bike to work, I'll save money on gas.

What will you do if you move to California?

TCD4, 29
SCD44 **A** **LISTEN.** Mark these sentences to predict the thought groups. Then listen and check.

1. If I get up at five o'clock, I can go running.

2. If you work more, you'll make more money.

3. Where will you go if you get time off?

4. What'll Ed do if he quits his job?

5. If she has a baby, will she work?

6. My boss gets angry if I am late.

TCD4, 30 **B** **LISTEN** again and repeat.

---

4 LISTEN and read.

A: Why are you so busy lately?

B: I'm trying to build a stronger résumé, so I've been taking a professional development course. To cover the costs, I've been working extra hours, too.

A: You must be tired.

B: Well, I have to work hard if I want to reach my goals.

A: But if you work this hard, you need to relax, too! We should get together if you have time this weekend.

B: <u>You're probably right</u>. I'll call you if I don't have to work.

A: Good.

5 PRACTICE the conversation from Activity 4 with a partner. Use the conversation strategy.

6 WHAT ABOUT YOU? ⃝Circle a goal below, then write your own ideas about what to do and how to relax as you work toward your goal.

Conversation Strategy
Expressing Agreement
You're probably right.
Good point!
I see what you mean.
I hadn't thought of that.

GOALS:
- conduct a job search
- get a promotion
- make more money
- learn a new skill

WHAT TO DO:

- _____

- _____

- _____

HOW TO RELAX:

- _____

- _____

7 ROLE-PLAY. Discuss your notes from Activity 6 with a partner. Then do a role-play, following the model in Activity 4. Talk about your goal and what you are doing. Your partner will give suggestions about how to relax.

Why have you been so busy lately?

I'm trying to learn some computer programming skills, so I've been taking some classes at the community college.

LESSON 4: Grammar and Vocabulary

 1 **GRAMMAR PICTURE DICTIONARY.** What would happen if these people made some changes at work? Listen and read.

TCD4, 32
SCD46

1
If Maria completed her accounting program, she could ask for a raise and **negotiate better benefits**. She could also be a strong **candidate** for other jobs.

2
If Margo had better **people skills**, she wouldn't have a hard time in her interviews. She would **make a better impression** with **interviewers**.

3
If Isaac spent more time **networking**, he could **have good connections** at many companies.

4
If the manager **encouraged teamwork**, the employees would have better ideas.

5
Eliza couldn't work with her friend if she **transferred** to a different **department**.

6
If Steven made a **career change**, he would become a chef. For now, he still likes his job in computer programming.

2 **READ** the sentences in Activity 1 with a partner.

3 **NOTICE THE GRAMMAR.** Circle *if* and underline the clause that follows. In the *if*-clause of each sentence, what verb form is used?

Present Unreal Conditional

Use the present unreal conditional to describe an imaginary situation and the result of that situation. Use the past tense in the *if-clause* and *would* or *could* in the main clause. The *if*-clause can come before or after the main clause without changing the meaning. When the *if*-clause comes first, use a comma.

Statements and Questions

If-Clause	Main Clause
If I *had* a car,	I *would drive* to work.
If Sharon *didn't have* a meeting,	she *could help* you.
If she *lost* her job,	what *would* she *do*?
If you *had* more money,	*could* you *quit* your job?

With present unreal conditionals, it is correct to use *were* instead of *was* for *I, he, she, it*, and singular nouns. However, *was* is commonly used in spoken English.

Example: If I **were / was** better at my job, I could get a promotion.

4 **COMPLETE** the present unreal conditional sentences with the correct form of the verbs in parentheses.

1. If Oscar _____*had*_____ (have) more time, he _____*would update*_____ (update) his résumé.

2. If Anna _____ (become) a manager, she _____ (encourage) teamwork.

3. Luz _____ (negotiate) better benefits if she _____ (have) better people skills.

4. If Alex _____ (make) a better first impression, he _____ (be) more successful at networking.

5. Joseph _____ (be) a stronger candidate for the job if he _____ (complete) his business program.

6. Sam _____ (transfer) to the sales department if he _____ (has) better connections with the department interviewers.

5 **WHAT ABOUT YOU?** Complete the sentences about yourself.

1. If I were a manager, I _____.

2. I _____ if I had more money.

3. If I _____ I would have more time.

4. I would make a career change if _____.

5. If I went back to school, I _____.

6. If I were the mayor, I _____.

7. If I were a language teacher, I _____.

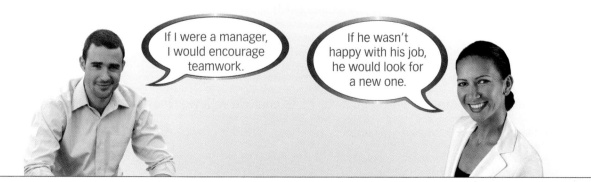

If I were a manager, I would encourage teamwork.

If he wasn't happy with his job, he would look for a new one.

LESSON 5: Grammar Practice Plus

TCD4, 33

1 **LISTEN** to the conversation between two interviewers, and look at the résumé for Steven. Put a check ☑ by the sections that are strengths. Circle the sections that are weaknesses.

> **STEVEN J. HOPKINS**
> 1734 MAPLE LANE
> SALT LAKE CITY, UTAH 84600
> 801-555-7896
>
> ✓ WORK EXPERIENCE
> 2003–Present   Senior Sales Representative, BusinessPro International
> 1998–2003   Sales Representative, Superior Business Consultants
>
> EDUCATION
> 1999   Certificate in Business Management   City College of Franklin
> 1998   Associate Degree, Business   Clarksville Community College
>
> SKILLS
> Microsoft Office and Macintosh computer programs, computer networking,
> interpersonal relations, finance

2 **LISTEN** again. Complete the evaluation form by checking ☑ Steven's strengths and weaknesses. Then write a comment and a recommendation.

Position: *Team Manager*			Interviewer name: *Lilia Smith*
Applicant name: *Steven J. Hopkins*			Interview date: *Dec. 5*

Area	Strength	Weakness	Comments:
Work experience			
Education and training			
Technical skills			
People skills			
Leadership skills			
Teamwork			
Recommendation			

3 **WRITE.** If you were Steven, what would you do to improve your weaknesses? Write at least three things.

Example: *If I were Steven, I would complete a continuing education course in management.*

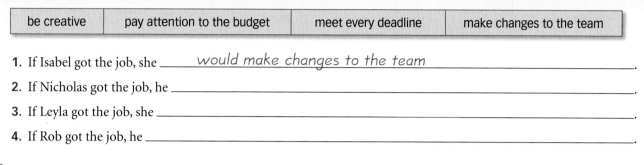

4 LISTEN to the interviews. Write one thing each person says he or she would do for the company. Use the ideas below.

TCD4, 34

| be creative | pay attention to the budget | meet every deadline | make changes to the team |

1. If Isabel got the job, she _____ *would make changes to the team* _____.

2. If Nicholas got the job, he _____.

3. If Leyla got the job, she _____.

4. If Rob got the job, he _____.

5 WRITE answers to the questions. Then compare your answers with a partner's.

1. 1. What would the other employees do if Isabel got the job?

   If Isabel got the job, the other employees would be afraid of getting fired.

2. What would the managers do if Nicholas got the job?

3. What would happen to the projects if Leyla got the job?

4. What would Rob's family do if he got the job?

5. Who would you hire if you were the interviewer?

Math: Bar Graph and Percentages

READ the information in the graph. Match the phrases with the correct information.

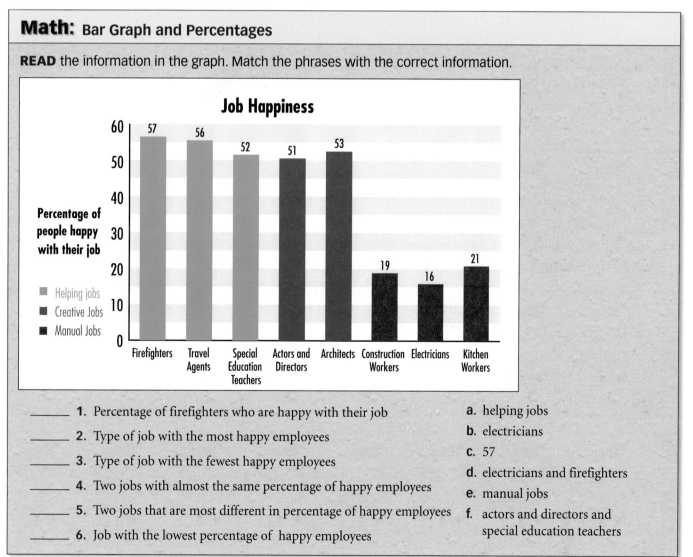

_____ 1. Percentage of firefighters who are happy with their job

_____ 2. Type of job with the most happy employees

_____ 3. Type of job with the fewest happy employees

_____ 4. Two jobs with almost the same percentage of happy employees

_____ 5. Two jobs that are most different in percentage of happy employees

_____ 6. Job with the lowest percentage of happy employees

a. helping jobs

b. electricians

c. 57

d. electricians and firefighters

e. manual jobs

f. actors and directors and special education teachers

LESSON 6: Reading

1 **THINK ABOUT IT.** What should someone do to prepare for a job interview? List three things.

1. _____

2. _____

3. _____

2 **BEFORE YOU READ.** Scan the article on the next page. Look at the headings. How many tips does the article give?

Reading Strategy Summary
Scan for specific information.
Use context to guess the meaning of new words.
Identify issues and advice.

3 **READ** the article. (Circle) each issue and <u>underline</u> the advice given.

4 **AFTER YOU READ.**

A. **ANSWER** the questions.

1. What is the main idea of this article?
2. What suggestions does the article make about how to dress for an interview?
3. What is one kind of research you should do before an interview?
4. What should you talk about in an interview if you are making a career change?
5. How can networking help you get a job?
6. What does the phrase *sell yourself* mean?

> **READING FOCUS: Identify issues and advice**
>
> Some reading texts tell about issues and ways to address the issues. As you read an article, notice issues that are mentioned. Find the advice that is given for each issue.

B. **COMPLETE** a T-chart. Write issues and advice from the article.

Issues	Advice
You want to look your best.	Make sure your clothes are neatly pressed. Wear simple dark-colored clothing.

C. **VOCABULARY.** Use context clues to help understand meaning. Find each idiom below in the article. Reread the paragraph. Then match the idiom with its meaning.

_____ 1. put your best foot forward   **a.** to say something nice about someone

_____ 2. stand out from the crowd   **b.** to stop you from doing something

_____ 3. put in a good word   **c.** to make the best impression you can

_____ 4. get in your way   **d.** be noticed more than the other people

How to Have a Successful Interview

Getting ready for a job interview can be tough. Sometimes you get nervous, and you may not put your best foot forward. If you want to make a great impression on the interviewer, you can
5 follow these tips.

Dress to Impress

Naturally, you will want to look your best. Make sure your clothes are neatly pressed. Many employers like a clean-cut* look, so you might
10 "want to wear dark-colored, simple clothing and little jewelry.

Show You Care

Potential* employers are impressed when you are interested and know something about the
15 company. Show them that this opportunity is more than "just a job" for you.

Know the Company

Prepare by doing research before the interview. Take the initiative and find out more about the
20 company. Read their website, and prepare a list of questions to ask about the company or the job.

Relate Your Experiences

Changing careers can be difficult. You may feel like no one will give you a chance in a new kind of
25 job. If you are making a career change, be prepared to tell how your skills and experiences will fit with the new career. If you want to become a landscaper, you can tell your interviewer about the gardens you designed for your neighbors. If
30 you hope to become a travel agent, you can tell how your previous* job at a resort hotel taught you about travelers.

Use Your Connections

You may ask yourself, "How can I stand out
35 from the crowd?" Don't forget to take advantage of* your networking connections. If you know someone in the company, you may have a better chance of being hired. Ask your acquaintance* to put in a good word for you!

40 ### Sell Yourself

Finally, don't let shyness get in your way. Sometimes job-seekers* think that they should not brag*. A job interview is your time to tell about why you are a good worker and why the company
45 should hire you. Sell yourself! You don't want to say to yourself after the interview, "If I had another chance, I could do better." Tell the interviewer about your good qualities.

Good luck!

---

clean-cut (adj.): looking neat, clean, and respectable

potential (adj.): possible

previous (adj.): former; in the past

take advantage of (idiom): use for your benefit

acquaintance (n.): friend or somebody that you know

job-seekers (n.): people who are looking for jobs

brag (v.): to talk proudly about what you have done

LESSON 7: Writing

1 **THINK ABOUT IT.** What jobs have you had in the past? What skills did you learn at each job? What were your achievements at each job? Tell a partner.

2 **BEFORE YOU WRITE.**

A. MAKE NOTES about your skills and achievements or awards at work, at school, or in other activities.

My Skills	My Achievements/Awards

> **WRITING FOCUS: Give specific details**
>
> When you write a résumé, it is important to include specific details about your experience, education, and qualifications.

B. READ part of a résumé that a job-seeker wrote. What facts does she state? What details does she give to support the facts?

MONROE COUNTY HOSPITAL   June 2008 – March 2009
Volunteer, Children's Unit

- Assisted nurses with childcare tasks: read aloud, played games, transported children

- Helped hospital guests: directed visitors to rooms, checked identification

- Completed administrative work: filed paperwork, updated charts, stocked supplies

> **WRITING FOCUS: Use résumé style**
>
> Begin your résumé with a heading that includes your name, address, telephone number, and email address.
>
> Most résumés use phrases rather than complete sentences. Compare:
>
> > Complete sentence: *I won the award for Employee of the Month.*
> >
> > Phrase: *Won award for Employee of the Month*
>
> Résumés also use bulleted lists instead of paragraphs.

3 **WRITE** your résumé. Follow the steps and the example outline below.

1. Write a heading with your name, address, telephone number, and email address.
2. Write the name of each place you worked or volunteered.
3. Write your job title and the dates that you worked or volunteered there.
4. Write about your duties and responsibilities. Tell facts and give evidence.
5. Write the name of each school you attended. List any degrees or certificates you have.

Name
Address
Phone number
Email address

PROFESSIONAL EXPERIENCE

Business or place   Dates
Job title
• Duties and responsibilities
•
•

Business or place   Dates
Job title
• Duties and responsibilities
•
•

EDUCATION

School   Degree
School   Degree

---

4 **AFTER YOU WRITE.**

A. **EDIT** your résumé. Ask yourself these questions.

1. Did I include every job and every school?
2. Is the information in the right order?
3. Did I give facts and evidence?
4. Did I use phrases and bulleted lists?
5. Is the spelling correct? Check the words in a dictionary if you are not sure.
6. Is the punctuation correct? Check commas, apostrophes, and periods.

B. **REWRITE** your résumé. Make revisions and corrections.

C. **DISCUSS** your résumé with a partner. Talk about how you can make the résumé stronger. Did you describe your duties clearly? Is there enough evidence to support your facts?

Career Connection

1 **THINK ABOUT IT.** Look at the picture. What do you think is happening? Do you think Sara knows the man who is interviewing her? Why or why not?

2 **LISTEN** to the interview between Sara, a part-time restaurant employee, and her supervisor, Mr. Wilson. Does Sara sound confident when she discusses the following topics, or a little uncomfortable? Write **C** for *confident,* or **U** for *uncomfortable* for each.

TCD4, 35

1. _____ Educational background   4. _____ Retirement

2. _____ Work experience   3. _____ Vacation and sick pay

3. _____ Salary

3 **DISCUSS.** Look at the vocabulary below. How important are these benefits to you? Number them in order of importance (1–5). Compare your list with a partner's.

_____ Health insurance / Dental care   _____ Personal leave / Sick leave

_____ Retirement plan   _____ Flexible schedule

_____ Vacation time

4 **ROLE-PLAY.** Look at these examples of language Sara used when she was talking with Mr. Wilson. With a partner, use the list you made in Activity 3 to practice negotiating a better benefits package.

> *I was wondering if …*   *I was wondering about …*
>
> *I guess what I'm saying is …*   *I was hoping it would be possible to …*

Sara: I was hoping it would be possible to count my three years of part-time work here towards the extra week of vacation time.

5 **WHAT ABOUT YOU?** What kind of job would you like to have five years from now? Would this job be a promotion for you, a career change, or the same job you have now? What could you do in the next five years to get a promotion, or better benefits? Talk with a partner.

Check Your Progress!

Skill	Circle the answers.	Is it correct?
A. Use real conditionals.	**1.** If I help her, she will **get / gets / got** a promotion. **2.** If she **arrive / arrives / will arrive** early, what will she do? **3.** My boss gets mad if I **turned / turn / will turn** something in late. **4.** Do your coworkers mind if you **leave / left / will leave** early?	☐ ☐ ☐ ☐

Number Correct | 0 | 1 | 2 | 3 | 4

Skill	Circle the answers.	Is it correct?
B. Use present unreal conditionals.	**5.** If Ed **will have / has / had** more money, he could quit his job. **6.** I could get a promotion if I **will take / take / took** more initiative. **7.** **Will / Did / Would** you apply for that job if you had the right skills? **8.** What **would / did / will** you do if your boss fired you?	☐ ☐ ☐ ☐

Number Correct | 0 | 1 | 2 | 3 | 4

Skill	Circle the answers.	Is it correct?
C. Talk about jobs and performance.	**9.** Could you help me **conduct / pursue** a job search? **10.** You should be assertive and **make / take** initiative more often. **11.** I need to **pursue / update** my résumé before I apply for a job. **12.** Would you **tell / give** me some feedback on my résumé?	☐ ☐ ☐ ☐

Number Correct | 0 | 1 | 2 | 3 | 4

Skill	Circle the answers.	Is it correct?
D. Talk about careers and skills.	**13.** I'm not happy. I want to **transfer / negotiate** to a new department. **14.** I don't want the **interviewers / connections** to think I'm shy. **15.** If you're friendly, you'll **have / make** a better impression. **16.** The new manager is encouraging **benefits / teamwork** in the department.	☐ ☐ ☐ ☐

Number Correct | 0 | 1 | 2 | 3 | 4

COUNT the number of correct answers above. Fill in the bubbles.

Chart Your Success					
Skill	Need	Okay	Good	Very Good	Excellent!
A. Use real conditionals.	⓪	①	②	③	④
B. Use present unreal conditionals.	⓪	①	②	③	④
C. Talk about jobs and performance.	⓪	①	②	③	④
D. Talk about careers and skills.	⓪	①	②	③	④

LESSON 1: Grammar and Vocabulary

1 **GRAMMAR PICTURE DICTIONARY.** What are people's plans? Listen and read.

TCD4, 36
SCD47

1

A: I'm going to be attending a business presentation next Wednesday. Do you want to come?

B: Oh, sorry. Next week, I'll be sightseeing in California. I'm **accompanying** my aunt.

2

A: What are you working on?

B: I'm going to be **coordinating** the **campaign** for Lina Hancock. She's a **candidate** for city mayor this year.

3

A: Why is Natalie taking so many business classes?

B: In a few years, she's going to be **taking over** her parents' business. She'll be **running** the finances and marketing, so she has a lot to learn.

4

A: I'm **selecting** my classes for next semester. Can you help me? Which classes are you taking?

B: Next semester? I won't be taking any classes! I'm going to be **enjoying** a semester off from school.

2 **PRACTICE** the conversations in Activity 1 with a partner.

3 **NOTICE THE GRAMMAR.** Underline *will be* and *be going to be* in the conversations above. Circle the verbs after *be* that end in *-ing*. Double underline the time phrases.

Future Continuous

Use the future continuous to talk about something that will be in progress in the future, or will happen over a period of time in the future.

Statements

Subject	*will / be going to*	*be*	Verb + *ing*	Time Expression
I	will		*teaching* the workshop	this semester.
David	will not / won't	be	*taking* the online course	next week.
You	are going to		*giving* the presentation	tomorrow.

Questions

(Question word +) *will*	Subject	*be*	Verb + *ing*	Time Expression
Will	I	be	*teaching* the workshop	tonight?
Where will	you		*giving* the presentation	on Sunday?

(Question word +) *be*	Subject	*going to be*	Verb + *ing*	Time Expression
Are	you	going to be	*teaching* the workshop	this weekend?
Why is	he		*taking* the online course	this month?

> Use time phrases to state or ask specifically when something will be happening.
> Jason will be attending the workshop *at the end of the month*.
> Are you going to be taking an English class *next semester*?

---

4 **COMPLETE** the sentences with the future continuous using the words in parentheses.

1. Next week, Claire _____*will be enjoying*_____ (will / enjoy) her vacation in Hawaii.

2. Steven _____ (be going to be / accompany) Michael on his campaign next month. Michael is a candidate for senator.

3. Next month, Rosa _____ (will / take over) a project from her sister. She _____ (be going to be / coordinate) an anniversary party for her parents.

4. Russ and Kathie _____ (will / sightsee) in Alaska in June.

5. In three years, Chris _____ (will / run) the company by himself.

6. This afternoon, the students _____ (be going to be / select) a gift for their advisor who is retiring.

5 **WHAT ABOUT YOU?** What will you be doing in the future? Write sentences about yourself. Use the future continuous. Then read your sentences to a classmate.

> Next week, I'll be studying for my final test.

1. Next week, I . . .
2. Next month, I . . .
3. In a year, I . . .
4. In five years, . . .

LESSON 2: Grammar Practice Plus

1 COMPLETE. Read this email to a Pleasant City administrator. Complete the email with the future continuous with *will*.

To: jbradley@pleasantcity.gov
From: asmith@mpcp.org
Date: 10/09/08
Subject: Let's work together!

One Day at a Time
Making Pleasant City Pleasant

Dear Mr. Bradley:

As we all know, the quality of life in Pleasant City has declined* in recent years. You are a candidate for mayor of Pleasant City, so I wanted to write you about an organization called "Making Pleasant City Pleasant." Next month, I (1)_____ (take over) the leadership of this organization. "Making Pleasant City Pleasant" works hard to improve our city, and we would love to see the city administration get involved.* Later this year, we (2)_____ (coordinate) a fundraiser for food and shelter for homeless families, and we (3)_____ (offer) reading classes to children and adults. Can you contribute* any supplies to our programs? Or can you help us acquire the materials for our classes? We can accomplish so much if we cooperate.* Ten years from now, I think our citizens (4)_____ (enjoy) their lives here in Pleasant City and the government (5)____ (run) the city well. But this will happen only if we work hard now. I look forward to hearing from you.

Sincerely,

Allison Smith

---

declined: decreased in quality

get involved: find ways to participate

contribute (something): give or donate money or supplies

cooperate: work together for a common goal or purpose

2 WRITE. Brainstorm ideas for Pleasant City's plan for city improvement. Write an idea for each year.

YEARLY FOCUS	PLAN
Next year — Traffic	We will be offering new solutions for public transportation problems.
In 2 years — Pollution	
In 3 years — Crime	
In 4 years — Education	
In 5 years — Our Citizens	

3 **TALK** about the picture. What will life in Pleasant City be like in five years? What will people be doing?

4 **WRITE** an article for the "Making Pleasant City Pleasant" website. Write more predictions about Pleasant City in five years. Use vocabulary from this unit and your own ideas.

5 **WHAT ABOUT YOU?** What are some problems in your community, your city, or your country? What will be different in the future? Talk with a partner about what you think citizens and leaders will be doing in the future.

LESSON 3: Listening and Conversation

1 **LISTEN** to the question. Then listen to the conversation with the candidate for mayor of Pleasant City. Listen to the question again. Fill in the correct answer. Replay each item if necessary.

1. Ⓐ Ⓑ Ⓒ   4. Ⓐ Ⓑ Ⓒ

2. Ⓐ Ⓑ Ⓒ   5. Ⓐ Ⓑ Ⓒ

3. Ⓐ Ⓑ Ⓒ   6. Ⓐ Ⓑ Ⓒ

2 **LISTEN** to the candidate again. Put the correct number in the box on the campaign button.

TCD4, 43

Free health exams for the elderly!

Help your neighbors. Give to the poor!

Let's help keep the air clean!

Neighbors, keep our streets safe!

Our future is about public services!

Improve our schools today!

Pronunciation: Intonation and Emotion

TCD4, 44

Native speakers often use intonation to express emotion. Listen to the following examples. Notice how intonation changes the emotion expressed in each example.

I'm going to be coordinating the fundraiser.   **disappointment**

I'm going to be coordinating the fundraiser?   **surprise**

I'm going to be coordinating the fundraiser!   **excitement**

TCD4, 45 SCD48 **A** **LISTEN** to the statements. Circle the emotion that is expressed.

1. I'm going to be working all night.	disappointment	surprise	excitement
2. We'll only be in Houston for one day.	disappointment	surprise	excitement
3. Danny is going to be staying with me.	disappointment	surprise	excitement
4. They will be traveling with a baby.	disappointment	surprise	excitement

TCD4, 46 **B** **LISTEN** again and repeat.

TCD4, 47
SCD49

3 **LISTEN** to the conversation. Mr. Lewis is a candidate for mayor.

A: Mr. Lewis. Could you please explain your plans for improving education?

B: Yes, of course. Schools right now are too crowded. Teachers need more classrooms and supplies.

A: What do you plan to do about it?

B: If I am elected, the education committee and I are going to provide more supplies for teachers. We will also be coordinating our efforts to build two new schools in the area.

A: What about the cost?

B: We are going to study our budget very carefully. I also want to ask community businesses and organizations to contribute to the schools.

4 **PRACTICE** the conversation in Activity 3 with a partner. Then make a new conversation. Write the problem and some solutions below each picture. Then use the information to practice the conversation.

1.

Problem

[ ]

Solutions

[ ]

2.

Problem

[ ]

Solutions

[ ]

3.

Problem

[ ]

Solutions

[ ]

5 **INTERVIEW** three other classmates to find out their solutions to the problems in Activity 4.

6 **WHAT ABOUT YOU?** What will you be doing at different points in the future? Tell a partner.

1. A month from now
2. A year from now
3. Five years from now
4. Ten years from now

Five years from now I'll be working as an accountant.

LESSON 4: Grammar and Vocabulary

 1 **GRAMMAR PICTURE DICTIONARY.** Cutting Edge has many plans to improve employees' quality of life. Listen and read.

TCD4, 48
SCD50

1

Cutting Edge, Inc. is changing its policies to enhance the **quality of life** for its employees.

2

The company is offering gym memberships to **promote** better health and to **minimize stress** for employees.

3

To **emphasize** the importance of a good **balance** between work and home, the company is giving workshops on time management.

4

Cutting Edge, Inc. is making changes to **expand** its **efforts** to help the environment.

5

To **address the issue of** paper waste, Cutting Edge is putting recycling bins in each office.

6

The company is also purchasing new, energy-saving equipment to **avoid the problem of** high electricity costs.

2 **READ** the sentences in Activity 1 with a partner.

3 **NOTICE THE GRAMMAR.** Underline the main verbs and circle the infinitives.

Infinitives of Purpose

Use infinitives to give a reason for an action. The infinitive can come before or after the main clause, but it is more common to put the infinitive after the main clause. If the infinitive comes first, use a comma.

Action	Infinitive of Purpose
I run every day	*to lose* weight.
She rode her bike to work	*to save* money.
David is going to Miami	*to meet* with the company.

Infinitive of Purpose	Action
To keep warm in winter,	I wear a sweater in the house.
To emphasize being punctual,	my boss hung new clocks in the office.

To express a purpose, you can also use *in order* + infinitive. This is more common in formal language.

She rode her bike *in order to save* money.

In order to address the issue of recycling, the governor is proposing new laws.

4 **WRITE.** Use infinitives of purpose to combine the sentences.

1. Cutting Edge, Inc. is going to use email more often. The company wants to reduce the amount of paper it uses.

   Cutting Edge, Inc. is going to use email more often to reduce the amount of paper it uses.

2. Cutting Edge is allowing employees to work from home more often. It wants to minimize stress and help employees balance work and home.

3. The company is trying to enhance quality of life for employees now. It hopes to improve employee satisfaction.

4. Cutting Edge is using conference calls more often. The company intends to avoid the high cost of travel.

5. Vending machines are being replaced with a café that serves fresh fruit and vegetables. The management wants to promote better health for employees.

6. The managers are offering computer training classes. They plan to emphasize better use of technology.

5 **COMPLETE** the sentences with your own ideas. Then discuss with a partner.

1. Many people are exercising more *to improve their quality of life* .

2. Parents are reading food labels more carefully _____ .

3. Community members are donating money _____ .

4. In order to address the issue of pollution, _____ .

5. We should make changes now _____ .

6. To save money, _____ .

LESSON 5: Grammar Practice Plus

1 **LISTEN** to the radio report. Check ☑ the company that promises to make each change for its employees. Then listen again and write the reason the companies are making the changes.

AREA	Cutting Edge	Macro Comp	Go Auto	Zip Travel	WHY?
We are offering free gym memberships.			✓		to promote better health
We are allowing more flexible work hours.					
We are addressing the issue of manager-employee relations.					
We are holding more conference calls.					
We are investing in new training programs.					

2 **WRITE.** Use the chart above. Write sentences about what each company in Activity 1 is doing and why.

Example: *Go Auto is going to be offering gym memberships to promote better health for its employees.*

Math: Reading Pie Charts

READ. Pie charts show comparisons among items. The charts below show how employees felt about the changes their companies made. Match each company with a description. Write the correct letters on the lines.

1. _____ Most of their employees thought this company was not successful.

2. _____ and _____ Most of their employees thought the company was very successful.

3. _____ Half of their employees thought the company was successful.

4. _____ One quarter of the employees thought the company was unsuccessful.

Employees' Opinions about Their Companies

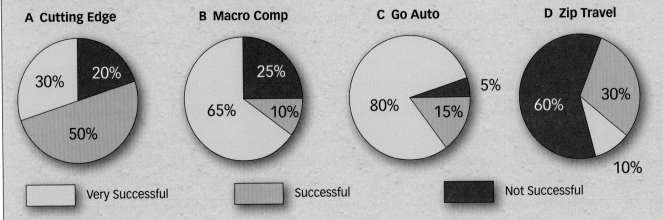

A Cutting Edge — 20%, 30%, 50%
B Macro Comp — 25%, 10%, 65%
C Go Auto — 5%, 15%, 80%
D Zip Travel — 30%, 60%, 10%

☐ Very Successful   ▦ Successful   ■ Not Successful

Infinitives That Follow Adjectives

Use an adjective with an infinitive to describe feelings about an action or the quality of an action.

Adjectives	Examples of Adjective + Infinitive
happy	I'm **happy to work** here.
thrilled	She was **thrilled to start** her new job yesterday.
pleased	I'm **pleased to meet** you.
surprised	They were **surprised to find out** about her promotion.
discouraged	He would be **discouraged to know** he didn't pass the test.
fun	It would be **fun to go** to dinner with you.
easy	It will be **easy to call** my sister in Japan.
difficult	It's **difficult to balance** work and home responsibilities.

3 **WRITE** about the people below. How does the person feel about the company change in Activity 1? Are they happy or unhappy to support the changes at the company where they work? Why? Read your sentences to a partner.

Example: *Tina works for Zip Travel. She loves to travel, so she is discouraged to find out about the new company travel policy. She's unhappy to be traveling less often. It's easy to find a new job in the travel business, so she's going to interview at some other travel agencies.*

1. Sara / Go Auto / runner

2. Jimmy / Cutting Edge / family and friends in a different country

3. Mark / Zip Travel / father of three

4 **ROLE-PLAY** a conversation between a person in Activity 3 and a coworker. Use the example as a model.

A: Did you hear about the new company policy?

B: Yeah, I sure did.

A: Aren't you excited?

B: Are you kidding? It's difficult to spend more time in the office. I would be happy to travel all the time.

A: Oh . . . for me, I wouldn't like to travel because it takes me away from my family. I like to spend more time at home.

LESSON 6: Reading

1 THINK ABOUT IT. How often do you think about the future? Do you make plans about what to do with your life? How far in the future do you plan for—next month, next year, the next five years? Tell a partner.

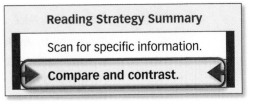

Reading Strategy Summary

Scan for specific information.

◄ **Compare and contrast.** ►

2 BEFORE YOU READ. Scan the personal statements on the next page. <u>Underline</u> key information about these people's plans.

3 READ the personal statements. Think about Terry and Perla. How are their goals and lives similar or different? Do they have similar or different goals and lives? Tell a partner.

4 AFTER YOU READ.

A. TALK with a partner. Take turns asking and answering the questions.

1. What are Terry's two main goals this year?
2. How is life changing for Terry's wife?
3. What will Terry do to help his wife and family?
4. What three things will Terry do to reduce stress?

5. Who are the members of Perla's family?
6. What is Perla going to do next month?
7. What are Perla's plans for work this year?
8. How does Perla feel about the upcoming year? Why?

B. COMPARE. Complete the chart below using information from the personal statements. Then discuss your answers with a partner and compare and contrast Terry and Perla's lives and goals. Use words and phrases such as *however, like, unlike, both, similar, different*.

> **READING FOCUS: Compare and contrast**
>
> When reading about two or more topics, think about how they are alike and different. Is the key information for each topic similar or different?

Examples:
Both Terry and Perla . . .   Like Terry, Perla . . .
Unlike Terry, Perla . . .   Terry and Perla are similar/different because . . .

		Terry	Perla
1.	More or less time spent at work in the upcoming year?	*less time*	
2.	Like working for the company?		
3.	Number of children?		
4.	Important to spend time with family?		
5.	Married?		
6.	Main goals?	1. 2.	1. 2.

PERSONAL STATEMENT: Terry Charles

This has been a hectic* year for me, so my main goals are to address the issue of stress and to improve my home life. This year, my wife will be running her own business. To promote the business, she will have to spend more time away from our three children. To minimize the stress on our family, I am going to be spending more time at home to help manage the household. Either I will be reducing my work hours to part-time, or I'll be telecommuting from home. I'm going to speak with human resources in the next few days to decide what will work best for both me and the company.

The doctor says I really need to work on my stress levels to avoid having a heart attack. A man my age needs to take care of his health. I've thought of many ideas to help reduce stress. This week, I'm purchasing a treadmill* so that I can get more exercise. I also will be spending more time relaxing. I work too much! I'm going to take the kids sightseeing around the city. There is so much to do here, but my wife and I have never had much time to explore it with the children. Finally, I am going to be donating some of my time to help out at the men's shelter* in our neighborhood. Giving back to the community is the best way for me to feel good about life and the future! It reminds me of how lucky I really am.

PERSONAL STATEMENT: Perla Ramos

I'm very excited about the upcoming* year. Now that my daughter is in kindergarten, I will be going back to school to get my degree. It has been hard being a single mom, but now I am looking toward the future. Next month, I will be selecting a college. My older sister will accompany me as I visit different schools. I couldn't have survived the last five years without her!

I also have a lot to accomplish* here at work. To expand my knowledge of the business, I am going to attend a technology convention this spring. To emphasize my commitment* to the company, I will be volunteering for new duties, too. I know it might be a lot to handle: starting school, doing more at work, and still taking care of my daughter. But I think it will be a very exciting time for me. I guess I will just need to practice coordinating all the parts of my life!

hectic (adj.): busy and stressful

treadmill (n.): an exercise machine for walking or running

shelter (n.): a place where people can stay overnight, have a meal, or get help

upcoming (adj.): next

accomplish (v.): do; complete a job or task

commitment (n.): strong desire to be together with someone or something

LESSON 7: Writing

1 THINK ABOUT IT. Have you ever decided to change something in your life, like learn something new, or stop a bad habit? What did you do? Did the change improve your life? Why or why not? Tell a partner.

2 BEFORE YOU WRITE.

> **WRITING FOCUS: Organize Ideas**
>
> When you need to write about a certain topic, you can begin with brainstorming. Write all of your ideas down quickly without thinking about whether they are good or bad. After you're done brainstorming, organize your ideas. You can organize ideas by topic, in time order, by comparing and contrasting, or in some other way. You may not always decide to use all of your ideas in your final draft.

A. READ the brainstorming notes one student wrote about the topic *Things I Want to Learn*. Then look at how he organized his ideas. Finally, read his finished paragraphs. Which brainstorming ideas were not used in the paragraphs?

Things I Want to Learn

golf – Paolo – summer

cooking class – next month

learn Spanish – next year?

Scuba diving – not sure when – next few years?

Hobby	How?	When?
cooking	class	next month
golf	Paolo will teach me.	this summer
Spanish	?	next year?
SCUBA diving	?	next few years

There are many hobbies I want to try or learn to do. The ones I'm most interested in are cooking, golf, and scuba diving. To improve my cooking, I'm going to take an Italian cooking class next month. My friend Paolo promised to teach me how to waterski, too. By the end of this summer, I'm going to be waterskiing like a pro!

Another thing I want to learn is SCUBA diving. Since I don't live near the ocean, I won't be SCUBA diving this year, but I hope to learn in the next few years.

B. BRAINSTORM AND ORGANIZE your ideas about the topic *How I want to improve my life.*

1. Choose three topics from the list below and write them in your notebook.
   Topics: Family, Health, Education, Leisure, Travel, Work, Community, Money

2. For each topic, brainstorm ideas and write them down. Think about your personal goals for each topic. Also think about when you might do each thing: in the next month, the next year, the next five years?

3. Complete the chart. Organize your ideas. Write one topic at the top of each column. Then write each of your ideas in the right place in the chart.

	Topic 1:	Topic 2:	Topic 3:
In the next month			
In the next year			
In the next five years			

3 **WRITE.** Choose one of the topics from your chart. Write 2-3 paragraphs that explain your goals for that topic over the next five years.

4 **AFTER YOU WRITE.**

A. **EDIT** your paragraphs.

1. Are there any sentences that don't belong?
2. Did you forget to include any important information?
3. Could you add details to help explain your ideas better?
4. Did you use future continuous correctly?
5. Did you use time phrases correctly?
6. Is your spelling, capitalization, and punctuation correct?

B. **REWRITE** your paragraph with corrections.

Career Connection

1 THINK ABOUT IT. How do you make important decisions in your life? Do you make lists, think things over by yourself, or talk with your family? Discuss in a group or with a partner.

2 READ about Jonathan, an employee in the field of Information Technology.

Jonathan has worked at IT-2000 for five years. He is not happy with his current job and recently applied for a position at another company: A-Z Internet. A-Z Internet has made an offer of employment to Jonathan. IT-2000 has made a counter-offer* of a $2,000 raise.

Now read the notes Jonathan wrote about the two jobs. As you read, circle the positive things about each company (pros) and underline the negative aspects (cons).

Issue	A-Z Internet, *Duluth, Minnesota*	IT-2000, *Miami, Florida*
Size / Growth potential	A-Z is a small company that will probably be doubling in size in the next two years. The company is going to be offering promotions to its best employees.	IT-2000 is a large company that probably will not be growing in the near future. I probably will not be receiving a promotion.
Technology	A-Z is going to be investing in state-of-the-art* technology. I would be thrilled to work with the new machines and software they'll be buying.	Management has no plans to expand the computer programming department, or to improve our current technology.
Management	I was pleased to learn that management emphasizes how to avoid major problems through careful planning.	I was discouraged to discover that management will not be addressing the issue of our outdated* computers.
Responsibilities Transfer of skills	If I accept A-Z's offer, I will have more responsibilities, like supervising others. I will be using skills I already have, but I'll also be learning new skills.	IT-2000 doesn't provide the opportunity to learn new skills or take on new challenges to its employees.
Salary / Benefits	$62,000 per year. 10 days vacation. Retirement package and health insurance are not great—the family plan is very expensive.	$70,500 per year, plus $2,000 raise. 15 days vacation. Excellent retirement package (already fully vested) and health insurance. Paid for my M.Sc. degree.

counter-offer (n.): an offer made by an employer in response to
   one from another company
state-of-the-art (adj.): the most current and advanced
outdated (adj.): not up-to-date

3 TALK with a partner about the pros and cons of the two positions above. What will happen if Jonathan takes the job at A-Z Internet? What will happen if he stays at IT-2000?

4 WHAT ABOUT YOU? Which is more important to you: growth potential, or benefits and salary? What issues would influence your decision to accept or turn down a job? Talk with a partner.

Check Your Progress!

Skill	Circle the answers.	Is it correct?
A. Use the future continuous.	**1.** In a month, we'll be **run** / **running** the company ourselves. **2.** They will **finishing** / **be finishing** the project next month. **3.** Am I **going to** / **going to be** sightseeing with the others? **4.** When are they going to be **giving** / **give** the presentation?	☐ ☐ ☐ ☐

Number Correct | 0 | 1 | 2 | 3 | 4

Skill	Circle the answers.	Is it correct?
B. Use infinitives of purpose.	**5.** I exercise every morning **to** / **for** lose weight. **6.** **To promote** / **Promote** exercise, the company will open a gym. **7.** We're making changes to **minimizing** / **minimize** stress. **8.** They use conference calls **to save** / **for saving** money.	☐ ☐ ☐ ☐

Number Correct | 0 | 1 | 2 | 3 | 4

Skill	Circle the answers.	Is it correct?
C. Talk about personal plans and goals.	**9.** Are you going alone, or will she be **accompanying** / **coordinating** you? **10.** I need to go online. I want to **select** / **campaign** my classes. **11.** Ann is going to be **taking under** / **taking over** her father's store. **12.** I'm going to be **running** / **enjoying** a long vacation next summer.	☐ ☐ ☐ ☐

Number Correct | 0 | 1 | 2 | 3 | 4

Skill	Circle the answers.	Is it correct?
D. Talk about business goals.	**13.** They want to expand their **efforts** / **issues** to have a strong company. **14.** I take vacations to **emphasize** / **minimize** stress for myself. **15.** The company emphasizes quality **for** / **of** life for its employees. **16.** To **promote** / **avoid** employee satisfaction, they gave the workers some time off.	☐ ☐ ☐ ☐

Number Correct | 0 | 1 | 2 | 3 | 4

COUNT the number of correct answers above. Fill in the bubbles.

Chart Your Success

Skill	Need Practice	Okay	Good	Very Good	Excellent!
A. Use the future continuous.	⓪	①	②	③	④
B. Use infinitives of purpose.	⓪	①	②	③	④
C. Talk about personal plans and goals.	⓪	①	②	③	④
D. Talk about business goals.	⓪	①	②	③	④

Grammar Reference Guide

Simple Present and Present Continuous Review

- Use the simple present to make general statements of fact and to talk about repeated actions or habits.
- Use the present continuous to talk about actions in progress right now, or actions that are temporary.

Simple Present

I **enroll** for classes every semester.

Do you **register** online?

He **doesn't study** on the weekends.

The office **accepts** online applications.

Twice a week, we **practice** pronunciation.

Where **do** they **study** at night?

Present Continuous

I'**m not using** the computer right now.

He **isn't eating** lunch now.

We'**re writing** an email to our teacher.

Is she **studying** for finals this week?

Are you **working** a lot these days?

Where **are** they **going**?

Time Expressions

Time expressions usually come at the beginning or the end of a sentence. If the time expression comes at the beginning, it is usually followed by a comma. If it comes at the end, do not use a comma.

Every day, she goes to class.

These days, I'm studying French.

She goes to class **every day.**

I'm studying French **these days.**

Correlative Conjunctions

Both . . . and, either . . . or, and *neither . . . nor* are correlative conjunctions. Use them to link similar types of phrases in a sentence.

Sam dislikes **both** algebra **and** accounting.

Both Jorge **and** Maria like algebra.

Erica takes **either** the bus **or** the train.

Either Ms. Jones **or** Mr. Lopez teaches accounting. I can't remember.

Paulo reads **neither** magazines **nor** newspapers.

Neither Wei **nor** Gina is in my nursing class.

Neither . . . nor is used more often in writing than in speaking.

Expressing Future Time with *Will*, *Be Going To*, and the Present Continuous

Use *will*, *be going to*, or the present continuous to talk about the future.

Use **will** to make plans, commitments, and offers at the moment of speaking.

> We**'ll work** on the applications tonight.
> I**'ll be** home at six o'clock every night.
> Sure, I**'ll help** you carry it.

Use **will** to ask for favors.

> **Will** you **help** me with this?
> **Will** you **study** with me tonight?

Use **will** to talk about definite future events or results.

> She **will** earn three credits for her class.
> If she takes this class, she**'ll** have enough credits to graduate.

Use **will** and **be going to** to make predictions about the future.

> They **will do** well on the test next week.   They**'re going to do** well on the test next week.
> The library **will be** full this weekend.   The library **is going to be** full this weekend.

Use the present continuous or **be going to** to talk about plans you've already made.

> A: What **are** you **doing** tomorrow?   A: What **are you going to do** tomorrow?
> B: I**'m studying** for my history test.   B: I'm **going to study** for my history test.

Use *be going to* when plans are already made, or something is sure to happen: *I'm going to attend class tomorrow*.

Use *will* when you're not sure if it will happen, or if it's only possible or probable: *I*

Past Time Clauses with *After, When, As Soon As, Before,* and *Until*

Join time clauses in the past to main clauses in the past to say when events happened. The time clause can come after or before the main clause. If it comes before the main clause, it has a comma.

Main Clause	Time Clause
Kristin followed up with the team	after she talked to her boss.
I listened to my voicemail	when I got to the office.
Did Andrew join the conference call	as soon as he left his other meeting?
Why did he accept the assignment	before he understood it?
Samuel and Tyler didn't ask for a day off	until they met their deadline.

Time Clause	Main Clause
After Kristen talked to her boss,	did she ask for a day off?
When Rachel got sick,	Chris covered for her.
As soon as Natalie listened to her voicemail,	she called her boss.
Before I followed up with the team,	I reviewed our schedule.
Until Andrea pulled together all her materials,	she couldn't make the presentation.

Simple Past and Present Perfect Review

Use the simple past to talk about events or actions that occurred and ended at a specific time in the past.

Simple Past

Adam **attended** several workshops *last year*.
Ed **didn't show** good leadership skills *yesterday*.
Did Mei **receive** a promotion *a month ago?*
Who **was** at the office party *last night?*
Kevin **worked** there *for nine years.*

Simple Past Time Expressions

a month / week / year ago
already
for (number) days / weeks / months / years
in 2007 / August
last week / month / year / Monday / summer
yesterday

Use the present perfect to talk about events or actions that:
- occurred at an unspecified time in the past.
- began in the past and continue to the present.

Present Perfect

Adam **has** *already* **attended** several workshops.
Ed **has shown** good leadership skills *so far.*
Has May *ever* **received** a promotion?
Have you **been** to any office parties *yet*?
They **haven't received** any new reports
　　since last year.
He **has** *never* **missed** a deadline.

Present Perfect Time Expressions

already
ever (in questions)
for a week / a month / six hours / ten years
since Tuesday / last month / year / summer / 2005
so far
yet (in questions and negatives)
never

Past Perfect

You can use the past perfect with the simple past to talk about two events in the past. Use the past perfect to show which event happened first. Use the simple past for the second event.

Subject	had (not)	Past Participle		Simple Past Time Clause
I		bought	tickets	*before* I *went* to the film festival.
They	had (not)	made	a reservation	*before* they *went* to the restaurant.
He		eaten	dinner	*when* the pizza *arrived.*

Use *already* or to emphasize that one event happened before another.

　　The film had *already* started when we arrived at the theater.

By the time means "some time before, but not after." When the phrase *by the time* is followed by the simple past, the next clause is often in the past perfect.

　　By the time we arrived at the film festival, the show had already started.

Past Perfect Continuous

The past perfect continuous describes an action that had been in progress before another event happened. We often use *for* to talk about how long the first event had been happening.

Past Perfect Continuous Statement				Time Clause (optional)
Subject	***had***	***been*** + Verb + ***ing***	***for*** + time	***when*** + **Subject** + **Simple Past**
I	had	been jogging	for an hour	*when* it started to rain.
They	had	been talking	for a while	*when* Tom showed up.

In addition to *when*, time expressions using *by the time, until,* and *by* are also common with the past perfect continuous..

By the time they arrived with the keys, we **had been waiting** in the cold for over 30 minutes.

Scott became a professional tennis player in 2005. *Until then,* he **had been working** at an amusement park near Chicago.

Of course Mike was tired when you got here! He**'d** already **been working** for six hours *by then.*

> The past continuous is often used instead of the past perfect continuous, especially when the order of events is clear to the listener.
> *I was standing in line when it started to rain.*

Past Modals: *Should (not) / Must (not)* + *have* + the Past Participle

Use a modal + *have* + past participle to express regret, give advice, and express certainty about things in the past.

Past Regret and Advice

Use *should / should not* + *have* + past participle to give better solutions (advice) or when you want to express a wish that the event had happened differently (regret).

Subject	Modal (not)	*have* + Past Participle	
I	should	have saved	more money. Now I'm broke.
You	shouldn't	have paid	your bill late. Now you have to pay a penalty.

Past Certainty

Use *must have* + the past participle to say you are sure or very certain that a past action happened or didn't happen.

Subject	Modal (not)	*have* + Past Participle	
Someone	must	have stolen	my credit card!
He / She	must not	have paid	the bill by the due date.

Tag Questions

To emphasize an idea, or to check or confirm your understanding of something, put a tag question at the end of the statement.

When the statement is **affirmative**, the tag is **negative**.

When the statement is **negative**, the tag is **affirmative**.

Be Careful!
With the subject pronoun *I*, we use *am* in the affirmative tag, but we use *are* in the negative tag. For example:
I'm not funny, **am** I?
I'm funny, **aren't** I?

	Statement + Question Tag
Simple Present	**It has** a great interest rate, **doesn't it**?
	You like that bank, **don't you**?
	My credit score isn't too low, **is it**?
Simple Past	**She made** the mortgage payment, **didn't she**?
	Paul didn't mail the check, **did he**?
Present Perfect	**They've been** here before, **haven't they?**
	He hasn't seen the budget, **has he**?
Modals	**Lisa should balance** her checkbook, **shouldn't she**?
	I shouldn't send my account number, **should I**?

Affirmative	Negative
Yes, it does.	No, it doesn't
Yes, I do.	No, I don't.
Yes, it is.	No, it isn't.
Yes, she did.	No, she didn't.
Yes, he did.	No, he didn't.
Yes, they have	No, they haven't.
Yes, he has.	No, he hasn't.
Yes, she should.	No, she shouldn't.
Yes, you should.	No, you shouldn't.

Active and Passive Voices (Simple Present and Simple Past)

Sentences in the active voice focus on the noun that does the action of the verb. Sentences in the passive voice focus on the noun that receives the action of the verb. Use the passive voice when you want to focus on the receiver of the action.

Active Voice

Subject	Active Verb	Object
Ted Lam	advises	the mayor.
The president	doesn't write	laws.
The governor	approved	the budget.
The mayor	didn't give	a speech.

Passive Voice

Subject	Passive Verb		by + Agent
	be	Past Participle	
The mayor	is	advised	by Ted Lam.
Laws	aren't	written	by the president.
The budgets	were	approved	by the governor.
A speech	wasn't	given	by the mayor.

In passive sentences, you can use *by* before the person or people who did the action (the agent). If you don't know who the agent is, or it's not important to mention the agent, don't use *by* + agent. For example:

The article about the governor was written by a local reporter.

A president is elected every four years.

Yes/No and Information Questions in the Passive Voice

Yes/No Questions

be	Subject	Past Participle		(by + Agent)
Was	the defendant	found	guilty?	
Are	attorneys	provided	to some defendants	by the court?

Information Questions

Question Word	be	Subject	Past Participle		(by + Agent)
What	was	the jury	asked	to do?	
Where	is	the defendant	taken	after the trial?	
When	were	you	chosen	to serve on the jury?	
Why	wasn't	the man	found	guilty	by the jury?
How	are	the decisions	made?		

Articles

Indefinite articles *a*, *an*, and *some* are used to talk about general or not specific things. The definite article *the* is used to talk about specific things or things already known by the listener or reader.

Indefinite Articles

Use indefinite articles to make general statements.

> *A gas leak* is very dangerous.

Use indefinite articles when you are not thinking of an exact person, place, or thing.

> I need *a new battery* for my phone.
> The repairman dropped *some tools* in the driveway.

Use *a* or *an* with singular count nouns. Use *a* before consonant sounds, and *an* before vowel sounds.

> a gas leak   a weak signal   an error   an estimate

Use *some* or no article with plural count nouns and with noncount nouns.

> (some) tools   (some) phones   (some) gas   (some) money

Definite Articles

Use the definite article *the* when you are discussing a specific person, place, or thing.

> Did you call *the repairman* again?
> *The men* on *the street* are checking *the power lines*.

Use *the* when a noun is talked about for the second time.

> They found a leak in the furnace last week. *The leak* had been there for a long time.

Use *the* with superlative adjectives.

> June wants *the best* cell phone she can buy.

Embedded Questions with *If, Whether,* and Other Question Words

> If the main clause begins like a question, use a question mark. *Do you know whether they allow pets?*

An embedded question is a question within a sentence. You can use an embedded question to ask for information politely or to say that you don't know something. Questions can be embedded (included in) a statement or a question.

Direct Questions		Sentences with Embedded Questions			
	Main Clause	**Question Word**	**Subject**	**Verb**	
Did they give their consent?	I wonder	if	they	gave	their consent.
Should I call a lawyer?	I'd like to know	whether	I	should call	a lawyer.
Who is the landlord?	I'm not sure	who	the landlord	is.	
What is the policy?	I don't know	what	the policy	is.	
Where did the landlord go?	Do you know	where	the landlord	went?	
How can I file a complaint?	Can you tell me	how	I	can file	a complaint?

Adjective Clauses with Relative Pronouns as Subjects

An adjective clause comes after a noun and gives additional information about the noun.

An adjective clause has its own subject and verb. The subject of an adjective clause can be a relative pronoun: *who* or *that*. An adjective clause always comes immediately after the noun it describes. When the noun is the subject of the main clause, the adjective clause comes *inside* the main clause.

Main Clause	Adjective Clause		Main Clause
Subject	**Relative Pronoun**	**Verb (+ Object)**	**Verb (+ Object)**
The **man**	who/that	robbed the store	was convicted.
The **car**	that	caused the collision	was red.

When the noun is the object of the main clause, the adjective clause comes *after* the main clause.

Main Clause		Adjective Clause	
Subject + Verb	**Object**	**Relative Pronoun**	**Verb (+ Object)**
I saw	the **man**	who/that	robbed the store.
The man drove	the **car**	that	caused the collision.

> The relative pronoun *which* is also used to refer to nouns. However, *that* is much more common.

Adjective Clauses with Relative Pronouns as Objects

A relative pronoun, *who*, *whom*, or *that*, can serve as the object of an adjective clause. When it is the object, it comes before the subject of the adjective clause. *Who* and *whom* refer only to people. *Whom* is more formal and is not as common as *who*. *That* refers to things and people.

Main Clause	Adjective Clause			Main Clause
	Relative Pronoun	Subject	Verb	
The **columnist**	who(m)/that	Lisa	met	was British.
The **story**	that	I	heard	isn't true.

Main Clause		Adjective Clause		
		Relative Pronoun	Subject	Verb
She's	the **columnist**	who(m)/that	Lisa	met.
That's	the **story**	that	I	heard.

When the relative pronoun is the *object* of the adjective clause, it can be omitted.

Correct ✔: She's the columnist **whom** Lisa met.

Correct ✔: She's the columnist Lisa met.

Gerunds as Objects of Prepositions

Form a gerund with the base verb + *-ing*. A gerund can follow *be* + adjective + preposition.

Subject	*be*	Adjective + Preposition	Gerund + Phrase
I	am not	nervous about	**driving** in the torrential rain.
She	was	serious about	**finding** shelter.
They	are	concerned about	**having** a blackout.
Sara	was	afraid of	**getting** lost in the storm.
The managers	were	interested in	**knowing** more.

Be careful! We cannot use infinitives instead of gerunds in this kind of sentence.

Correct ✔: I'm nervous about driving.

Incorrect ✗: I'm nervous about to drive.

Gerunds as Objects of a Verb + Preposition

A gerund can follow a verb + preposition.

Subject	Verb + Preposition	Gerund + Phrase
They	focus on	**saving** the environment.
I	plan on	**helping** the victims.
He	works on	**solving** the global warming problem.
She	cares about	**protecting** our water.
I	believe in	**helping** other people.
They	help with	**cleaning** up after a tornado.

Causative Verbs

Use a causative verb to show that someone caused, helped, or allowed something to happen.

Most common causative verbs are followed by object + infinitive. Some examples are *allow, enable, permit,* and *require.*

Subject	Verb	Object	Infinitive	
The teacher	requires	his students	to study	for an hour every day.
The parents	allow	their sons	to ride	bikes to school.

The causatives *let, make,* and *have* are always followed by object + base form.

Subject	Verb	Object	Base Form	
Janet	let	her daughter	take	the bus yesterday.
She	made	her son	study	for the exam.
Tom	had	the mechanic	change	the tires.

Help can be followed by object + infinitive or by object + base form.

The crossing guard *helps* pedestrians **to cross / cross** the street.

Passive Causatives *Get* and *Have*

Use *get* and *have* to show that someone made another person do something.

Subject	Verb	Object	Past Participle
I	had	my hair	done.
He	got	his car	repaired.
We	are having	our house	painted.

Verbs That Take Gerunds or Infinitives

Many verbs can take a gerund or an infinitive with no change in meaning. With some verbs, the meaning changes. The verbs *forget*, *remember*, and *stop* change in meaning with a gerund or infinitive.

Verb + Infinitive	Verb + Gerund
I always **stop to look** for traffic. (I stop doing one thing in order to do another.)	I **stopped driving** my son to school. (I used to drive him, but I don't anymore.)
I **remembered to bring** the letters. (I didn't forget to bring them.)	I **remember mailing** the letters. (I remember the act of mailing the letters.)
I **forgot to go** to the Visitor Center. (I intended to go, but I forgot.)	I'll never **forget seeing** it for the first time. (I will always remember this.)

Reported Speech

When you want to report what someone said, you can use reported speech. Use *said* to introduce the person's words and ideas. The verb usually changes when you use reported speech. *That* can be omitted in reported speech without changing the meaning.

Direct Quotation	Reported Speech
Simple Present ➡	**Simple Past**
Jan said, "I *have* some cabinet locks." She said, "You *can borrow* my cabinet locks."	Jan said (that) she *had* some cabinet locks. She said (that) I *could borrow* his cabinet locks.
Present Continuous ➡	**Past Continuous**
Ed said, "I'm *talking* to the doctor." Stan said, "We're *having* a fire drill."	Ed said (that) he *was talking* to the doctor. Stan said (that) they *were having* a fire drill.
Future with *Be Going to* and Will ➡	***Was/Were Going to* and *Would***
Joe said, "I'm *going to do* it later." May said, "I'll *help* you."	Joe said (that) he *was going to do* it later. May said (that) she *would help* me.
Simple Past ➡	**Past Perfect**
Ann said, "He *took* a safety class." David said, "You *weren't* too noisy."	Ann said (that) he *had taken* a safety class. David said (that) we *hadn't been* too noisy.
Present Perfect ➡	**Past Perfect**
Lee said, "I've *been* here before." Bo said, "He *hasn't asked* for my advice."	Lee said (that) he *had been* there before. Bo said (that) he *hadn't asked* for her advice.

You may have to change words like pronouns, possessives, and *here* to report the speaker's original meaning. For example: Jack said, "**My** brother and **I** have eaten **here** several times." Jack said (that) **he** and **his** brother had eaten **there** several times.

Reported Speech with *say* and *tell*

Use *said* or *told* to introduce a person's words and ideas. Follow *told* with a noun, a name, or an object pronoun (me, you, him, her, us, them).

Doris **said**, "The candy is a choking hazard.."
Doris **said** (that) the candy was a choking hazard.
Doris **told** her daughter (that) the candy was a choking hazard.
Doris **told** Mia (that) the candy was a choking hazard.
Doris **told** her (that) the candy was a choking hazard.

Phrasal Verbs

A phrasal verb is a two- or three-word verb that includes a main verb and a particle.
A particle looks like a preposition, but it isn't a preposition when it's part of a phrasal verb.

Some phrasal verbs cannot be separated in a sentence. If an inseparable phrasal verb takes an object, the object comes after the the phrasal verb.

Inseparable Phrasal Verbs

count on (trust)	I can **count on** her to buy healthy food.
fall for (believe)	Sue didn't **fall for** his excuses.
come back (return)	I **came back** from the gym at 5:30.
show up (arrive)	Ed **showed up** early for the yoga class.

Some phrasal verbs can be separable or inseparable. Notice the placement of the object.

Separable Phrasal Verbs

With most separable phrasal verbs, an object noun can come either after the particle, or between the verb and the particle. If the object is a pronoun, it must come between the verb and the particle.

use up (use completely)	I **used up** all my cell phone minutes this month. I **used** all my cell phone minutes **up** this month. I **used** them **up** this month.
look up (look for information)	We **looked up** the information online. We **looked** the information **up** online. We **looked** it **up** online.

With some phrasal verbs, the object must come between the verb and the particle.

talk into (convince)	Dan **talked** me **into** going for a run.
start over (begin again)	Let's **start** the exercise **over**.

Real Conditionals: Present and Future

Real conditionals describe a situation and the result of the situation. Real conditionals include an *if*-clause and a main clause. The *if*-clause can come before or after the main clause. When the *if*-clause is first, use a comma after it.

Statements and Questions about the Present

Use the present tense in the *if*-clause and in the main clause to describe something that usually happens in a specific situation.

If-Clause	Main Clause
If I **am** late,	my boss **gets** mad.
If Melissa **works** hard,	she **finishes** her tasks quickly.
If you **leave** early,	do your coworkers **get** angry?

Statements and Questions about the Future

Use the present tense in the *if*-clause and the future tense or a modal in the main clause to describe something that will happen in the future if something else happens first.

If-Clause	Main Clause
If Carlos **works** on his typing skills,	he's **going to get** a promotion.
If Melissa **doesn't check** her email,	she **won't get** the news from our meeting.
If he **gets** a raise,	he **can buy** a new car.
If we **don't turn in** the assignment,	what **will** the boss **say**?

Present Unreal Conditional

Use the present unreal conditional to describe an imaginary situation and the result of that situation. Use the past tense in the *if-clause* and *would* or *could* in the main clause. The *if*-clause can come before or after the main clause without changing the meaning. When the *if*-clause comes first, use a comma.

Statements and Questions

If-Clause	Main Clause
If I *had* a car,	I *would drive* to work.
If Sharon *didn't have* a meeting,	she *could help* you.
If she *lost* her job,	what *would* she *do*?
If you *had* more money,	*could* you *quit* your job?

With present unreal conditionals, it is correct to use *were* instead of *was* for *I, he, she, it*, and singular nouns. However, *was* is commonly used in spoken English.

Example: If I **were / was** better at my job, I could get a promotion.

Future Continuous

Use the future continuous to talk about something that will be in progress in the future, or will happen over a period of time in the future.

Statements

Subject	*will/be going to*	*be*	Verb + *ing*	Time Expression
I	will		*teaching* the workshop	this semester.
David	will not / won't	be	*taking* the online course	next week.
You	are going to		*giving* the presentation	tomorrow.

Questions

(Question word +) *will*	Subject	*be*	Verb + *ing*	Time Expression
Will	I		*teaching* the workshop	tonight?
Where will	you	be	*giving* the presentation	on Sunday?

(Question word +) *be*	Subject	*going to be*	Verb + *ing*	Time Expression
Are	you		*teaching* the workshop	this weekend?
Why is	he	going to be	*taking* the online course	this month?

Use time phrases to state or ask specifically when something will be happening.
Jason will be attending the workshop *at the end of the month*.
Are you going to be taking an English class *next semester*?

Infinitives That Follow Adjectives

Use an adjective with an infinitive to describe feelings about an action or the quality of an action.

Adjectives	Examples of Adjective + Infinitive
happy	I'm **happy to work** here.
thrilled	She was **thrilled to start** her new job yesterday.
pleased	I'm **pleased to meet** you.
surprised	They were **surprised to find out** about her promotion.
discouraged	He would be **discouraged to know** he didn't pass the test.
fun	It would be **fun to go** to dinner with you.
easy	It will be **easy to call** my sister in Japan.
difficult	It's **difficult to balance** work and home responsibilities.

Irregular Verbs

Have

Base Form	Simple Past	Past Participle	Base Form	Simple Past	Past Participle
be	was/were	been	keep	kept	kept
become	became	become	know	knew	known
begin	began	begun	leave	left	left
bleed	bled	bled	lend	lent	lent
break	broke	broken	lose	lost	lost
bring	brought	brought	make	made	made
buy	bought	bought	meet	met	met
choose	chose	chosen	pay	paid	paid
come	came	come	put	put	put
cost	cost	cost	read	read	read
cut	cut	cut	ring	rang	rung
do	did	done	run	ran	run
drink	drank	drunk	see	saw	seen
drive	drove	driven	sell	sold	sold
eat	ate	eaten	send	sent	sent
fall	fell	fallen	set	set	set
feel	felt	felt	shake	shook	shaken
fight	fought	fought	shut	shut	shut
find	found	found	sleep	slept	slept
forget	forgot	forgotten	speak	spoke	spoken
fry	fried	fried	speed	sped	sped
get	got	gotten	spend	spent	spent
give	gave	given	take	took	taken
go	went	gone	teach	taught	taught
grow	grew	grown	tell	told	told
have/has	had	had	think	thought	thought
hear	heard	heard	wear	wore	worn
hold	held	held	write	wrote	written
hurt	hurt	hurt			

Audio Script

Pre-Unit

LANGUAGE IN THE CLASSROOM   Activity 1 (Page 2)

missing

A: Hi. My name's Soo-hee.

B: Oh, hi. My name's Alex.

A: Nice to meet you, Alex. Where are you from?

B: From?...oh, yes. I'm from Russia. How about you?

A: I'm from Korea.

B: I see.

A: Hey, Marissa! Hi!

C: Hi, Soo-hee! How's it going?

A: Great. Marissa, this is Alex. He's from Russia.

C: Hi, Alex. Nice to meet you.

A: Nice to meet you, too, Marissa. Where are you from?

C: Me? Oh, I'm from Peru.

A: Oh.

C: Yeah. You're going to like it here. The class is great. The teacher is friendly…

A: Sounds good.

C: Yeah. So, why are you taking an English class, Alex?

B: Oh, well. I'm getting ready to take a big exam, so I can get a new job.

A: Oh, I see. I'm trying to get into the community college next year.

B: And how about you, Marissa?

Marissa: I need English for my job. I have to read and write a lot of email in English now, so…

Marissa: Here comes Mr. Davis. Great to have you here, Alex.

Alex: Thanks!

Unit 1

LESSON 2 Grammar Practice Plus Activity 2 (Page 8)

1. Carlos is in the business program at the community college. He is taking <u>accounting</u> and <u>business management</u>.

2. Rebecca, his wife, also attends the community college. She is in the <u>nursing</u> program. This semester, she is studying <u>Medical Assisting Skills,</u> and she's also taking Introduction to <u>Health Care online.</u>

3. Ana is a high school student, but she is already thinking about college. She's looking into <u>early childhood education</u>, <u>restaurant management</u>, and <u>hotel and hospitality</u>.

4. Luis is in middle school, but he likes to fix things. He's looking through two books—one about <u>electrical work</u> and one about <u>air conditioning science.</u>

5. Paulo is in elementary school, but he really likes cars and computers. He's looking at the pictures in a book about <u>auto body repair.</u> He also has a book about <u>computer</u> programming.

LESSON 3 Listening and Conversation Activity 1 (Page 10)

1. Why does Linda want to talk to her husband Tom about schedules?

   missing

   A: Hi, Tom.

   B: Hi, honey. How was your day?

   A: It was good. I'm registering for classes this week, so we need to talk about our schedules.

   B: Sure.

   Why does Linda want to talk to her husband Tom about schedules?

   A. She's worried about being too busy.

   B. She's registering for classes.

   C. She's happy about her work schedule.

2. What is Linda signing up for?

   A: So, you're taking a continuing education course on Tuesday and Thursday afternoons, right?

   B: That's right. So you need to pick Sam up from school on Tuesdays and Thursdays.

   A: Okay. I can do that. I'm signing up for an English class that meets on Monday and Wednesday nights.

   B: That's fine.

   What is Linda signing up for?

   A. a continuing education course

   B. an English class

   C. a class that meets Tuesday and Thursday nights

3. What online course is Linda looking into?

   A: I'm also looking into an online course in American history.

   B: That sounds interesting.

   A: Yes, I'm excited about taking it. It only meets once a week, but we have lots of work online. And it satisfies the history requirement for my program.

   B: Great.

   What online course is Linda looking into?

   A. an English class

   B. a class that satisfies a requirement for her program

   C. a class that sounds boring

4. What is the problem with the online course?

   A: When does the online course meet?

   B: It meets on Friday afternoons.

   A: Uh oh. You have to take Sam to his new swim class on Friday afternoons.

   What is the problem with the online course?

   A. It meets at the same time that Linda has her English class.

   B. It meets at the same time that Linda has to work.

   C. It meets at the same time that Linda has to take Sam to swim class.

5. What is Linda's problem?

   A: Oh no! I forgot about Sam's swim class!

   B: Can you take the online class at a different time?

   A: No, I can't. I'm working a lot right now, so I don't have a lot of flexibility in my schedule.

   What is Linda's problem?

   A. She doesn't have a lot of flexibility in her schedule.

   B. She wants to make plans for Saturdays.

   C. She can take the online course on a different day.

6. What does Tom say?

   A: Okay. I understand. Maybe Sam can take the bus to his swim class with his friends.

   B: Sure. He'll like that. Good idea.

   What does Tom say?

   A. Linda needs to change her schedule.

   B. Sam can play with his friends.

   C. Sam can take the bus.

Activity 2 (Page 10)   *missing*

A: Hi, Tom.

B: Hi, honey. How was your day?

A: It was good. I'm registering for classes this week, so we need to talk about our schedules.

B: Sure.

A: So, you're taking a continuing education course on Tuesday and Thursday afternoons, right?

B: That's right. So you need to pick Sam up from school on Tuesdays and Thursdays.

A: Okay. I can do that. I'm signing up for an English class that meets on Monday and Wednesday nights.

B: That's fine.

A: I'm also looking into an online course in American history.

B: That sounds interesting.

A: Yes, I'm excited about taking it. It only meets once a week, but we have lots of work online. And it satisfies the history requirement for my program.

B: Great. When does the online course meet?

A: It meets on Friday afternoons.

B: Uh oh. You have to take Sam to his new swim class on Friday afternoons.

A: Oh no! I forgot about Sam's swim class!

B: Can you take the online class at a different time?

A: No, I can't. I'm working a lot right now, so I don't have a lot of flexibility in my schedule.

B: Okay. I understand. Maybe Sam can take the bus to his swim class with his friends.

A: Sure. He'll like that. Good idea.

LESSON 5 Grammar Practice Plus Activities 2 & 3
(Page 14)

A: Rebecca, you are doing very well in our program.

B: Thanks, Ms. Jones. I'm really working hard.

A: I can tell! You have very good grades for many of your courses.... in Patient Information and Medical Assisting Skills II, especially. Nice work!

B: Thanks.

A: You still have a few more courses to take though. Are you going to take Medical Office Procedures this summer?

B: Yes, I'm enrolling in that course for summer, then Medical Technology in the fall.

A: Good...You will need those before your internship. And Mrs. Carson is teaching that this summer.

B: Oh, great! She's my favorite professor. I'm looking forward to it.

A: Then, let's see.... you will need Medicine Doses and your internship.

B: Yes, I'll take Medicine Doses in the fall, too. Then I'm going to do my internship in the spring. How am I going to find my internship?

A: I'll help you with that. And it'll be your last requirement for the program!

B: I know! I'm going to finish in only three more semesters.

A: Congratulations! You're going to really enjoy your work as a medical assistant.

CAREER CONNECTION Activities 2 & 3 (Page 20)

A: Hi, Sally. How did registration go yesterday?

B: Great! But I think we're going to need another new teacher.

A: Another one?

B: Yes. We had several new enrollments yesterday. Eight new children will start here on Monday.

A: Wow! That's great.

B: Yes. Six of them are four-year-olds. And there were two toddlers: a one-year-old and a two-year old.

A: Oh, that's excellent news!

B: I agree. But we have a problem…

A: What's that?

B: Well, there aren't enough teachers for all the children. I just looked at the schedule. Jenny is going on vacation for two weeks.

A: Oh, yes, that's right. Well, let's see…we'll have 78 children in the program on Monday. We have five teachers. So we'll need to hire one more teacher, and we'll also need to find someone to cover Jenny's class. Any ideas?

B: Hmm… Maybe we could ask Regina to cover Jenny's class?

A: That's one solution. Unfortunately, Regina doesn't have much experience with three- and four-year-olds. She's been here for two years, but she's still working on her degree.

B: True. You're right, she isn't qualified yet, and she only has experience with toddlers. But she is organized and very patient. She could probably take care of the three- and four-year-olds for a couple of weeks.

A: Hmm… Is there anyone else?

B: Maybe Marcia. She has worked here for three years now. She's very flexible and talented. She also has a bachelor's degree in Early Childhood Education.

A: OK. Please ask both Marcia and Regina. I'm sure one of them can help. And we still need one more new teacher.

B: Well, we're in luck. Two women applied here last week, and one of them seems really good. Her name is Cynthia. I put her resume on your desk. She has a master's degree in education and five years of teaching experience. She's also creative and artistic.

A: Wow, she sounds great! I'll call her to set up an interview.

B: OK, I'll speak with Marcia and Regina and see who can help take care of the three- and four-year-olds while Jenny's on vacation.

Unit 2

LESSON 2 Grammar Practice Plus Activity 2 (Page 24)

1. Luke is careful with his papers and assignments. He's very organized.
2. Thomas is tired of his job. He's burned out.
3. Lorenzo has a lot of work to do. He's really overwhelmed.
4. Silvia always arrives at her meetings on time. She's very punctual.
5. Jenny often takes care of her coworkers. She's very helpful.
6. Donna has a lot of new ideas. She's very creative.

LESSON 3 Listening and Conversation Activity 1 (Page 26)

1. What are the people talking about?
   A: Hey, Ana.
   B: What's up, Chris?
   A: Did you complete that project for Sam this morning?
   B: No, I didn't, but I'm going to finish it after I eat lunch.
   A: Okay, thanks!

   What are the people talking about?
   A. a project
   B. a phone call
   C. a meeting

2. When did Natalie call Chris?
   A: Natalie, did you call Chris this morning?
   B: Yes, I did.
   A: Great, thanks. When did you call?
   B: Um . . . about 9:30 A.M. I called as soon as I got to the office.
   A: Perfect.

   When did Natalie call Chris?
   A. in the evening
   B. in the morning
   C. in the afternoon

3. What does Tyler tell the speaker?
   A: Hi, Tyler. How's your day going?
   B: Just fine! What can I do for you?
   A: I was just wondering . . . did you schedule the meeting for next week?
   B: Yes. I scheduled the meeting as soon as I talked to Mrs. Jones.
   A: Thanks!

   What does Tyler tell the speaker?
   A. He scheduled the meeting after he talked to Mrs. Jones.
   B. He scheduled the meeting before he went home.
   C. He forgot to schedule the meeting.

4. Why is Natalie tired?
   A: Natalie, are you okay?
   B: I'm just tired.
   A: Did you complete the project you were working on?
   B: Yes, I did, but I didn't go to bed last night until I finished it. I went to bed at 4:00 A.M!
   A: Now you need to ask for a day off.

Why is Natalie tired?
A. She stayed up until 4:00 working on a project.
B. She didn't finish the project.
C. She took a day off.

5. Why didn't Paul cover for his coworker?
A: Paul, did you cover for me last night?
B: I'm so sorry. No, I didn't. I got an emergency call from my sister after you left.
A: Oh, no!!
B: I'm really sorry, but I had to go help her.
A: Well, I understand. It's okay.

Why didn't Paul cover for his coworker?
A. He forgot.
B. He had to go to class.
C. He had to help his sister.

6. When will Lorenzo follow up with Andrew?
A: Lorenzo, did you follow up with Andrew about his assignment?
B: Um . . . no . . . What assignment?
A: The sales report?
B: Oh, right! I'm sorry. I'll call him before I go home today.
A: Thank you.

When will Lorenzo follow up with Andrew?
A. after he gets home
B. before he goes home
C. tomorrow

LESSON 5 Grammar Practice Plus Activities 4 & 5 (Page 31)
A: Lorenzo, you've done a great job here since you came to the company.
B: Thank you very much. I've worked hard and tried to manage my time well.
A: Well, you really have. In fact, your time management meets expectations nicely. Let's take a look at your evaluation form.
B: Okay.
A: You've shown good leadership skills and you meet expectations there. Maybe you can attend a workshop on leadership.
B: Good idea. I'll look into it.
A: Great . . . especially because your teamwork has exceeded expectations. You really get along well with others and are very helpful. Your communication skills are great. They exceed expectations, too.
B: Wonderful! It's really important to me to work well with my coworkers and talk about problems.
A: You do a good job. There's one area, though, that could use improvement.
B: Okay . . . ?
A: I think your preparation has been below expectations. You do a very good job working with everyone, but you need to do a better job at pulling together materials before you need them.
B: Okay. I'll try to work on that.

Unit 3
LESSON 2 Grammar Practice Plus Activity 2 (Page 40)
1. The hostess had already given Uma and Rajiv menus before the server came to the table.
2. Tom and Tammy had studied dinosaurs in school before they went to the Natural History Museum.
3. Joey had never ridden a rollercoaster before.
4. Andy and Amy had already picked up their tickets at the box office before they arrived at the concert hall.
5. Mark and Jill had bought tickets to the play before it sold out.
6. Tony, the usher, was still standing at the door of the auditorium because some people hadn't sat down yet.
7. Before she went to the modern art museum, Jane had already read about the exhibit in her events brochure.

LESSON 3 Listening and Conversation Activity 1 (Page 42)
1. A: What did you think of the symphony's debut performance?
B: I didn't attend the concert. By the time I arrived at the box office, the tickets had sold out.

Which is the best response?
A. Oh, that's too bad.
B. Well, that's good news.
C. Did you buy the tickets?

2. A: You know, I think I lost my concert tickets. I can't find them anywhere.
B: Did you look inside the events brochure? I saw you put the tickets in the brochure.

Which is the best response?
A. There's nothing I want to see in that brochure.
B. That's a good idea. I hadn't thought of looking there.
C. I can't figure out where I put them.

3. A: Would you like to go to the film festival instead of renting a movie?
B: Great idea! Can you still get tickets?

Which is the best response?
A. No, I sold my tickets online.
B. I'll call the box office to find out.
C. OK, I'll go to the video store.

4. A: Mike was great in the Shakespeare performance last night.
B: I didn't know he was an actor! Was that the first time you'd seen him in a play?

Which is the best response?
A. No, I've read a lot of Shakespeare plays.
B. No, I've seen him play a lot of games.
C. Yes, it was. I had never seen him perform before.

5. A: Would you like to go to the new Italian restaurant for dinner tonight?
B: That sounds great. What time should we go?

Which is the best response?
A. I'll make a reservation for seven o'clock.
B. I'll talk to the usher after the show.
C. We should get there in time.

6. A: I took my kids to the Natural History Museum last week.
B: That sounds great. What did you see?

Which is the best response?
A. We saw a lot of interesting modern art.
B. We saw an incredible dinosaur exhibit.
C. We heard a very nice symphony orchestra.

Activity 2 (Page 42)
A: Could you hand me the entertainment section of the newspaper please?
B: Here it is. Are we still going out tonight?
A: That's what we'd planned, right?
B: Yes, but it's six o'clock now and we'd also talked about staying home. Is there anything interesting on TV tonight?
A: Hmm. There's a game show on at 7:00. What about that?
B: Nah. You can watch it if you want.
A: Do you wanna watch a history program? There's one called the *History of the American West* at eight o'clock.
B: Not really. What about that reality show I was watching a few weeks ago...what's it called...something about people sleep-walking...? It seemed interesting.
A: Yeah, that's on later. It's called *The Sleepover House!* Boring! (yawns)
B: Very funny. Are there any comedy shows on tonight?
A: *Fun Times with Mr. Doozy*, makes its debut tonight at 8:30.
B: Oh, I've heard about that show. Mr. Doozy is a children's program. I don't want to watch a kids' show!
A: Okay. What about a drama? *Crime Scene Detectives* is on at 9:00.

B: Forget it. Last week when I was watching it, I realized I'd already seen that one before. It wasn't new—it was a rerun. Ugh!

Activity 3 (Page 42)
A: Well, since you didn't like anything on TV, let's go to the movies. They're having a film festival at the Town Theater. Ooh, I'd love to see a thriller. *Jaws* is playing at 7:10.

B: Ew! I can't stand films about big, scary sharks. How about an action film?

A: Let me see…Our only choice is the *Terminator*, but 10:20 is too late for me. (sighs) We can't go to *The Lion King*—it was at 2:20 so it has already ended. Um, would you like to see *E.T*? It's playing at 8:10.

B: Ugh! Science fiction? No way.

A: Okay. Our last choice is *You've Got Mail* at 8:15.

B: Hmm. I don't think I've ever seen *You've Got Mail*. Isn't that the one about the woman and guy who met online before they met in person?

A: Oh yeah, it's so romantic. I loved that movie.

B: All right. Let's just go!

LESSON 5 Grammar Practice Plus Activities 2 & 3 (Page 46)

1. *A:* I gave the boys some cotton candy, but I don't think they liked it. They looked kind of sick.
   B: Well, that's because they'd been riding the rollercoaster all morning at the amusement park.
   A: Oh, I see.

2. *A:* Hi, Suzie. Where did you go with Pete last night?
   B: We went to a great little sidewalk café.
   A: That sounds great! Did you have a good time?
   B: Well, not really. we'd only been sitting there for five minutes when it started to rain!
   A: Oh, no!

3. *A:* How was the street fair, Holly?
   B: Hmm. Not so great.
   A: Really? Why?
   B: Well, I was walking around, having fun, and then I saw my ex-boyfriend Dave.
   A: That's too bad.
   B: Yeah, I know. I had been having such a good time until then.

4. *A:* So the boys won their soccer game?
   B: Yeah. I can't believe it!
   A: Me neither. I know they'd been practicing really hard for the last month, but I never thought they'd win!

5. *A:* Did you win your big tennis match, Hugo?
   B: No. I broke my tennis racket.
   A: Really? That's too bad.
   B: Yeah, and I'd been playing really well until that time. Now I have to buy a new racket!

6. *A:* Hey, Marcie. Did you hear that storm last night?
   B: Yeah. My power went out. I was really scared!
   A: Scared? Of a storm?
   B: Well, maybe it was because I'd been watching a really scary movie on TV at the time.
   A: Mm-hmm.

LESSON 7 Writing Activity 2B (Page 50)
A: Chim Doc? Is that you?
B: Juanita! I can't believe it's been 10 years already. Time flies!
A: I know. You look great. What have you been doing?
B: I just moved to Miami and opened another art gallery. I sell my own paintings in my art gallery.
A: Another art gallery? That's great. But I thought you were living in Los Angeles.
B: I have a gallery there too, and one in New York. I travel a lot.
A: I always knew you would be a successful painter. I'm very happy for you.
B: Thanks! Now, tell me about you. What are you doing now?

A: Oh, I'm a sixth grade teacher. I'm also the coach of the girls' soccer team.
B: Wow, that's wonderful. It's great to see all our friends again.
A: It sure is. Hey, look! Is that Doug over there?
B: I think so! Let's go talk to him.

CAREER CONNECTION Activity 2 (Page 52)
A: Marcel, come in, Marcel.
B: This is Marcel. Go ahead.
A: Uh, yes, this is Mr. Hanif. What's your location?
B: I'm on the first floor. I was just giving directions to some patrons.
A: We've got a problem on the third floor. Can you get upstairs and check on it for me?
B: I'm on my way up now.
A: OK, great.
B: What happened?
A: We had some kind of problem up there this afternoon. I just got Horace's report.
B: OK, I understand. What happened?
A: Well, some curious patrons went into the restricted work area. Apparently, the warning signs had fallen down. The alarm went off after the visitors crossed the barricades.
B: Was anyone hurt?
A: No, fortunately, no one was hurt.
B: That's a relief. Was there any damage to the exhibit?
A: I'm not sure. By the time Horace got upstairs, two of the kids had already knocked over part of the dinosaur display. They didn't realize we'd put up those barricades to keep our visitors safe and protect the exhibit.
B: All right. I'll check on it. Did Horace reset the alarm system?
A: No. You'll need to reset it. Horace didn't have time to do it before his shift ended.
B: OK. I'm here now. I see the situation. First, I will reset the alarm system. Then, I'll put the signs up again, in a better place. After that, I'll secure the barricades. When I'm done, I'll come down to your office. I should read Horace's security report and make sure all the areas are safe. I can take care of the things he didn't have time to do.
A: Great, Marcel, I knew I could count on you.
B: Always glad to help, Mr. Hanif. Talk to you later.

Unit 4

LESSON 2 Grammar Practice Plus Activity 2 (Page 56)
1. Millie needed to cash a personal check, but she couldn't.
2. Tamir got in the business accounts line to make a withdrawal.
3. Sarah noticed unusual charges on her credit card, and she's worried about credit card fraud.
4. Bart wanted to make a deposit to his personal checking account.
5. Winnona saw a suspicious man leaving the bank.
6. Juan and Rosa spoke to the financial advisor about getting a mortgage loan.
7. Paolo got a receipt for insufficient funds in his checking account.

LESSON 3 Listening and Conversation Activity 1 (Page 58)
1. *A:* Why do you look so disappointed?
   B: I just got a notice for insufficient funds in my checking account.

   Which is the best response?
   A. You should have balanced your checkbook last week.
   B. You shouldn't have used your credit card.
   C. You must have saved a lot of money.

2. *A:* You seem upset. What's wrong?
   B: We got a penalty charge on our credit card statement.

   Which is the best response?
   A. Oh. We didn't see the statement.
   B. Too bad. We need a better interest rate.
   C. You're right. We should have paid the bill on time.

3. *A:* I'm very worried. There is a lot of unusual activity on my credit card statement. I don't remember making all those purchases.
   B: Really? What do you think happened?

   Which is the best response?
   A. Maybe someone stole my credit card information.
   B. I used my credit card to buy our concert tickets.
   C. I couldn't remember my password.

4. *A:* You know, we should have talked to a financial advisor about our savings plan last year.
   B: You're right. We should have gotten a better interest rate. What should we do now?

   Which is the best response?
   A. We can't go to the bank.
   B. We had better wait.
   C. We should make an appointment.

5. *A:* Oh wow. Look at the offer in this bank brochure. We could have invested in a certificate of deposit.
   B: You're right. We could have earned more interest.

   Which is the best response?
   A. Next year, let's get a CD.
   B. This statement is outrageous.
   C. I should have opened a savings account.

6. *A:* Hello. I need to make a deposit to my personal checking account.
   B: Sorry, this is the line for business accounts. You should get in that line over there.

   Which is the best response?
   A. Oh, okay. Thanks for your help.
   B. You shouldn't tell me that.
   C. I'd better talk to you.

Activity 2 (Page 58)

A: Hello. How can I help you?
B: Hi, I would like some information on investing money.
A: Well you could get a savings account with a four percent interest rate.
B: I see. And how about a certificate of deposit?. How does that earn money?
A: The CD we offer earns five percent interest over 18 months.
B: Is that a high interest rate?
A: Yes it is. It is a very good rate. I think you could earn more money with a CD.
B: I can withdraw the money whenever I want, can't I?
A: Well, you can, but with a CD there's a high penalty if you withdraw the money before 18 months.
B: Maybe I'd better open a savings account and a CD.
A: That's a good idea. Here's a brochure with more information.
B: Okay. I'll read it over. Thank you for your help.

LESSON 5 Grammar Practice Plus Activity 4 (Page 63)

A: Nancy, we should go over our budget now.
B: Good idea. Let's see . . . Our car payment is $250, but we spent $100 dollars on gas this month. So for March, that's $350 total for car and gas expenses.
A: Right. Maybe we should have made fewer trips to the supermarket and bought less. You saved our receipts, didn't you?
B: Yes. They're here. You're right. We spent $400 on food this month.
A: Yep, and we also spent $200 on movies, music CDs, and dining out.
B: Well, you know I love going to nice restaurants. But, maybe we could have stayed home and I could have cooked more.
A: With a $1,700-monthly mortgage payment, we'd better stay home more often.
B: I agree. Our phone bill is high this month, isn't it?
A: Yes. It's $165. We should have made calls on the weekends when we have free minutes.
B: True, but I had to call my sister for her birthday, didn't I?

A: I guess so. But we could have put that extra money into the savings account. This month we don't have anything for our savings.
B: Gee. I probably shouldn't have bought those new clothes.
A: Probably not. And I shouldn't have bought a new computer, but I needed it! Ugh! Our credit card bill is outrageous.
B: We'd better transfer money from our savings account.
A: I think that's the best solution. We'll manage better next month, won't we?

LESSON 7 Writing Activity B (Page 66)

A: Hello. This is Access Credit Card Company, Ms. Suresh speaking. How may I help you?
B: Hello. I have a problem with my credit card statement. There's a charge on it for something I didn't buy.
A: OK. What is your name?
B: John Green.
A: And your credit card number?
B: 365 922 076.
A: Thank you. And what is the date of the incorrect charge?
B: November 17th. It's for $300 at Wash-Co Appliance Store. I've never bought anything there!
A: OK, don't worry. You need to send us a letter about this. Write to the Billing Inquiry address on your statement. The address is on the back of your statement. In your letter, include your account number and what you think the incorrect charge is. Then we'll investigate.
B: OK.
A: And make sure to pay your bill on time. You don't need to pay the disputed charge, but you do need to pay the rest.

Unit 5

LESSON 2 Grammar Practice Plus Activity 2 (Page 72)

1. Garbage was collected by the Public Works Department.
2. A chair was knocked over by a dog.
3. A speech was given by the mayor.
4. First aid kits were handed out by the free clinic.
5. Free bike helmets were provided by a police officer.
6. The party was sponsored by the Public Safety Department.

LESSON 3 Listening and Conversation Activity 1 (Page 74)

1. *A:* Good afternoon. Senior Services. How can I help you?
   B: Hello. My name is Bill Jones. I have a doctor's appointment at 3:00, and the van isn't here yet to take me to the doctor's office. The ride was scheduled last week by my grandson.

   Which is correct?
   A. Bill Jones is calling to schedule a ride for next week.
   B. A ride was scheduled by Bill Jones's doctor last week.
   C. Bill Jones's grandson scheduled a ride for him last week.

2. *A:* 911 operator. What is the emergency?
   B: A man was just hit by a car! I think his leg is broken. Send an ambulance to Third Street and Avenue A!

   Which is correct?
   A. A car hit a man.
   B. The caller broke his leg.
   C. The caller was in a car accident.

3. *A:* Public Works Department. How may I help you?
   B: Hi. I just moved to 578 Oak Street. Is the garbage collected on Mondays in this neighborhood?
   A: No, it isn't. It's collected every Wednesday morning.

   Which is correct?
   A. Public Works doesn't collect garbage on Oak Street.
   B. Garbage is collected on Mondays on Oak Street.
   C. Garbage is collected on Wednesdays on Oak Street.

4. *A:* Mission Community Center. How can I help you?
   B: Hi. I just signed my son up for your after-school program. Do you provide snacks for children in the program?

A: Yes, we provide fruit, sandwiches, juice, and milk.

Which is correct?
A. Snacks are provided by parents.
B. Snacks are provided by the community center.
C. Snacks are not provided.

5. *A:* Free Clinic. How may I help you?
B: How often is your nutrition class offered?
A: We have a nutrition class once a month. It's always on the first Monday of every month. Would you like to sign up for the next class?

Which is correct?
A. The Free Clinic offers nutrition classes at the community center.
B. The Free Clinic offers a nutrition class every month.
C. The Free Clinic offers nutrition classes every day.

6. *A:* Good afternoon. Animal Control. What can I do for you?
B: Hello. The bicycles in my garage were knocked over last night. I think there is an animal hiding in my garage.
A: We'll send someone over. Can I have your address, please?

Which is correct?
A. There is a dog in the caller's garage.
B. Someone took bicycles out of the caller's garage.
C. The caller wants Animal Control to help him find an animal.

Activities 2 & 3 (Page 74)

A: Public Works. This is Erin Colby. How can I help you today?
B: I'm calling because the stop sign at the corner of Maple Street and 3rd Avenue was knocked over this morning.
A: I see. How did that happen?
B: It was hit by a car. I was standing two feet away from the sign when it happened.
A: Was anyone injured?
A: I wasn't injured, but the driver hit his head.
B: Did you talk to the driver of the car?
A: No, he drove away right after he hit the sign.
B: Did anyone else witness the accident?
A: Yes, there were three other people there. I can provide their phone numbers if you want them.
B: Thank you. We'll send someone out to talk to you and repair the sign as soon as possible.

LESSON 5 Grammar Practice Plus Activity 5 (Page 79)

1. Carlos Tejada's social security number is 987–65–4320.
2. Carlos's address is 1472 South Ocean Drive.
3. Carlos's zip code is 91368.
4. The zip code for the Sunshine Catering Company is 94132.
5. One thousand seven hundred fifty-eight dollars was withheld for federal taxes.

CAREER CONNECTION Activity 2 (Page 84)

A: As you know, Dylan Anderson is starting work here today as Chief Supervisor. This position was created because our plant is growing. With so many new employees, we need a strong leader who can step in and help manage the floor so that I can focus on administrative work. It was decided last week by a unanimous vote of the Board of Directors that Mr. Anderson is the right person for the job. And I know he's going to be a great new member of our team. Please welcome Mr. Dylan Anderson.
B: Thank you, Ms. Rivers, or should I say "boss." I'm very glad to be here with such a great group of people… Well, I don't like to give speeches, so I'll just get right to business.
  First of all, I want to talk about how the management here will be changing. Previously, we had three shift supervisors who oversaw operations on the floor. Last week, two more line workers were promoted to new shift supervisor positions as well. Alexis Moran and Mike Woodford, could you raise your hand? Give them a round of applause, everyone! All five shift supervisors report to me and are responsible for day-to-day operations in their department.

As you know, many of you were assigned to a new shift supervisor because of this change. Updated staff charts were provided for everyone this morning, and by now you've all had a chance to meet with your new supervisors. The maintenance team was assigned to Mr. Woodford, and the warehouse team was assigned to Ms. Moran. We know that this is a big change for many of you, but it's really going to improve things around here in the long run. We hope you'll all agree.

Unit 6

LESSON 2 Grammar Practice Plus Activity 2 (Page 88)

1. The wall in the kitchen is cracked.
2. Water is dripping from the faucet.
3. The paint is peeling from the ceiling.
4. The doorknob on the door is broken.
5. The carpet is stained.

LESSON 3 Listening and Conversation Activity 1 (Page 90)

1. *A:* Union Bell Telephone Company. May I have your name and home phone number please?
B: Hello. My name is Sara Lopez, and my phone number is 818-555-8747.

Which is correct?
A. Sara's phone number is 818-555-8747.
B. Sara is calling 818-555-8747.
C. The number for the telephone company is 818-555-8747.

2. *A:* How may I help you?
B: I'm calling because there are some errors on my telephone bill.
A: I'm sorry about that. Were the errors on this month's bill?
B: Yes, they were.

Which is correct?
A. Sara didn't receive her most recent bill.
B. Sara made some errors on her most recent bill.
C. The phone company made some errors on her bill.

3. *A:* Okay. I have your bill on my computer screen. What is the first error?
B: I was charged for a call to New York on March 3. But I didn't call New York.

Which is correct?
A. Sara called New York.
B. Sara was in New York.
C. Sara didn't call New York.

4. *A:* Is it possible that someone else in your home called New York?
B: No, I live alone.

Which is correct?
A. Sara lives by herself.
B. Sara lives with one roommate.
C. Sara's roommate made the phone call to New York.

5. *A:* All right. Is there anything else?
B: Yes. There's a charge for a call to Los Angeles on March 8, but I didn't make that call. I was out of town that day.

Which is correct?
A. Sara was in Los Angeles on March 8.
B. Sara wasn't home on March 8.
C. Sara got a voicemail message from Los Angeles.

6. *A:* Hold one moment, please, while I check your call history. [pause] Thank you for holding, Ms. Lopez. I apologize for the errors. I've taken the charges off of your bill. You will receive an updated bill in a couple of days.
B: Thank you very much.

Which is correct?
A. The phone company will not take the charges off the bill.
B. The phone company is going to send Sara a new bill.
C. Sara has to pay for the changes to her bill.

Activity 3 (Page 90)

A: Union Bell Telephone Company. May I have your name and home phone number please?

B: Hello. My name is Sara Lopez, and my phone number is 818-555-8747.

A: How may I help you?

B: I'm calling because there are some errors on my telephone bill.

A: I'm sorry about that. Were the errors on this month's bill?

B: Yes, they were.

A: Okay. I have your bill on my computer screen. What is the first error?

B: I was charged for a call to New York on March 3. But I didn't call New York.

A: Is it possible that someone else in your home called New York?

B: No, I live alone.

A: All right. Is there anything else?

B: Yes. There's a charge for a call to Los Angeles on March 8, but I didn't make that call. I was out of town that day.

A: Hold one moment, please, while I check your call history. [pause] Thank you for holding, Ms. Lopez. I apologize for the errors. I've taken the charges off of your bill. You will receive an updated bill in a couple of days.

B: Thank you very much.

LESSON 5 Grammar Practice Plus Activity 5 (Page 95)

A: Hello, and thanks for calling the Renter's Rights Radio Show. What's the problem?

B: Hi. Well, I'm having a problem with one of my neighbors. Every time he does his laundry, he spills soap all over the floor and doesn't clean it up. He's not very friendly, so I'm afraid to talk to him about it. Can you tell me what I should do?

A: You should ask your landlord or your apartment manager to talk to your neighbor about the problem. If your neighbor doesn't start cleaning up his mess, your landlord should make sure that the laundry room is clean.

B: Okay. Thank you.

A: Let's have another call. Hi there. What's the problem?

C: Hi. My problem is with my landlord. He says he is going to evict me for paying my rent late. It's due on the first of each month, and I paid it on the third. That's only two days late! Then he changed the locks so I can't get into my apartment. I don't know what I should do.

A: Your landlord doesn't have the right to evict you for paying your rent two days late. You should call a lawyer. This is a serious issue.

C: Okay, I will. Thank you.

A: We have time for one more call. Hello, caller. What's the problem?

D: Well, there are cockroaches in my apartment. I told my landlord about them two weeks ago, but he still hasn't done anything about them.

A: Because this is an important health issue, your landlord should have taken care of this problem right away. Write him a letter and keep a copy of the letter for yourself. It's best if you send the letter by certified mail so you have proof that he received it. In the letter, tell your landlord that you are going to call a health inspector to file a complaint. If he still doesn't take care of the issue, file a complaint with a health inspector.

Unit 7

LESSON 2 Grammar Practice Plus Activity 4 (Page 105)

1. Officer King is the person who is talking to the owner of the butcher shop.
2. Officer Dill is the person who has a theory about the robbery.
3. Robin Gale is the person who looks surprised.
4. Tina Ruiz is the person who identified the thieves.
5. Tom Lee is the person who owns the butcher shop.

6. Lee West is the person who is looking for his dog.

LESSON 3 Listening and Conversation Activity 1 (Page 106)

1. A: Did you read about the man who found 500 coins in the walls of his house?
   B: Yeah, I did! The coins are 200 years old!

   Which is correct?
   A. A man found 200 coins in his house.
   B. A man found 500 coins in his house.
   C. A man found coins that are 500 years old.

2. A: Did you read about the bus drivers who are demonstrating?
   B: Yes, I did. They've been demonstrating for two weeks. They're asking for higher pay and better health care.

   Which is correct?
   A. Bus drivers want higher salaries and better health insurance.
   B. Health care workers have been demonstrating for two weeks.
   C. Bus drivers demonstrated two weeks ago.

3. A: Did you hear about the 20-car collision that happened this morning?
   B: No, I didn't. What happened?
   A: Someone's car broke down on the freeway. The driver who was behind that car didn't see it, so he hit it. Then 18 more cars crashed.
   B: Oh, that's terrible!

   Which is correct?
   A. Eighteen cars crashed on the freeway this morning.
   B. A driver of a car that broke down caused a 20-car collision.
   C. Twenty cars broke down on the freeway this morning and caused a collision.

4. A: Hi, Bill. Are you going to get a flu vaccination this year?
   B: Yes, I am. I heard there might be a flu epidemic. My doctor told me about it.
   A: Let's get our vaccinations together. I know about a hospital that offers free vaccinations.

   Which is correct?
   A. Bill is going to visit a doctor because there may be a flu epidemic.
   B. Bill visited a doctor because he wanted to get a flu vaccination.
   C. Bill is going to get a flu vaccination because there might be a flu epidemic.

Activity 2 (Page 106)

1. A: Did you read about the man who found 500 coins in the walls of his house?
   B: Yeah, I did! The coins are 200 years old!

2. A: Did you read about the bus drivers who are demonstrating?
   B: Yes, I did. They've been demonstrating for two weeks. They're asking for higher pay and better health care.

3. A: Did you hear about the 20-car collision that happened this morning?
   B: No, I didn't. What happened?
   A: Someone's car broke down on the freeway. The driver who was behind that car didn't see it, so he hit it. Then 18 more cars crashed.
   B: Oh, that's terrible!

4. A: Hi, Bill. Are you going to get a flu vaccination this year?
   B: Yes, I am. I heard there might be a flu epidemic. My doctor told me about it.
   A: Let's get our vaccinations together. I know about a hospital that offers free vaccinations.

Activity 3 (Page 106)

A: Did you read the article about the couple that got married at the airport last month?

B: No, I didn't. What happened?

A: Well, they met each other thirty years ago at the airport gift shop, but they didn't speak again after that. They both married different people, and years later, they both got divorced. But they never forgot each other. Then, last year, they saw each other at a restaurant that's next to the same gift shop!

B: Really? And they recognized each other?

A: Yeah. They remembered each other, so they said hello. They started dating, and now they're married!

B: I can't believe it!

A: It's true!

LESSON 5 Grammar Practice Plus Activity 3 (Page 111)

Mike Jennings of Plainfield, Illinois had a problem. He was overweight, dangerously overweight. And, he spent too much time on the computer. His doctor said he needed to get out of the house and exercise more, but Jennings didn't do it.

"I had gotten used to spending all of my free time in front of the computer, surfing the net. It was hard to just stop doing it," he explained. Then one day Jennings found a website that quickly changed his mind and his health.

"I like to read blogs, so I decided to look for some health blogs. I found some really interesting stuff. There are some great blogs out there that are written for people like me." Jennings is talking about a growing number of health-related blogs that include tips for losing weight, eating right, and preparing easy and healthful meals.

"I started to read tips and ideas from people who were trying to lose weight, like I am. I tried the exercises and recipes I read about. Before I knew it, I had lost ten pounds. I felt great. Now I spend a lot less time on the Internet. But when I am surfing the net, I read health blogs. I told my doctor about the blogs, and she's going to tell her other patients about them."

For people like Mike, blogs can be a good source of information and support for the difficult tasks of losing weight and staying healthy.

CAREER CONNECTION Activity 2 (Page 116)

A: Welcome to the food education and safety training session. At least once a year, local Health Inspectors visit restaurants to make sure employees are following the health codes. As you know from recent news stories, a few restaurants have been shut down because their customers got sick from the food. First of all, it's important for *all* employees to wash their hands after using the restroom. Employees who don't wash thoroughly might spread germs and bacteria, such as E. coli. You've all heard of E. coli, right?

B: Yeah. E. coli can give people food poisoning.

A: Right. E. coli is a type of bacteria that causes food poisoning. You can get abdominal cramps, fever, and an upset stomach. E. coli is very contagious. It can cause an epidemic because it spreads easily from person to person. Does anyone know how E. coli spreads?

C: I do. E. coli can spread if you have the bacteria on your hands and then touch food or another person.

A: That's right. If you have bacteria on your hands and don't wash properly, you can contaminate anyone or anything you touch. You can also spread E. coli by handling raw food or unwashed vegetables and touching clean food. Did you know that foods like raw eggs, and uncooked meat, chicken, or shellfish contain bacteria? [*audience makes response sounds*] Well, it's true. Both cooked food and uncooked food that haven't been stored at the correct temperatures can contain E. coli and other types of bacteria. So that's why proper refrigeration is very important! Fruits and vegetables may also contain bacteria, so, cleaning them properly can help prevent the spread of food poisoning.

B: Is E. coli the same thing as salmonella?

A: Good question. They're both bacteria and cause similar symptoms. Like E. coli, salmonella can cause abdominal cramps, fever, and vomiting. People can also spread salmonella by the improper handling of food. That's why it's important to follow the health codes. Thoroughly wash your hands, cooking utensils, and food preparation surfaces. Also, all food preparation staff must wear plastic gloves while handling food. Employees who have long hair must wear a hair net in the kitchen. This helps prevent food contamination and the spreading of illnesses. Remember: You can help prevent food poisoning outbreaks by following these health codes! We want to keep all of you and the customers safe and happy! That's it for today. Thanks for your participation.

Unit 8

LESSON 2 Grammar Practice Plus Activity 1 (Page 120)

1. Residents have been concerned about returning to their homes after lightning started a fire in the area. It has taken firefighters three days to control the intense fire.

2. There has been a drought with no rain or snow and low water levels for over four months. State government officials are serious about reducing water use. They are asking citizens to conserve water.

3. People in the area are nervous about traveling on highways in the heavy snowstorms and freezing temperatures. If you have to drive today, drive very slowly and carefully or wait until the blizzard ends.

4. There have been torrential rains in the northern part of the state this week, especially on the coast. The local government is asking residents to leave the area if the ground starts to move and there is a mudslide.

5. Residents of the coast are worried about experiencing sudden, high levels of water near their homes. Local government officials are asking residents to take precautions and leave the area because they think there might be flash floods.

6. Because of the tornado warning, people should be serious about finding shelter or a safe place in their homes immediately. The weather service reports that there are extremely high winds in several parts of the state.

7. There were three small earthquakes today in the southern area of the state. Scientists think there is a small possibility of another one later today. Take precautions if you feel the ground begin to shake. For example, you can wait under a strong table or desk until the shaking is finished.

8. Today's forecast is for 100-degrees with poor air quality. People should be cautious about spending time outdoors. We are advising people to stay inside and drink plenty of water.

9. Severe thunderstorms and extremely high wind gusts have been reported in the area today. A hurricane warning has been issued. Many residents are concerned about protecting their homes from the high winds and torrential rain.

LESSON 3 Listening and Conversation Activity 1
(Page 122)

1. *A:* What's the weather forecast for today?

   B: I'm not sure. I heard that there might be a severe thunderstorm.

   A: Uh-oh. I'm worried about driving to Boston in the rain.

   Which is the best response?

   A. Maybe you should take the train.

   B. You should go to the airport and wait.

   C. You should find shelter immediately.

2. *A:* How was your trip to Wisconsin?

   B: There was a tornado when I was there. It was scary!

   A: Wow. I saw a tornado there last year too. I'd never seen a one before.

Which is the best response?
A. Neither had I.
B. So had I.
C. I did too.
3. A: In New York City, we had a power outage for five hours.
B: I heard about that. There were power outages all over the state.
A: Well, now people are cautious about using energy during the extreme heat.

Which is the best response?
A. Droughts happen all the time.
B. People should use less electricity when it is so hot.
C. Everyone should turn the air conditioning on high.
4. A: There was a drought in Atlanta last year.
B: I didn't know about that. What happened?

Which is the best response?
A. Atlanta had torrential ran.
B. They had no rain for six months.
C. People had to evacuate.
5. A: It's really snowing a lot now.
B: I hate driving in snow. It's hard to see, and the roads are bad.
A: The weather report said we should be cautious about traveling in this blizzard.

Which is the best response?
A. I heard that, too. We should be cautious of flash floods.
B. I heard that, too. We should drive slowly with the lights on.
C. I heard that, too. We should prepare for a hurricane.
6. A: There isn't a smog advisory today, is there?
B: Yes, I think there is. Why do you ask?
A: I'm worried about exercising outdoors, but I want to go running.

Which is the best response?
A. You should exercise at the gym.
B. You shouldn't drive in bad weather.
C. You should go running in the park.

Activities 2 & 3 (Page 122)
Hello, I'm Mary Armstrong with your national weather and emergency preparedness report. In the Northeast, residents have been concerned about flash floods because of the severe thunderstorms that moved through the area yesterday. Government officials recommend getting to higher ground right away if you live on the coast or near the rivers because of the very high water levels. In the Southeast, there is a hurricane warning in effect. As always, residents are advised to protect their homes from the high winds and find a safe place on the first floor in preparation for the possible hurricane. Throughout the Midwest there has been a tornado advisory today. We have reports of wind gusts of up to 100 miles per hour. The weather service recommends finding shelter as soon as possible if there are tornadoes in the area. In the Northwest, the torrential rains last week have caused extremely wet, shifting ground. Residents should be prepared to leave the area quickly if there are mudslides. Finally, due to the extremely dry temperatures in the Southwest, forest rangers and firefighters have been on alert. They have been concerned about fighting the wildfires that have spread across the region. Government officials have told residents to evacuate the area immediately until the fires are completely under control and it is safe to return. Tune in tonight at 6 P.M. for an update.

LESSON 5 Grammar Practice Plus Activities 3 & 4
(Page 127)
A: This is Juan Perez and you're watching "The Solutions Hour." Today, I'm happy to welcome Ms. Eva Erickson, an expert on natural disaster preparedness. Eva, thank you for being here. Tell us about environmental and disaster relief organizations and what they do.
B: Thanks, Juan. First, I'll talk about the National Resources Defense Council. They've really focused on improving the environment after Hurricane Katrina. They've also been cleaning up the neighborhoods and making sure the water is safe to drink. They try to keep areas where children play free from toxic waste.
A: I see. There were wildfires in Northern California a few years ago. Who usually helps during this type of disaster?
B: Well Juan, the U.S. Department of Agriculture is concerned about protecting our wildlife, and they are also concerned about preventing wildfires. The USDA may also investigate the causes of the fires and take precautions to prevent them, especially during extreme heat or drought conditions.
A: That's great information to know. Now, I remember that one year, Wisconsin had more than sixty tornadoes. Who helps people rebuild their homes after this type of disaster?
B: Habitat For Humanity is an organization that goes to many areas of the country to help build homes for victims of natural disasters. Several teams of volunteers in Wisconsin built houses for people after their homes were destroyed by tornadoes.
A: In 2003 New York had a serious problem with thc power outages. Who helped and what did they do?
B: During the power outages, the city's food supply was in danger. So the American Red Cross made sure that residents had water and food. Volunteers were on the streets of New York during the crisis, giving out bottles of water and meals to the residents.
A: That's all the time we have for today. Thanks for being here with us today Eva, and giving us some important information about these groups.

Activity 2B (Page 130)
What do you know about green groups? Today we're going to talk about three green groups that support finding solutions to global warming, protecting our wildlife, and saving our environment. The first group is Greenpeace. Greenpeace activists often have demonstrations against the government. They want politicians and government leaders to pay attention to the issue of global warming and other environmental problems.

The Nature Conservancy is another well-known green organization. They're against extreme logging and cutting down trees in our forests. They also support helping our forests by planting trees after wildfires. Like Greenpeace, the Nature Conservancy is also concerned with solving our problems with global warming.

Another group that you might have heard of is The National Wildlife Federation. This organization cares about protecting wildlife. They believe in protecting nature for the children's future. They're against killing wildlife that are endangered, or at risk. The National Wildlife Federation supports protecting wild animals such as elephants, polar bears, and tigers. They are also interested in finding solutions to global warming.

These groups are important to our society. You can make a donation to one of these groups or register to volunteer by visiting their websites.

Unit 9

LESSON 2 Grammar Practice Plus Activity 2 (Page 136)
1. A guide dog helps Rita cross the street.
2. Luz is a driver education teacher. She is making her student practice parking at a parking meter.
3. The traffic rule does not allow Tony to turn left at the intersection during rush hour.
4. Carla is a traffic officer. She made Sue pay a fine for parking in a tow-away zone.

5. Martina is letting her son Ben ride the bus by himself today.
6. Lina is helping Ralph go around the road construction.
7. The wheelchair access ramp allows Tom to get to his classes on time.
8. The traffic law does not permit Howie to park so close to a fire hydrant.

LESSON 3 Listening and Conversation Activity (Page 138)

1. What did the woman tell the man?
   A: Excuse me. You're not allowed to park here.
   B: Oh really?
   A: Well, there's a wheelchair access ramp here.
   B: Oh, I'm sorry. I didn't see the ramp.

   What did the woman tell the man?
   A. He is not handicapped.
   B. He can't park there.
   C. He's allowed to park there.

2. What happened to the man's car?
   A: Could you drive me to work in the morning?
   B: Sure. Where's your car?
   A: It broke down while I was driving home yesterday. Last night I had to take it to a mechanic to get it fixed. It will be ready this afternoon.

   What happened to the man's car?
   A. It is at his home.
   B. He has to take it to a mechanic.
   C. The mechanic is fixing it.

3. What is the teacher helping the man do?
   A: Did you take your learner's permit exam?
   B: Yes, I passed it weeks ago! Since then, I've been practicing for my driver's test.
   A: That's great. What have you been doing in your driving class?
   B: Well, the teacher has been helping me practice parking on the street.

   What is the teacher helping the man do?
   A. Practice parking on the street.
   B. Practice parking in a parking lot.
   C. Practice for the learner's permit exam.

4. Why was the woman late?
   A: Hey, where have you been? I've been waiting here at the restaurant for half an hour.
   B: There was road construction, so there was a big traffic jam.
   A: Well, I already ordered some soup because I was very hungry.
   B: That's okay. I should have called but I left my cell phone at home.

   Why was the woman late?
   A. Because her car broke down.
   B. Because she forgot her cell phone.
   C. Because there was road construction and a traffic jam.

5. What is the man's new job?
   A: Ok. Here are some tips about your new job. The first thing is to get the drivers to slow down in the school zone.
   B: Right.
   A: Also, I usually make the children hold hands before they cross the street. And, I have them walk, not run.
   B: Thanks. Those are good tips.

   What is the man's new job?
   A. He's a bus driver.
   B. He's a crossing guard.
   C. He's a driver education teacher.

6. What is the woman going to do?
   A: Ugh! I can't stand driving in rush hour traffic.
   B: I know that, but you have to be patient. Just stay calm.
   A: Let's listen to the radio. The music makes me feel better.
   B: Good idea. Since you're nervous about driving, I'll let you listen to your favorite music.

   What is the woman going to do?
   A. Drive the car.
   B. Listen to music she likes.
   C. Let the man listen to music that he likes.

Activities 2 & 3 (Page 138)

A: Hi. Where have you been? I thought you'd be home at 3:30.
B: Oh, you won't believe this. There was an accident at the intersection of Main Street and South Street.
A: That must have been a bad traffic jam!
B: Yeah, it was! But that's not all. It was 3 o'clock, so all the school buses were on the roads. I was behind a bus, so of course, we had to stop and wait every time it stopped.
A: Well, I can understand that.
B: Oh, but that's not the worst part. My car broke down. I had to have it towed to the gas station. Then I had the mechanic drive me here.
A: That's terrible. You know, my hair appointment was for 4 o'clock. I had to cancel it because you weren't here with the car.
B: Sorry about that.
A: [Laughs] Well, I won't get my hair done before the party tonight!
B: Don't worry. You'll still look great.

LESSON 5 Grammar Practice Plus Activities 2 & 3 (Page 142)

1. A: Hi Jack. I have to buy paint supplies and light fixtures. Do you know where the hardware store is?
   B: Sure Sam, it's on the west side of town. Take Main Street and turn left on North. Go past the Stardust Hotel and you'll see it on the corner of North Street and West Street. [C]
   A: Thanks!
   B: You're welcome.

2. A: Excuse me. Do you know where the post office is?
   B: Sure. Go up Main Street and around the statue. It's on the corner of First Street and State Street. It should be on your right. [A]

3. A: Hello. I need to get my car registration renewed. Is there a Department of Motor Vehicles near here?
   B: Yes. It's on South Street between Elm Street and West Street. [B]
   A: Oh, thanks.
   A: Don't mention it.

4. A: Excuse me, is there a parking lot around here?
   B: Sure. Go up Main Street and turn right on Pine. It's across the street from the shopping mall. [G]
   A: Thanks for your help.
   B: No problem!

5. A: Excuse me. Is there a moving van rental service here on Main Street?
   B: Yes. Just go up Main Street and take a left on First Street. It's across the street from the auto repair shop. [E]
   A: Thanks!

6. A: Excuse me. I need to get information about a business license. Do you know where I should go for that?
   B: Yes, I do. You can get advice at the Chamber of Commerce. It's located at the corner of Main and Hope Streets. The entrance is in front of the statue. [D]

7. A: Excuse me. Do you know where I can find a convenience store around here?
   B: I remember seeing one near the school on State Street. Go straight up Main Street and turn right on Pine. Go past the shopping mall, and I think it is on State Street across from the school. [F]

Activity 5 (Page 143)

A: Hi, Mrs. Peterson.
B: Hello Sam. It looks like you're really getting things done today.
A: Yes, but I forgot to do some things this morning.

B: Oh, well. I always forget things. This morning I forgot to take my keys with me. I had to call my son at work and get him to bring his set of keys.

A: Oh. Yesterday, I went to the Department of Motor Vehicles and forgot to bring my proof of insurance. I had to go all the way back to my apartment to get it.

B: Oh, we're quite the pair! What else do you have to do today?

A: Well, I forgot to buy a winter coat before I moved here. Do you know where I can find a nice coat?

B: Hmm. I remember seeing sale signs at the shopping mall. There's a good department store there.

A: Thanks. I also need some information about a business license. Do you know where I can get that?

B: Oh, yes. Go to the Chamber of Commerce. It has a lot of information about small businesses. Then, stop at Town Hall to pick up the application. [sighs] Town Hall is such a beautiful building. I remember getting my marriage license there 40 years ago.

A: Wow, you've really lived here a long time, haven't you?

B: Yes. I remember seeing this town for the first time when I was twenty years old. I thought the houses were so beautiful. Now I only see the town by bus because I stopped driving last year. You probably have a car, don't you?

A: Well, yes, but my car is getting fixed at the auto shop. I have to remember to call the mechanic this afternoon. I should add that to my to-do list.

LESSON 7 Writing Activity 2B (Page 146)

A: Hello?

B: Hi, Mom. It's Tom. I just got in a car accident.

A: Oh, no! Are you okay?

B: Yes, I'm okay, don't worry.

A: How many people were in the other car? Is anyone else hurt?

B: Well, there was a woman driving and her two children in the back seat. The kids were scared, but they stopped crying once they were out of the car. Luckily everyone is okay.

A: Oh, thank goodness. What happened?

B: Well, I just got out of school and was driving to work. It was almost 3:30, so I was worried I was going to be late. I was sitting at a stoplight behind another car. The light turned green and she started to go. But then she saw a pedestrian in the crosswalk and stopped suddenly. I put on my brakes, but wasn't able to stop in time. I hit her from behind. We both pulled over and like I said, her kids were crying, but we are all okay.

A: Did you get her name and contact information?

B: Yeah—after she calmed her kids down, we exchanged names and insurance information. Her name is Maria Chang. I got her phone number and email address, but forgot to get her home address.

A: Did the police come?

B: Yes, an officer from the Miami Police Department came. He took a report and had us move our cars off the road.

A: Is your car okay?

B: No, actually, the whole front of my car is dented in. I'm having it towed to Pete's Body Shop on Main Street.

A: Well, the most important thing is that you are okay. We can fill out an insurance claim when you get home.

B: Okay, mom. See you soon.

A: Bye.

CAREER CONNECTION Activities 2 & 3 (Page 148)

A: Hey, Ray, what's going on? Where are those car parts? I needed them 15 minutes ago.

B: Yeah, hey, Carl, we've got a machine that's broken down on the production line.

A: Oh, no. I need the parts for this shipment.

B: But we only have three completed here, Carl.

A: But I need ten...

B: Well, I don't know what to say. It's broken. We just have to wait for an engineer to come and fix the machine.

A: But that could take over an hour! We have to get this machine working again right away. I need to get the shipment of parts out by six o'clock tonight... Let's ask Nancy. I think she knows how to fix this machine... Nancy, do you know how to fix this thing?

C: I don't know, guys. I worked on this machine a long time ago. I'm not sure if I remember how to fix it. I guess I could try, but... [hesitating]

B: If you don't want to wait for an engineer, let's ask the supervisor if we can call Gary. Gary's the lead engineer on this machine. He can definitely tell us how to fix it. Let's ask the supervisor for Gary's number.

C: But Gary's in Germany. He's on vacation. Remember? It's kind of late to call him there now. I don't want to wake him up.

A: Aw, c'mon, Nancy, can't you just try to fix the machine?

B: Listen, Carl. I don't think it's a good idea for Nancy to work on the machine. What happens if she can't fix it? Then no one can help us, and your order won't go out on time. Let's just call Gary. He said we can call him any time.

A: Well, if we're going to call him, let's do it now. If we wait until later, it'll really be too late to call him. I'll get his number.

Unit 10

LESSON 2 Grammar Practice Plus 2 Activity 2 (Page 152)

1. A: Please don't leave this bowl of candy on the table.
   B: Why not?
   A: Jimmy can get up on the chair and reach these. Didn't I tell you they're a choking hazard?
   B: Oh yeah, you did.

2. A: Whoa! Who left this toy on the stairs?
   B: Oh, I bet one of the boys did that.
   A: We need to put these child-safety gates up. And please tell them to keep their toys off the stairs.
   B: All right.

3. A: Wow. You have too many electrical cords plugged in here!
   B: Do you think so?
   A: Yeah. I heard we shouldn't have more than two plugged in at one time. You've got four things plugged in here! It could start a fire.
   A: Oh, OK. I'll take care of it.

4. A: Miriam, did you say you bought new locks for the cabinet doors?
   B: Yes, they're in the living room.
   A: We need to lock these cabinets. There are toxic cleansers inside, and I don't want the boys to get in there.

5. A: Who left these pans on the stove like this?
   B: I did. Why?
   A: I told you last time you need to turn the handles toward the wall. It's a real burn hazard if the boys pull these pans off the stove.

6. A: Billy, stay away from that outlet. Susan--they said we have to put covers on the electrical outlets. It's dangerous if they're not covered, especially if the children can reach it easily.
   B: OK, I'll get some more covers for the outlets.

LESSON 3 Listening and Conversation Activity 1 (Page 154)

1. A: Do you have electric heat in your house?
   B: No, we use a kerosene heater.
   A: You need a carbon monoxide detector.

   Which is correct?
   A. She told him he needed a smoke detector.
   B. He told her he had a carbon monoxide detector.
   C. She said he needed a carbon monoxide detector.

2. A: Does your family practice fire drills?
   B: Yes, we practice twice a year.

Which is correct?
- **A.** She told him her family practiced twice a year.
- **B.** He told her she needed to practice fire drills.
- **C.** She told him he needed to practice fire drills twice a year.

3. *A:* Did you buy some cabinet locks?
   B: No, I didn't have time. I'll buy them tomorrow.

   Which is correct?
   - **A.** He told her she needed to buy cabinet locks tomorrow.
   - **B.** He told her he'd buy cabinet locks tomorrow.
   - **C.** She told him she would buy cabinet locks tomorrow.

4. *A:* I think the smoke detector is broken.
   B: No, it isn't. It just needs a new battery.

   Which is correct?
   - **A.** He told her that he had to put a new battery in the smoke detector.
   - **B.** She told him that the smoke detector needed a new battery.
   - **C.** She told him that the smoke detector was broken.

5. *A:* I can't find the bathroom cleanser. Did you move it?
   B: I put all the toxic cleansers in a high cabinet.
   A: Oh, that's a good idea.

   Which is correct?
   - **A.** She told him she put the bathroom cleanser in a high cabinet.
   - **B.** He told her he put the toxic cleansers in a high cabinet.
   - **C.** He told her she should move the toxic cleansers.

6. *A:* We need a new child-safety gate.
   B: I can buy one tomorrow on my way home from work.
   A: That would be great. Thanks.

   Which is correct?
   - **A.** She told him that they needed a new child-safety gate.
   - **B.** He told her that he bought a child-safety gate.
   - **C.** She told him that she could buy a child-safety gate tomorrow.

Activities 2 & 3 (Page 154)
A: Brown and Miller. This is Laura speaking.
B: Hi, Laura. It's Jack.
A: Hi, Jack. Are you coming to work today?
B: No, I'm not. That's why I'm calling. I fell this morning and broke my ankle.
A: Oh no! How did you fall?
B: I tripped on some toys on the stairs.
A: That's terrible. Are you feeling okay?
B: It hurts a lot, but I'll be fine.
A: Are you at home now? Do you need a ride to the hospital?
B: No, I'm at the hospital now. Mia drove me here. Will you let Stan know what happened?
A: Sure, I'll give him the message. Well, take it easy, and I'll call you later to find out how you're doing.

LESSON 5 Grammar Practice Plus Activity 4 (Page 159)
When I was in college, I used to exercise every day. I went to the gym every morning, and my friends could always count on me to play basketball or soccer with them in the afternoons. I used to be in really great shape. But now, I'm about thirty pounds overweight. I'm not used to taking care of myself anymore. Instead, I'm used to eating fast food for dinner and watching TV every night. I started a diet three months ago, but I didn't follow through with it. I gave up after a week. I tried to go jogging last week, but I'm not used to exercising anymore. I got tired after three minutes! I used to be able to run five miles without getting tired! I need to get back in shape. I just signed up with the gym in my neighborhood, and I'm going to start exercising three days a week starting tomorrow. Well, maybe I'll start next Monday.

Unit 11
LESSON 2 Grammar Practice Plus Activity 2 (Page 168)
1. Luis is very demanding of his employees. He expects a lot of them and gets upset if they make mistakes.
2. Jana is very professional. She does a good job with her work. She's punctual and has good training.
3. Allison works for the company. She is impressed by Kent.
4. Maria is prepared for her interview with Chris. She has her résumé, business card, and references.
5. Kirk is sloppy. He looks disorganized and his clothes don't look clean. He might have a hard time getting an interview.
6. Kent is assertive. He's not afraid to do new things or meet new people. He is confident about himself.

Activity 5 (Page 169)
1. Kent is assertive and very confident. He has taken the initiative and has been conducting a job search so he can make a career change in a new city. He has good communication skills, but he needs to build a stronger résumé. If the company wants him to have more work experience, he might ask to do an internship with the company.
2. Maria is very organized, so she's always prepared. She is a hard worker, but usually, she works too much. She often gets sick because she is so tired. Unfortunately, she's not very assertive, but when she goes to interviews, she is still given good feedback.

LESSON 3 Listening and Conversation Activity 1 (Page 170).
1. *A:* Let's talk about Jim first. What do you think is his greatest strength?
   B: Well, he's always ready and prepared. For example, if I ask him to give a presentation at a meeting, he comes with all of the information he needs.
   A: Yeah. That's true. And he's organized, too.
   B: Right. If I ask him for information about sales or whatever, he knows just where to find it.

   Which response is correct?
   - **A.** Jim is assertive.
   - **B.** Jim is prepared.
   - **C.** Jim is demanding.

2. *A:* Okay, let's talk about Jan.
   B: She's had a good year.
   A: She sure has. The thing I like about Jan is that she's confident. She's not afraid to take initiative. If she hears about a project that she wants to work on, she'll come to me and tell me she wants to do it.
   B: That's great. If she continues to do well, she'll receive a promotion.

   Which is correct?
   - **A.** Jan is impressed.
   - **B.** Jan is sloppy.
   - **C.** Jan is assertive.

3. *A:* All right, on to Sam.
   B: Oh yeah. Sam. Hmmm.
   A: What are we going to do about him? I like him. He's friendly, but he's always late. And when he does show up for meetings, he doesn't have the materials he needs.
   B: And his reports always have mistakes in them.
   A: If he wants to keep his job, he needs to take some steps to improve immediately.

   Which is correct?
   - **A.** Sam is demanding and aggressive.
   - **B.** Sam is unprepared and sloppy.
   - **C.** Sam is punctual and helpful.

4. *A:* So what about Ann?
B: Well, she definitely has some strengths, but she has her weaknesses, too.
A: True. I mean she's very nice and everyone likes her.
B: Yes. And that's so important.
A: And she always offers to assist her coworkers.
B: But she needs to build her confidence. She's a little shy. She doesn't speak up enough.

Which is correct?
A. Ann is helpful but unassertive.
B. Ann is professional but sloppy.
C. Ann is organized but demanding.

5. *A:* Let's talk about Ed. How did he do this year?
B: Well, he does great work. He's had good training, and he's smart.
A: But . . .
B: But he makes his coworkers a little nervous. He expects a lot from everyone, sometimes too much.
A: I see. If that continues, we'll need to give him some feedback about that.

Which is correct?
A. Ed is sloppy but prepared.
B. Ed is assertive but unprepared.
C. Ed is professional but demanding.

6. *A:* Okay. The last person to talk about is Mary.
B: Mary took a professional development course this year, and it really helped her.
A: Really? How?
B: Well, she used to come to meetings without the information she needed. And she used to make a lot of mistakes in her work.
A: And now?
B: Well, now she's like a new person. She's always on time, and she always has the reports she needs. She's really improved.

Which is correct?
A. Mary used to be unprepared, but now she's prepared.
B. Mary used to be demanding, but now she's nice.
C. Mary used to be organized, but now she's sloppy.

Activity 2 (Page 170)

A: Let's talk about Jim first. What do you think is his greatest strength?
B: Well, he's always ready for anything. For example, if I ask him to give a presentation at a meeting, he comes with all of the information he needs.
A: Yeah. That's true. And he's organized, too.
B: Right. If I ask him for information about sales or whatever, he knows just where to find it.
A: Okay, let's talk about Jan.
B: She's had a good year.
A: She sure has. The thing I like about Jan is that she's confident. She's not afraid to take initiative. If she hears about a project that she wants to work on, she'll come to me and tell me she wants to do it.
B: That's great. If she continues to do well, she'll receive a promotion.
A: All right, on to Sam.
B: Oh yeah. Sam. Hmmm.
A: What are we going to do about him? I like him. He's friendly, but he's always late. And when he does show up for meetings, he doesn't have the materials he needs.
B: And his reports always have mistakes in them.
A: If he wants to keep his job, he needs to take some steps to improve immediately. So what about Ann?
B: Well, she definitely has some strengths, but she has her weaknesses too.
A: True. I mean she's very nice and everyone likes her.

B: Yes. And that's so important.
A: And she always offers to assist her coworkers.
B: But she needs to build her confidence. She's a little shy. She doesn't speak up enough.
A: Let's talk about Ed. How did he do this year?
B: Well, he does great work. He's had good training, and he's smart.
A: But…
B: But he makes his coworkers a little nervous. He expects a lot from everyone, sometimes too much.
A: I see. If that continues, we'll need to give him some feedback about that. Okay. The last person to talk about is Mary.
B: Mary took a professional development course this year, and it really helped her.
A: Really? How?
B: Well, she used to come to meetings without the information she needed. And she used to make a lot of mistakes in her work.
A: And now?
B: Well, now she's like a new person. She's always on time, and she always has the reports she needs. She's really improved.

Activity 3 (Page 170)

A: Let's talk a little more about Mary.
B: Okay.
A: I know she took that professional development course this year, right?
B: Yes, and it's really helped her.
A: I agree. Do you think she's ready for a little more responsibility?
B: [*sounding surprised*] Do you want to give her a promotion?
A: No… not a promotion, at least not yet. I'd like for her to take over a major project in our department. Do you think she would be okay with more responsibility? If we give it to her, we will have to make sure it goes well.
B: Well, she really has improved. I'm not sure she has very much experience with leadership though.
A: That's a good point. But I do think she has more confidence and better organization. If we ask her to do more, I think she will take the initiative to learn what she needs to know. She needs more experience
B: All right, then. I'll meet with her tomorrow.

LESSON 5 Grammar Practice Plus Activities 1 & 2
(Page 174)

A: So, Lilia, tell me about the interview.
B: Well, Marcos, the other interviewers, and I met with Steven Hopkins today. He made a good impression.
A: Really?
B: Yes, I think he is a great candidate. I'm looking at his résumé right now. He's only had two jobs since he finished his degree, but I think he got a lot of great work experience at both places.
A: What about his education?
B: Well, unfortunately, that's not as good. He earned his certificate in management over ten years ago. If I were Steven, I would have completed some continuing education courses since then. He will need to do that soon.
A: Good point.
B: His skills and interests look good though. He has good technical skills with computers. If we set up our new network next year, he could lead that project.
A: That's a good idea.
B: He's very easy to talk with, and I think he has good people skills. I'm not sure about his leadership skills, though. He's never really had to work with several people before. Teamwork might be new for him.
A: True, but if he has good people skills and good communication skills, I'm sure he'll encourage teamwork and make good connections.

B: I agree. Overall, I think he would make a great employee at our company. If we gave him the job, I think his coworkers would enjoy working with him. I would recommend him!

Activity 4 (Page 175)

1. A: Isabel, you have an excellent résumé. If you were hired at our company, what would you be able to contribute?
   B: Thank you. If I were hired at the company, I would be able to use my leadership experience in many ways. I would help my team find better ways of doing things. I would also make changes to the people who are on the team, maybe even firing one or two of them if necessary. Or transferring them to other departments. I think you have to have high standards to be a good leader.
   A: I see . . . [sounds dubious]

2. A: Nicholas, we are very impressed with your past work experience. Tell us—if you were hired at our company, what would you change or do differently?
   B: If I were hired, I would try to encourage everyone to be creative and think of new ideas. I think one of the most important things a team should do is always think of new ways of doing things. I know it sometimes takes longer and costs more money, but I think brainstorming and trying new things is very important.
   A: That's an interesting point… [sounds serious, ponderous]

3. A: Leyla, your résumé says you have skills in financial management. Tell us about that.
   B: Yes, I do! In my last job, I was responsible for the budget for our account. I am very careful with money, and I pay close attention to expenses. If I were hired at this company, I would make sure we covered the costs of our projects with the budget we were given.
   A: Excellent. [sounding pleased, like this is the first person that has shown any promise]

4. A: Rob, your past work experience makes you seem like a very hard worker.
   B: Oh yes, I am! I never let anything stop me from finishing my work. If I were hired at this company, I would meet every deadline and make sure all my coworkers did too. At my last job, I worked 12 to 14 hours a day to get things done. I didn't always get to see my family, but my boss always knew a project would be finished on time.
   A: You sound like a very hard worker. [sounding serious, but with a tinge of sarcasm]

CAREER CONNECTION Activity 2 (Page 180)

A: [friendly] So, Sara, tell me… Why should we hire you for the assistant manager position?
B: [confidently] Well, Mr. Wilson, I really want to pursue this opportunity because I think the job would be a great fit for me. Here's my updated resume. If you read the first section, you'll see that I am about to graduate with my degree in hotel and restaurant management.
A: Wow, that's great.
B: [confidently] And if you evaluate my credentials, you'll see that I'm in the top 5% of my class. Mr. Wilson, if you gave me the chance, I guarantee that you would not be sorry! I'd be very dedicated and hard-working.
A: I believe that, Sara. You've been one of our most reliable workers here for the last three years.
B: [hesitating slightly] Mr. Wilson, there's something I should tell you. I've been doing some networking around town, and one of my connections has offered me a job as a front desk manager at a hotel. The job would pay about 10% more than you're offering for the assistant manager position.
A: [thoughtfully] Oh, I see. So…
B: So, well, actually, if I had my choice, I'd rather stay here because I really want to concentrate on working in the restaurant business.

But with student loans to pay off, I have to be practical, too. [hesitating] I guess what I'm saying is… if I were promoted here, I'd need a higher salary than the one advertised.
A: I see… Well, I'll take that into consideration, Sara.
B: Thank you.
A: OK. As a full-time employee you'll be eligible for a full benefits package: healthcare, dental, retirement… Do you have any questions about them?
B: Well, I know that there is a retirement plan here, but I don't know when an employee is vested. I was wondering if you could tell me more about that?
A: Let's see… we pay 4% into the retirement plan, and you're fully vested in the plan after 5 years.
B: I see. OK. [hesitating] Um, I was also wondering about vacation and sick leave benefits.
A: You get two weeks' vacation to start, and one sick day every 3 months. You will earn another week of vacation time after three years of employment.
B: All right. Let's see… [hesitating] Uh, if I were hired as the assistant manager, I was hoping it would be possible to count my three years of part-time work here towards the extra week of vacation time.
A: Oh, well, we might be able to do something about that. I'll discuss that with Human Resources.
B: Thank you.
A: I appreciate your coming in today, Sara. We'll let you know our decision soon.
B: Thank you for your time, Mr. Wilson.

Unit 12

LESSON 3 Listening and Conversation Activities 1 & 2
(Page 186)

1. What will the candidate do about pollution?
   A: We've seen a lot of positive changes to Pleasant City recently. But some problems remain. For example, pollution is getting worse. As mayor, what will you do about this?
   B: Well, in the next few years, three more factories are going to be opening. So, as mayor, I will design a plan to help factories reduce pollution.

   What will the candidate do about pollution?
   A. close the factories.
   B. open new factories.
   C. help factories reduce pollution.

2. Why do the schools need help?
   A: There are so many different ways to help improve the city. What do you think is the most important problem right now?
   B: Well, I think our schools need a lot of help. In the next five years, hundreds of children are going to be entering our schools. We need more classrooms, more teachers, and more textbooks.

   Why do the schools need help?
   A. In five years, they will need more classrooms, teachers, and textbooks.
   B. In five year, hundreds of children will be leaving the schools.
   C. In five years, many of the schools will close.

3. Where is the candidate going to be speaking?
   A: Your campaign is just beginning. A lot of people want to hear what you have to say. Where do you plan to speak?
   B: Well, my campaign is all about improving public services. I'm going to be speaking at schools, firehouses, hospitals, and City Hall.

   Where is the candidate going to be speaking?
   A. at shopping malls and on television.
   B. in sports arenas and theaters.
   C. in places where teachers, nurses, and firefighters work.

4. How will the candidate help senior citizens?
   A: Many people in Pleasant City are senior citizens. Do you think we will have enough public services for them?
   B: No. Many older people in our city need better health care. If I am mayor, I will ask all health clinics to give all senior citizens a free health examination.

   How will the candidate help senior citizens?
   A. She'll ask them to work at the hospitals.
   B. She'll ask the health clinics to offer free exams.
   C. She'll ask them to buy better health insurance.

5. Who can help reduce crime in Pleasant City?
   A: Crime is still a big problem in some parts of Pleasant City. What do you plan to do about it?
   B: Well, tomorrow I'm going to be speaking at the police station about this. Citizens need to help our local police officers. We all need to watch our neighborhoods carefully and call the police if we see or hear anything strange or suspicious. Neighbors can really help fight crime.

   Who can help reduce crime in Pleasant City?
   A. people who own shops in Pleasant City.
   B. people who visit Pleasant City.
   C. people who live in Pleasant City.

6. How can the people of Pleasant City help the community?
   A: Do you think the people of Pleasant City can help the community?
   B: Absolutely. As mayor, I am going to be encouraging every person in Pleasant City to help the community.
   A: How so?
   B: Well, for instance, we can all help with donations. Anyone can donate food, clothes, and even money to community agencies. And people can volunteer to help in the schools and sports programs.

   How can the people of Pleasant City help the community?
   A. by encouraging the mayor to help.
   B. by donating and by volunteering in the community.
   C. by asking the police to volunteer.

LESSON 5 Grammar Practice Plus Activity 1 (Page 190)
You're listening to KYOK [k-y-o-k] radio, 99.1 FM. It's five o'clock and time for business news. A recent report in the *Business Journal* shows that several leading businesses are going to be making important changes this year to improve the quality of life for their workers.

Cutting Edge, Inc is going to be allowing more flexibility in employees' work hours to encourage workers to spend more time at home, away from the office. That sounds like a great policy to me. They'll also be trying to improve relationships between managers and employees.

Software giant, Macro Comp is going to be spending more money on employee training. To help its employees acquire more professional skills, the company will be sending them to professional workshops and paying for it.

Well-known auto manufacturer, Go Auto is going to be offering employees free gym memberships. To encourage better health habits, the company is paying for its employees' exercise classes.

And finally, everyone's favorite travel agency, Zip Travel is going to be decreasing employee travel. You heard that right. The travel agency is going to be buying a new conference calling system to reduce the amount of travel for employees.

We're going to be checking in with employees of these companies at the end of the year to see how their employers succeeded. Now, onto the stock market report for today…[fade]

Vocabulary

Numbers in parentheses indicate unit, then page numbers.

accept (1, 6)
access (6, 96)
accident (5, 74)
accompanying (12, 182)
accounting (1, 8)
accused of (5, 72)
activism (n) (8, 128)
activist (8, 128)
address the issue of (12, 188)
admissions office (1, 6)
advertisement (10, 160)
advise against (8, 122)
advisor (1, 14)
after (2, 23)
aggressive (2, 33)
air quality (8, 118)
already (3, 39)
amusement park (3, 40)
approve (5, 70)
arrested (5, 72)
as soon as (2, 23)
ask (for) (2, 22)
assertive (11, 168)
attorney (5, 76)
auditorium (3, 38)
authorities (9, 144)
auto body repair (1, 8)
automated payment (4, 60)
avoid the problem of (12, 188)
balance a checkbook (4, 54)
bar graph (7, 111)
basics (1, 16)
battery (10, 152)
be used to (10, 158)
before (2, 23)
believe in (8, 124)
big business (7, 112)
blizzard (8, 120)
blog (7, 108)
bodybuilding (3, 48)
both . . . and (1, 12)
box office (3, 38)
break my lease (6, 92)
broken (6, 86)
build a stronger resume
    (11, 166)
burned out (2, 24)
business (1, 8)
business management (1, 8)
by the time (3, 39)
calculate (3, 47)
candidate (11, 172)
capable (2, 33)
carbon monoxide detector
    (10, 150)
career change (11, 172)
cares about (8, 126)
cautious about (8, 120)
Celsius (8, 123)
certificate of deposit (CD)
    (4, 54)

certification (2, 28)
Chamber of Commerce
    (9, 142)
change of address (form)
    (9, 140)
checkbook (4, 54)
child-safety gate (10, 152)
child-safety locks (10, 150)
choking hazard (10, 152)
citizen (5, 70)
classified ads (7, 108)
collect (5, 72)
collision (7, 102)
column (7, 108)
columnist (7, 108)
come back (10, 157)
comfortable (2, 33)
committed a crime (7, 102)
communication skills (2, 28)
communicative (2, 33)
compare (12, 192)
competition (3, 48)
complete (2, 29)
computer basics (1, 10)
computer programming (1, 8)
concerned about (8, 120)
concert hall (3, 38)
condition (6, 92)
conduct a job search (11, 166)
confident (11, 170)
congressmen (5, 70)
congresswomen (5, 70)
consent (6, 92)
contacting (1, 12)
continuing education course
    (1, 6)
contrast (12, 192)
convenience store (9, 140)
coordinating a campaign
    (12, 182)
cotton candy (3, 46)
count on (8, 126)
court (5, 70)
cover (1, 6)
covered for (2, 22)
cracked (6, 86)
creative (2, 24)
credit card fraud (4, 56)
credit card information (4, 54)
credit card offers (4, 60)
credit report (4, 56)
credit score (4, 60)
credits (1, 12)
crisis (8, 124)
crossing guard (9, 134)
current (6, 94)
database (n) (4, 64)
dead (6, 86)
debit card (4, 54)
debts (4, 64)
debut performance (3, 38)

defendant (5, 76)
demanding (11, 168)
demonstration (7, 102)
demonstrators (7, 102)
denies (4, 64)
Department of Motor Vehicles
    (9, 142)
dependable (2, 33)
deposit (6, 96)
deposit slip (4, 56)
developed communication
    skills (2, 28)
dinosaur exhibition (3, 40)
disagreeable (2, 33)
disaster relief (8, 124)
discriminate against (6, 92)
donated (7, 102)
download (1, 16)
dripping (6, 86)
driver education (9, 134)
drop out (10, 158)
drought (8, 120)
early childhood education
    (1, 8)
earn (1, 12)
earn a living (1, 16)
earthquake (8, 120)
either . . . or (1, 12)
elected (3, 48)
electrical cords (10, 152)
electrical outlet (10, 152)
electrical work (1, 8)
emissions (3, 48)
emphasize (12, 188)
employment rights (5, 75)
encourage teamwork
    (11, 172)
encyclopedia (5, 81)
engine trouble (9, 140)
enjoying my semester off
    (12, 182)
epidemic (7, 102)
error (6, 86)
evacuating (8, 124)
evaluate your credentials
    (11, 166)
events brochure (3, 38)
evict (6, 94)
evidence (7, 104)
ex-boyfriend (3, 46)
expand efforts (12, 188)
extreme heat alert (8, 118)
Fahrenheit (8, 123)
fall for (10, 157)
fatalities (9, 144)
federal taxes (5, 78)
feedback (11, 166)
Ferris wheel (3, 44)
file a complaint (6, 92)
file tax returns (5, 72)
film festival (3, 38)

financial advisor (4, 54)
fire drill (10, 150)
fire hydrant (9, 136)
flash flood (8, 120)
flexibility (1, 6)
focus on (8, 124)
followed through with
    (10, 156)
followed up (2, 22)
forecast (8, 118)
format (1, 16)
fortunately (3, 38)
found out about (10, 156)
friendly (11, 170)
front page (7, 108)
futuristic (3, 48)
gas leak (6, 86)
get in your way (11, 176)
give a speech (5, 72)
give up (1, 16)
global warming (8, 124)
gotten along (2, 28)
governor (5, 70)
grade point average (GPA)
    (1, 15)
grow up (10, 158)
guide dog (9, 134)
guilty (5, 76)
gust of wind (8, 118)
hand out (5, 72)
handicapped passengers
    (9, 134)
handrails (10, 150)
hardware store (9, 142)
have good connections
    (11, 172)
headline (7, 108)
health care (1, 8)
helpful (2, 24)
hostess (3, 38)
hotel and hospitality (1, 8)
human-interest (7, 108)
hurricane (8, 120)
identify (7, 102)
identify strengths and
    weaknesses (11, 166)
identity theft (4, 60)
immigration (5, 75)
impressed (11, 168)
impressive (2, 33)
in effect (8, 121)
in order to (12, 189)
income tax (5, 78)
injury (5, 74)
innocent (5, 76)
insufficient funds (4, 54)
interest rate (4, 54)
internship (1, 14)
interviewer (11, 172)
invest in (4, 54)
investigating (7, 102)

issue (8, 118)
jackknifed (9, 144)
job interview (11, 176)
joined a conference call
(2, 22)
knock over (5, 72)
landlord (6, 96)
laws (5, 70)
leadership skills (2, 28)
lease (6, 94)
likeable (2, 33)
local (7, 108)
look forward to (10, 158)
look up (10, 157)
losing an internet connection
(6, 86)
made a presentation (2, 22)
maintained (2, 28)
make a better impression
(11, 172)
make improvements (1, 12)
managed time (2, 28)
mayor (5, 70)
medical assisting (1, 8)
meet with (1, 12)
met a deadline (2, 22)
minimize stress (12, 188)
miss out on (10, 158)
modern art museum (3, 40)
monitor (v) (4, 64)
monthly budget (4, 60)
mortgage loan (4, 56)
mortgage payment (4, 60)
moving van rental service
(9, 142)
mudslide (8, 120)
natural disasters (8, 124)
natural history museum (3,
40)
negotiate better benefits
(11, 172)
neither . . . nor (1, 12)
nervous about (8, 120)
networking (11, 172)
notice (6, 94)
nursing (1, 8)
obligations (6, 96)
on track (1, 12)
online course (1, 6)
opinion (7, 112)
organize (1, 12)
out (6, 86)
outlet covers (10, 150)
outrageous (4, 54)
overdrawn (4, 54)
overwhelmed (2, 24)
paid off (10, 156)

parking lot (9, 144)
parking meter (9, 136)
participants (8, 128)
parties (6, 96)
payment due date (4, 54)
pedestrians (9, 134)
peeling (6, 86)
penalty (4, 54)
people skills (11, 172)
personal injury (5, 75)
personality test (1, 12)
placement test (1, 6)
policy (6, 92)
post office (9, 142)
power (3, 46)
power outage (6, 86)
precautions (8, 118)
prepared (11, 168)
preparedness (8, 123)
president (5, 71)
prioritize (1, 12)
problem (11, 176)
professional (11, 168)
professional development
(11, 166)
professor (1, 14)
project (2, 22)
promote better health
(12, 188)
promotion (2, 28)
proof of insurance (9, 140)
provide (5, 72)
public service campaign
(8, 128)
pulled together materials
(2, 22)
punctual (2, 24)
pursue opportunities (11, 166)
put in a good word (11, 176)
put your best foot forward
(11, 176)
qualifications (2, 28)
quality of life (12, 188)
questionable (2, 33)
racket (3, 46)
raise awareness (8, 128)
reality TV show (3, 42)
reasons (7, 112)
received positive performance
reviews (2, 28)
recommend (8, 127)
refund (5, 79)
register (1, 7)
reliable (2, 33)
requested (2, 22)
rescued (7, 102)
research (1, 6)

reservation (3, 38)
resources (8, 124)
responders (9, 144)
restaurant management (1, 8)
road construction (9, 136)
road test (9, 140)
role model (7, 102)
roller coaster (3, 40)
running finances (12, 182)
rush hour (9, 134)
safety devices (10, 150)
salary increase (2, 31)
sales tax (3, 47)
savings account (4, 58)
scheduled (2, 22)
school administrator (1, 12)
school zone (9, 134)
selecting classes (12, 182)
sell yourself (11, 176)
semester (1, 14)
senator (5, 70)
sensitive (2, 33)
serious about (8, 120)
serve on a jury (5, 72)
severe thunderstorm warning
(8, 118)
show up (10, 157)
shown leadership skills (2, 28)
sidewalk café (3, 44)
sightseeing (12, 182)
sign up (10, 156)
signal (6, 86)
sloppy (11, 168)
smog advisory (8, 118)
smoke detector (10, 152)
soccer game (3, 44)
solution (11, 176)
spending allowance (4, 60)
spokesperson (8, 128)
sponsor (5, 72)
stadium (3, 44)
stained (6, 86)
stand out from the crowd
(11, 176)
start over (10, 157)
state taxes (5, 78)
street fair (3, 44)
street vendor (3, 38)
strengths (11, 168)
sublet (6, 94)
submit (1, 6)
suitable (2, 33)
suspect (7, 104)
take initiative (11, 166)
take steps (11, 166)
taking over (12, 182)
talk into (10, 157)

tasks (1, 12)
tax booklet (5, 78)
tax return (5, 78)
teller (4, 56)
tenant (6, 96)
tenant rights (5, 75)
tennis match (3, 44)
term (6, 96)
test out (1, 6)
theater (3, 40)
theory (7, 104)
think over (10, 156)
top story (7, 108)
tornado (8, 118)
torrential rain (8, 118)
tow truck (9, 140)
tow-away zone (9, 136)
Town Hall (9, 140)
toxic cleansers (10, 152)
toxic waste (8, 124)
transfer departments (11, 172)
trial (5, 76)
turn down (10, 158)
uncooperative (2, 33)
unfortunately (3, 38)
unsure about (8, 120)
until (2, 23)
update a resume (11, 166)
URL (7, 108)
use up (10, 157)
used to (10, 158)
usher (3, 38)
utilities (6, 96)
valuable (2, 33)
vehicles (9, 144)
versatility (3, 48)
Visitor Information Center
(9, 140)
visually impaired (9, 134)
voicemail (2, 22)
W-2 form (5, 78)
wages (5, 78)
weak (6, 86)
weaknesses (11, 168)
website address (7, 108)
wheelchair access ramp
(9, 136)
wheelchair lift (9, 134)
when (2, 23)
wildfire (8, 120)
withdrawal (4, 54)
withhold taxes (5, 72)
workshop (2, 28)
worried about (8, 120)

Index

Career Skills

Life Skills

Credits

Illustrators: Punto 5, Silvia Plata, Ismael Vázquez Sánchez, Juan Ramón Jasso Olvera, Jorge Break.

Photo credits:

10 D. Hurst / Alamy; **11** OJO Images / SuperStock; **17** Tetra Images / Getty Images; Content Mine International / Alamy; Image Source Black / SuperStock; WireImageStock / Masterfile; **27** Seth Joel / Getty Images; **33** Stockbyte / SuperStock; Somos Images LLC / Alamy; **34** Somos Images LLC / Alamy; **41** Flint/Corbis; **43** Photodisc / SuperStock; **46** age fotostock / SuperStock; Kevin Dodge / Corbis; Ladi Kirn / Alamy; BananaStock / SuperStock; Corbis RF / Alamy; John-Francis Bourke / zefa / Corbis; **47** Marcel Hartmann / Sygma / Corbis; Christopher Farina / Corbis; United Artists / Courtesy of Getty Images; **49** Robert Galbraith / Reuters / Corbis; De Laurentiis / The Kobal Collection; **50** Syracuse Newspapers / Li-Hua Lan / The Image Works; **52** Roy McMahon / Corbis; **56** Ned Frisk Photography / Corbis; Flint / Corbis; **59** Image Source White / SuperStock; Tetra Images / Alamy; **65** Digital Vision / Alamy; **66** b Digital Vision/Alamy; **73** Ned Frisk Photography / Corbis; **75** Stockbyte / Alamy; **77** Photodisc / SuperStock; **80** AP Photo / Matt Rourke; **81** Bettmann / Corbis; **82** Jay Syverson / Corbis; **84** Image Source Black / Alamy; John Lund / Nevada Wier / Getty Images; **91** Photodisc / SuperStock; **95** Ned Frisk Photography / Corbis; **98** SuperStock / Alamy; **103** Photodisc / SuperStock; **107** BananaStock/SuperStock; **124** Andrea Booher/FEMA News Photo / Getty Images; Adam Tanner / Reuters / Corbis; **121** UpperCut Images / Alamy; Colin McPherson / Corbis; Mark Wilson / Getty Images; Haas / Suddendeutsche Zeitung Photo / The Image Works; **123** BananaStock / SuperStock; Mark Antman / The Image Works; **124** Andrea Booher / FEMA News Photo / Getty Images; Mike Simons / Getty; Monica Graff / The Image Works; **126** Stephen Agricola / The Image Works; C.E. Meyer / USGS; Raymond Gehman/ Corbis; Jim West/ Alamy; **128** Ap Photo / Hidajet Delic; **129** Norbert von der Groeben / The Image Works; Time Life Pictures / USDA Forest Service / Time Life Pictures / Getty Images; **130** AP Photo / The Herald-Sun, Kevin Seifert; Jacksonville Journal Courier / Steve Warmowski / The Image Works; Angela Lubrano / ArenaPAL / Topham / The Image Works; **138** Angelo Cavalli / SuperStock; Andre Jenny / Alamy; age fotostock / SuperStock; SuperStock, Inc. / SuperStock; Goss Images / Alamy; **139** ColorBlind Images / Getty Images; **145** Wolfgang Lienbacher / Getty Images; **155** Don Mason / Blend Images / Corbis; **159** Pixtal / SuperStock; **161** Somos / Veer / Getty Images; **162** Somos / Veer / Getty Images; **171** Image Source / SuperStock; **177** Purestock / Getty Images; Glow Images / SuperStock; **178** Custom Medical Stock Photo / Alamy; **187** Corbis / SuperStock; **193** Businesspeople look at laptop; **194** Senthil Kumar / Corbis; **196** Pixland / SuperStock

Cover photo:
Man at desk with book: McGraw-Hill
Hand: Getty
Family with rabbit: Corbis
Girl graduating: Getty
Businessman giving presentation: Corbis
Smiling family: Getty